EXETER MEDIEVAL ENGLISH TEXTS AND STUDIES
General Editors: Marion Glasscoe and M.J. Swanton

# JUDITH

EXETER MEDIEVAL ENGLISH TEXTS AND STUDIES
General Editors: Marion Glasscoe and M.J. Swanton

A full list of titles in the Exeter Medieval English Texts and Studies series is available from University of Exeter Press, Reed Hall, Streatham Drive, Exeter, Devon EX4 4QR, UK.

# JUDITH

edited by
Mark Griffith

UNIVERSITY
*of*
EXETER
PRESS

First published in 1997 by
University of Exeter Press
Reed Hall, Streatham Drive
Exeter EX4 4QR
UK



**British Library Cataloguing in Publication Data**
A catalogue record for this book
is available from the British Library

ISBN 0 85989 568 8

Printed in Great Britain by Short Run Press Ltd, Exeter

For

Louise

# Contents

# Preface

The Old English poem now known as *Judith* is one of the finest surviving narrative poems from the Anglo-Saxon period and it has been much admired by critics of this literature. It has not, however, been edited very often, nor particularly well. There has only been one full scholarly edition—that by A.S. Cook—which first appeared in 1888 and which he condensed for the Belles-Lettres Series in 1904. The latter is now very difficult to obtain and the former is to be found only in the best academic libraries. B.J. Timmer re-edited the poem for the Methuen Old English Library Series in 1952, and this was reprinted with some revisions and corrections in 1978 by the Exeter Medieval English Texts Series. His edition has only a very brief introduction, a slight commentary and a selective bibliography and glossary. It is also greatly out of date. Though the present edition formally replaces Timmer's in the Exeter series, it does not follow Timmer's model. Rather, it is a modern edition in the style of P.J. Lucas's edition of *Exodus* for the same series, and I am happy, at this point, to acknowledge the general influence of that volume. Accordingly, I include an extensive introduction, a full commentary and a comprehensive glossary. The introduction focuses mainly on issues of literary interest, though I include sections on the orthography, phonology and dialect vocabulary for those who are interested in such areas. A traditional approach to O.E. phonology has been adopted on the grounds that no new approach has gained general acceptance, and the issues involved are too broad to be covered in a few pages dealing only with a single text. The conclusions in these areas are few and tentative, though the re-analysis of the poem's spellings shows it to be surprisingly consistent in this regard. Perhaps inevitably, these more technical parts are targeted at academics, whilst the literary critical sections appeal to a more general readership. Some, therefore, may find parts of the introduction and the commentary too technical for their liking, and others may find material too self-evident to be worthy of mention. In defence of this mixed mode, I can only say that my primary purpose in this edition has been to preserve the poem from further decline into obscurity by explaining the particular nature of its literary qualities, but I am aware too of the normal format of modern editions of O.E. poems, and have no wish to disappoint those who expect that. My regard for the poem has increased in the writing of this edition, and I now believe it to be, after *Beowulf* and *Exodus*, the best O.E. verse narrative. It does not have the subtle irony of *Beowulf* nor the stylistic exhibitionism of *Exodus*. Nevertheless, it lacks the main defects of many O.E. poetic narratives—excessive circumlocution and uneven structure—and it has virtues which are very rare or unique in this corpus: an independent and coherent interpretation of the source couched in a fresh and vigorous style, with touches of comic realism. *Judith* is a translation, but it is translation at its very best. If this edition manages to persuade the reader that the poem merits close and careful reading, or re-reading, it will have served its maker's purpose.

I should like to thank a number of colleagues and friends who have helped me in various ways. I am grateful to Dr Andrew Prescott of the British Library for arranging access to the manuscript. Professor Eric Stanley of Pembroke College, Oxford, read the introduction, commentary and bibliography and corrected them with his customary attention to detail. I have also particularly valued his unrivalled knowledge of the history of Anglo-Saxon studies. Mr Alan Ward of Wadham College, Oxford, made a number of contributions to the sections on spelling and phonology, and patiently answered a number of queries about points of phonological difficulty. I have greatly enjoyed conversations with him about Old English for the last twenty years. Professor Jane Toswell of the University of Western Ontario generously corrected a draft version of several parts. Professor Gerry Smith of New College, Oxford, made useful comments on the section on metre, and saved me from confusing hyphens with dashes. Mr Geoffrey de Ste Croix, also of New College, helpfully informed me about the Greek background to Judith. Mr David Leopold of Merton College, Oxford, introduced me to the mysteries of the Dell Pentium and Microsoft Word and never patronised me for my computer illiteracy. The formatting of this book owes much to his help and advice. Above all, my thanks are owed to my partner, Ms Louise Pickering of Wadham College, Oxford, who put up with a man obsessed with another woman. Any remaining mistakes are, of course, the responsibility of the editor. Those who notice errors or who have sensible suggestions for this work's improvement are welcome to communicate them to me.

New College, Oxford
July1997 Mark Griffith

# List of Abbreviations

Abbreviated bibliographical references (apart from those for dictionaries) are given in the Bibliography, at the end of relevant entries in square brackets. The abbreviations of the titles of journals in the Bibliography are conventional and may be found in Greenfield and Robinson. The short titles of O.E. verse texts in the footnotes and the commentary are those of Mitchell, *et al.* (1975 and 1979).

| | |
|---|---|
| acc. | accusative |
| adj(s). | adjective(s) |
| adv(s). | adverb(s) |
| *Alexander* | *Alexander's Letter to Aristotle* |
| A-S | Anglo-Saxon |
| BT | J. Bosworth and T.N. Toller, *An Anglo-Saxon Dictionary* (Oxford, 1882–98) |
| BTS | *Supplement* to Bosworth-Toller's *Dictionary* (Oxford, 1908–21) |
| C | the Commentary to this edition |
| *Christopher* | *The Life of St Christopher* |
| col. | column |
| comp. | comparative |
| conj. | conjunction |
| cpd(s). | compound(s) |
| dat. | dative |
| dem(s). | demonstrative(s) |
| DML | Dictionary of Medieval Latin from British Sources |
| DOE | Dictionary of Old English |
| EEMF | Early English Manuscripts in Facsimile |
| EETS os/ss | Early English Text Society, Original or Supplementary Series |
| fem. | feminine |
| gen. | genitive |

| | |
|---|---|
| Ger. | German |
| Grein | C.W.M. Grein, *Sprachschatz der angelsächsischen Dichter* (Heidelberg, 1912) |
| indic. | indicative |
| inf. | infinitive |
| Lewis and Short | C.T. Lewis and C. Short, *A Latin Dictionary* (Oxford, 1879) |
| lit. | literally |
| masc. | masculine |
| M.E. | Middle English |
| MED | Middle English Dictionary |
| MGH | Monumenta Germaniae Historica |
| M.H.G. | Middle High German |
| Mod.E. | Modern English |
| MS(S) | manuscript(s) |
| neut. | neuter |
| nom. | nominative |
| non-WS | non-West Saxon |
| O.E. | Old English |
| OED | Oxford English Dictionary |
| O.I. | Old Icelandic |
| OL | Old Latin version(s) of the Bible |
| O.N. | Old Norse |
| O.S. | Old Saxon |
| OT | Old Testament |
| pers. | person |
| pl. | plural |
| PL | Patrologia cursus completus, series Latina |
| prep. | preposition |
| pres. | present |
| pret. | preterite |
| pron(s). | pronoun(s) |
| sing. | singular |
| subj. | subjunctive |
| *Wonders* | *The Wonders of the East* |
| WS | West Saxon |
| x | (following a numeral) the number of occurrences of a particular feature |

# Introduction

## 1 The Manuscript

The unique text of *Judith* is found in MS Vitellius A XV in the Cotton collection in the British Museum. This volume consists of two originally separate codices, the Southwick and the Nowell, which were arbitrarily brought together by a binder, probably in the late sixteenth or seventeenth century.[1] The Nowell codex contains five texts, three prose (*The Life of St Christopher*, *The Wonders of the East* and *Alexander's Letter to Aristotle*) and two verse (*Beowulf* and *Judith*), which are arranged in this order, with *Judith* as the final text. Ker dates the codex to between the last quarter of the tenth century and the first quarter of the eleventh, a slightly later date than that he gives to *The Exeter Book* and *The Vercelli Book*, but about the same as that of *The Junius Manuscript*.[2] Nothing is known of its provenance or of its history before it came into Sir Robert Cotton's possession, except for the name of a previous owner, 'Laurence Nowell',[3] written at the top of (what is now and presumably also then was) its first page, along with the date 1563.

It is written in two distinct, but contemporary, hands; Scribe A, writing in an Insular script influenced by Caroline minuscule, is responsible for the prose pieces and for *Beowulf* up to the middle of verse 1939b, whilst Scribe B, using a late variety of

---

[1] See Ker, liv: Cotton 'separated manuscripts which belonged together and directed his binder to put unrelated manuscripts within the same cover'. Ker, 279–83, gives a brief description of both codices. For full description and discussion of the compilation of the Nowell codex, see Förster (1919), Malone, 1–118 (109–14 deal with the text of *Jud*), Dobbie, ix–xxxiii, Sisam (1953), 61–96, Taylor and Salus (1968), Boyle (1981), Gerritsen (1988), and Lucas (1990).

[2] Ker, 281; see, also, his introduction, xx, for explanation of the meaning of the dating. Cameron, *et al.*, 36–7, list other A-S manuscripts which Ker dates in the form 's. X/XI'.

[3] Laurence Nowell the antiquary, not his namesake who was Dean of Lichfield; see Lucas (1990), 463, n.3, for a bibliography on the subject. Nowell's place in the history of O.E. studies is traced by Ker, l–li.

square Anglo-Saxon minuscule, finished *Beowulf* and also wrote *Judith*. The text of the poem, incomplete at the beginning, occupies quire 14, folios 202r–209v in the current numbering, but the end of the poem did not originally coincide with the end of the quire as it has come down to us. The final six lines have been added to the bottom of f. 209v, presumably from a following leaf subsequently lost, by an early modern hand imitating Insular script. Though quire 14 is now the final one in the manuscript, as Ker shows, it cannot always have been so:

> A pattern of wormholes on ff. 192–201—but not on ff. 202–9—and marks of exposure on f. 201v. show that Beowulf was once at the end of the manuscript and not followed, as it now is, by Judith.[4]

Lucas, expanding on Boyle, points out that the end of quire 13 meets several of the criteria established by Robinson for the end of a manuscript booklet: the end of the booklet and the end of the text coincide; the last page shows the results of exposure; and the ten leaves in both quires 12 and 13, rather than the eight of quires 1–11, with 21 lines of text beside the usual 20. These features suggest that the scribe modified the page and quire structure in order to fit the text into the booklet.[5] If *Judith* was originally an integral part of the Nowell codex which ended with *Beowulf*,[6] then, given the inseparability of its first four texts, *Judith* can only have preceded the incomplete *Christopher* at its beginning. Lucas calculates from comparison with its Latin source that the missing two-thirds or so of the saint's life would have occupied 15 pages at the normal 20 lines per page, and concludes:

> Before Quire 1, therefore, we must posit a Quire *0. If this Quire *0 had the usual eight folios, then *Christopher* would have begun on fo. 1v. Only fo. 1r is unaccounted for. As we have already seen, at the end of *Judith* ... there

[4] Ker, 282.

[5] See Lucas (1990), 469–70, Boyle (1981), 24-31 and Robinson (1978), 232-3.

[6] Some have doubted its integrity; note Sisam (1953), 67–8, Malone, 118, Clubb, (1964), 562, and Kiernan (1981), 151, who regard *Jud* as a separate product added at some later date.

> must have been another leaf ... The possibility arises that Quire *0 came in between what is now Quire 14 and Quire 1, that it contained the end of *Judith* on its first page, that the rest of that page was left blank (as at the end of *Christopher*, *Marvels*, and *Alexander's Letter*), and that *Christopher* began on the second page and continued through the rest of the quire.[7]

If this is not the case, it is, as Lucas comments, a coincidence that the last lines of *Judith* and the missing portion of *Christopher* provide just the right quantity of text to fill the posited additional quire. Someone who read the texts of the manuscript in this order might have been more inclined to link the biblical Judith with saints than with heroes.

Because *Judith* occupies eight leaves and begins in mid-sentence towards the end of section 9 (the tenth numbered section opening in l.15), it is clear that quire 14, if it was, as it is now, a quire of eight leaves, cannot have begun the original manuscript, but must have been preceded by at least one other quire. If nine sections preceded the present beginning of the poem and were of approximately the average length of the three which survive, then just under a thousand lines of verse—perhaps three quires in all—are missing.[8] Although all of this material may have constituted the lost opening of the poem, the selective treatment of the biblical source (assuming that *Judith* dealt only with the story of Judith), and the fact that poems may be numbered in continuous series in O.E. poetic manuscripts (rather than each poem beginning with a new first section),[9] make it more probable that a

---

[7] Lucas (1990), 472. See, further, 473–4, for remarks on the absence of <*io*> from both *Jud* and *Christopher*; for other shared spellings (e.g. *swyrd*, *hyne*, the use of thorn and eth), see, below, on spelling.

[8] Sections 10, 11 and 12 average 112 lines. 9 x 112 = 1008, minus the 14 lines which survive from the ninth section gives a figure of 994 missing lines. Quire 14 contains 342 lines, so 994 lines would very nearly fill three quires (342 x 3 = 1026). The slight discrepancy does not pose a problem, for there is no necessity for these sections to be exactly the average length of the last three, and Cavill (1985), 157, demonstrates that there is considerable variation in section length within individual poems.

[9] The poems in *The Junius Manuscript* are so numbered. See Woolf (1986), 121–2, and Lucas (1990), 477–8. On the treatment of the source, see section 6.

great deal of the lost material was another poem or poems. Nevertheless, since no O.E. poem which has section numbers (and whose beginning has survived) starts in the middle of a numbered section, it seems likely, as Chamberlain has suggested, that at least the missing part of the ninth section, perhaps around a hundred lines, did belong to *Judith*.[10] The best guess that can be made, therefore, of the original length of the poem is that it comprised about 450 lines, and the lost opening presumably dealt in fairly brief fashion with Holofernes' assault on the Hebrews, the siege of Bethulia, Judith's journey to the Assyrian camp, and her first three (relatively uneventful) days there.[11]

The section numbers X, XI and XII are placed at the end of lines 14, 121 and 235; each is preceded in the manuscript by a mark of punctuation (twice a single point; once, at 235, by the end-of-section marker :~), and each is followed by a point and, at the start of the next line of script, by a single, large, unornamented capital opening the section. Though the sections do not end in any noticeably fashioned way, they begin, as often in *Beowulf*, either with a resumptive statement (XI and XII), or with 'the announcement of an action, especially of the "motion" of individuals or groups of men' (X).[12] Because their average length is considerably greater, but the variation in their length significantly less, than those in the part of *Beowulf* written by Scribe B, they may be supposed to have been copied from the scribe's exemplar, but we do not know whether the poet or an earlier scribe was responsible for their inclusion.[13] If *Judith* was

[10] Chamberlain (1975), 137.

[11] If this reasoning is correct, the notion that the verbal echo between the beginning and end of the existing text represents a rhetorical linking of the opening and conclusion of the poem must be discarded (on this see further pp.92–3). Opinions about the original length vary from Timmer's calculation, by comparison with the source, that the poem had 'about 1,344 lines' (p.2), to Woolf's view, (1986), 124, that, apart from a few details, 'none of the poem is missing'; the view that I give here is that of Lucas (1990), 478, n.40. Further speculation about the length and, accordingly, the content of the lost opening, *pace* Chamberlain (1975), 141–7, seems pointless.

[12] Klaeber (1950), ci, and n.2–3.

[13] Those complete sections following *Beo* 1939b average 72 lines, and vary from 45 to 141 lines in length; the same figures for *Jud* are 112, and 107 to 114; see Cavill (1985), 157. That section divisions in O.E. poetic manuscripts derive from the poets has been argued by Gollancz (1927), xxxii, Timmer (1952) and Cavill

preceded by other texts numbered in continuous series, then it follows that 'even if the divisions were authorial the scribe viewed [the numbers] in relation to manuscript compilation rather than individual poetic structure'.[14] The divisions occur in the poem at natural pauses in the narrative and some editors have recognised this by placing breaks at the same points,[15] but scribes as well as poets may be presumed to have had enough understanding of the structure of what they wrote to position them so. The sections may have been designed to be of convenient length for separate reading sessions.[16]

Apart from the large capitals, the following types of punctuation and abbreviation are used:

(i) Small capitals appear very rarely (only at l.28 *Swa*, 83 *Ic*, 143 *Swa*, and possibly 68 *Se*),[17] and are not, therefore, a guide to the metre or sentence structure. All four examples are verse-initial; the first two begin sentences (at the opening of a speech in l.83); the third is clause-initial, but sentence-initial only if *swa* is an adverb rather than a conjunction; the last is clearly mid-clause. Scribe B also uses them very sparingly in his portion of *Beowulf*, and they are much less frequent here than in any of the prose texts of the codex or in the other major poetic codices.[18] As always in Anglo-Saxon manuscripts, proper names are not capitalised.

(ii) Accent marks are visible (in the main, clearly) in 31 places:[19]

---

(1985); Klaeber (1950), ci, views those in *Beo* as authorial. That they are scribal in origin (at least in the Junius MS) is the view of Tolkien (1981), 33–4, and Lucas (1994), 11.

[14] Lucas (1994), 11.

[15] So Dobbie, Sweet, Hamer, and Cassidy-Ringler. On the function of the end-of-section mark as an indicator of a paragraph boundary, see Parkes (1992), 306, *positura*.

[16] Wells (1976), and Lucas (1994), 11–12, give summaries of this much-discussed view.

[17] 68 *Se* is noted by Malone, 23, but not by Dobbie, lxxi. The *s* is larger than normal (though there is some variation in the size of word-initial uncial *s*), and is preceded by a point. Because small capitals are often merely ordinary letters written larger, there is some difficulty in their identification.

[18] For details, see Dobbie, xxvi–xxvii and lxxi, and Malone, 20–5.

[19] In addition, Junius marks an accent in l.248 *búr-* (which can no longer be seen in the top line of folio 208r of the MS). More detailed analyses of these marks in the poem are given by Dobbie, xxxi–xxxiii, and Malone, 26–9.

7 *á*, 8 *wín-*, 16 *wín-*, 50 *cóm* (?), 82 *á-*, 109 *-róf*, 117 *nó*, 121 *hám*, 128 *blác-*, 133 *bá*, 140 *-gán*, 143 *ǽr*, 144 *-béad*, 146 *-róf*, 148 *wíf*, 149 *gán*, 190 *ár-*, 196 *dóm*, 197 *tír*, 236 *-tíd*, 257 *nán*, 276 *búr-*, 277 *-dráf*, 306 *tíd*, 307 *gár*, 310 *-hwón*, *-cóm*, 313 *hrǽw*, *rúm*, 316 *-réaf*, 318 *dóm-*.

This distribution is to some extent systematic. All of these occur over long monophthongs in primarily or secondarily stressed closed syllables of monosyllabic lexemes, except for 144 *-béad*, 316 *-réaf* (long diphthongs); 82 *á-* (unstressed prefix in an open syllable); 7 *á*, 117 *nó*, 133 *bá* (open syllables). Such syllables also occur plentifully without accents. Nevertheless, they are not found over short vowels and are less frequent over front vowels. Though they occur over the long stem vowels of monosyllabic lexemes when these form parts of compounds, they do not occur over them when such words are inflected (so 196, 266 *dóm*, but 299 *dome*; 109, 146 *-róf*, but 20 *rofe*, 53 *rofra*). The acute accents used by both scribes in *Beowulf* and by Scribe A in the prose pieces follow the same semi-systematic distribution (with few exceptions).[20] The Nowell codex accordingly belongs to that group of manuscripts in which the accent primarily falls on long monosyllables.[21]

(iii) Punctuation marks: the scribe, though a careful speller (or a careful copier of a well spelled exemplar), punctuated neither frequently, nor systematically, nor with any diversity of signs. With the exceptions of the single use of the mark :~ (which closes section XI) and marks of insertion, punctuation is confined to the point, or low dot, which is used very sparingly (except in the last lines, copied in the early modern period, where it occurs frequently but is of doubtful authenticity). Though points may become indistinct through fading, the text of *Judith* is relatively clear, and sixteen (excluding the three placed after the section numbers and the one immediately before section number XI) are visible. This number is proportionately less than in either scribe's

[20] For the exceptions in *Beo*, see Dobbie, xxxii, for those in *Alexander*, see Malone, 26–8.

[21] See Ker, xxxv. Usage in *The Exeter Book* and *The Vercelli Book* is similar, but with rather more exceptions; see respectively Krapp and Dobbie (1936), xxiv–xxv, and Scragg (1971). The accent's other functions, so far as these are discernible, are given by Ker, xxxv.

part of *Beowulf*, much less than in the second and third prose texts, but not very dissimilar from usage in *Christopher*. Most of the points both in *Beowulf* and in *Judith* are placed at the end of verses. They occur at the following places (after the word quoted):

f. 202r (l. 14b) *gesohte.*, 202v (21a) *dryhten.*, (32b) *gumena.*, 203r (40b) *iudithðe.*, 203v (59a) *besmitan.*, (60b) *gestyrde.*, (67b) *druncen.*, 204r (82b) *acwæð.*, 204v (90b) *-synta.*, 205r (121b) *leas.*, 205v (153b) *leng.*, 206v (190b) *sende.*, 208r (268a) *træf.*(?), 209r (306b) *gelyste.*, (312a) *-trod.*, (322b) *wæron.*

Apart from 32b, these are all verse final and may have metrical significance. However, 21a and 268a are also line final in the manuscript, and 153b and 322b are text final on folios 205v and 209r respectively. In addition, 14b and 121b close sections IX and X, 21a, 59a, 60b, and 90b coincide with the ends of clauses or sentences, and 82b is placed immediately before a speech. Only 40b, 67b, 190b, and 306b occur where there is strong enjambement between these and the following verses and no other kind of juncture. These four can only be interpreted as metrical in function. That in 32b is placed at the end of the first sense group and may indicate a caesura.[22]

(iv) There are several commonplace abbreviations: the ampersand *7* is used for *ond/and*, and the crossed thorn *ꝥ* for *þæt* (always for the conjunction, including *oðꝥ* for *oðþæt*, and generally for the demonstrative, but note *ðæt*, ll.10, 204); the tilde commonly stands for *m*, and is not used for *n* (mainly restricted by Scribe A to *m* in the dative plural *-um*, but more variedly used by Scribe B), overlined *þōn* (with the line half over *o* and half over *n*) is used once for *þonne* (l.329). Scribe B also uses a number of abbreviations not used by the first scribe. Overlined *g*

---

[22] The punctuation is generally viewed as metrical: see Malone, 29–32, but Dobbie, xxx–xxxi, (who counts seventeen points) denies this on the grounds of their infrequency. In view of the points which occur where there is strong enjambement in the sense, Parkes's opinion, (1992), 111 and 151, n.97, that the punctuation in Cotton Vitellius A XV 'indicates only the largest semantic units, the *sententiae*'—presumably based on the regularity of the marking of fitt boundaries—needs modification. On the pointing of caesurae, see Bliss, § 42, and Lawrence (1893), chapter 1. The origin of the point and its more regular metrical use in MS Junius 11 are discussed by Lucas (1994), 21–4.

is used for the prefix *ge-* (not before l.225, thereafter 21x, but written out in ll.287, 288, 290, 293, 294, 303, 308, 331, 338),[23] and once for *-ge* in *werige* (l.229); The tilde is also used above the final letter of *æft* for *æfter* (in ll.18 and 65, but not in 117), and of *dryht* for *dryhten* (in ll.21, 274, 299, but not in 61, 92, 198). A circumflex over the *n* of *holofern* indicates *holofernus* (in ll.7, 46, but not 21, 180, 250; cf. *holofernes*, 336). There is a tendency for these abbreviations to occur at the end of a manuscript line (e.g. in ll.18, 21, 46).[24] There is no evidence from folio 209v of an increased or more varied use of abbreviations, as there is on the final crowded leaf of *Beowulf*.[25]

## 2 Transcript and Editorial History

On the 23rd October 1731, a fire at Ashburnham House in Little Deans Yard, Westminster, where the Cotton library was then housed, destroyed part of the collection. Cotton Vitellius A XV escaped serious damage but suffered some scorching to its upper edges and side margins. Subsequent crumbling increased the textual loss, though *Judith* suffered less than *Beowulf*. Of particular value, therefore, for establishing letters and words lost as a consequence of the fire, is the surviving transcript made some time before the fire by Franciscus Junius (1589–1677), now Bodleian MS Junius 105.[26] A second, slightly later transcript by Humfrey Wanley (1672–1726) of a small part of the poem seems

[23] Occurrences of the abbreviation are listed by Cook, 88.

[24] Further details on the use of abbreviations in the codex are given by Dobbie, xxvii–xxix, Klaeber (1950), xcviii and Malone, 25–6.

[25] See Dobbie, xxix, Klaeber (1950), xcviii and n.3.

[26] A facsimile of the transcript is printed in Robinson and Stanley. The transcript is not dated; but Junius was in England from 1621–1651 (with spells abroad in 1642 and 1644–6), and again from 1674 until his death in 1677. Given that he was 85 by 1674 and resided mainly in Oxford from that date, the copy was almost certainly made before 1651. Madan, II, part II, 984, says only 'mid-17th cent.', but see Hetherington (1980), 222: Junius 'visited the libraries of Sir Thomas Cotton and Sir Simonds D'Ewes, among others, between 1646 and 1651, studying Old English manuscripts and making transcripts of them'. The twelve pages of copied text in Junius 105 are entirely devoted to the poem, and the remaining pages are blank. The heading on the first page is: 'Fragmentum historiæ Judith, descriptum ex Cottoniæ bibliothecæ MSto codice, qui inscribitur VITELLIUS. A.15. paginâ 199'.

not to have survived.[27] Excluding the last six lines of the manuscript, for which there is no authentic O.E. witness, the Junius transcript preserves nearly one hundred letters or marks of abbreviation which cannot be read in the manuscript, mainly from the top line of each leaf. Though Junius shares some of the weaknesses of early modern transcribers of O.E. texts, and made occasional errors, his copy of the poem, when compared with the surviving text, demonstrates a very high degree of reliability.[28] His only major departures from a principle of neutral copying are his addition of punctuation and omission of most of the accents.[29]

---

[27] See Heyworth (1989), 15–16 and n.15, Letter to Thomas Tanner, 19th April 1695: 'I copied almost a leaf & a half of the fragment of Judith, which is said to be written stylo Cædmoniano: I know no[t] when I shal copie the rest'. Heyworth notes that he was unable to trace this transcript.

[28] Most of Junius's errors are trivial. His knowledge of O.E. orthography sometimes caused him to use an available spelling variant: *þ* for *ð* and vice versa is frequent; *-ll* is used for *-l* (74 *þrymfull*, 141 *weall-*, 199 *snellra*), *i* for *y* (84 *wille*, 92, *drihten*, 168 *siððan*, 218 *Assirium*, 285, 286 *is*, and 346 *drihtne*, if the spelling *dryhtne* in the final copied lines is correct), *a* for *o* before a nasal (130 *hand*), *æ* for *a* in a position of low stress (7 *ðæm*), unvoiced *h* for final *g* (187 *burh-*). Twice he spelled *Ebreisce* for MS *Ebrisce* (241, 305), and once *Juditðe* for *Iudithðe* (40). He failed to cross a *d* to form *ð* in *weard* (155). He ignored corrections in the manuscript at 32 *baldor*, 54 *gebrohten*, 150 *forlæten*, 319 *fyrd*, and understandably gave *heo ildon* in 142 because he could not read the corrected *heoldon* (from *heordon*). Four changes by him may represent conscious emendations: 85 *þearfendre*, 163 *weras 7 wif*, 165 *ðeodnes*, 179 *starian* (85, 165, 179 are clearly correct). He has *gesceop* in 344 where the copied lines read *gesceow*. There are only eight serious errors: 67 *winessa* for *wine swa*, 182 *syðor* for *þ swyðor*, 205 *hluin mon* for *hlummon*, 215 *elðeodriga* for *elþeodigra*, 249 *bringan* for *þringan*, 325 *wundenloce* for *wundenlocc*, 325 *wagon* for *wægon*, 335 *sylfne* for *sylfre*. On Junius's general carefulness as transcriber, see Bennett (1938), 341–4.

[29] Junius preserved accents only in l.7 *á* and 133 *bá* (see also n.19). He used two punctuation marks, one which resembles a semi-colon, and a point or stop. The first always marks major syntactic pauses (more than thirty times). The second is used syntactically up to l.80 (at the end of verses 2a, 8a, 12a, 19a, 21a, 34a, 37a, 40a, etc.), but, thereafter, it is much more frequent and predominantly metrical, marking off one verse from another, though not without occasional errors, and with a return to the former syntactic use in ll.265–80. Extra spacing is also used throughout to separate verses. This system differs from that used in Junius 12, his transcript of *Met*, where the semi-colon is rare, and the point is used metrically only (see Robinson and Stanley, 5.1–5.32.2). Nonetheless, Bennett's remark, (1938), 75, that 'it seems doubtful whether ... anyone before Hickes and Wanley recognised [*Jud*] as verse', requires modification (and note also Wanley's remark, n.27 above, that *Jud* 'is *said* to be written stylo Cædmoniano'). Stanley (1997), 9,

The first edition of the poem was published in Oxford in 1698 as the final part of Edward Thwaites's principal publication, *Heptateuchus*.[30] The only earlier printing of a specimen of O.E. poetry in England is that of *Durham* in Roger Twysden's *Historiæ Anglicanæ Scriptores Antiqui*, 1652 (though Junius published his edition of the Cædmon manuscript in Amsterdam in 1655). Thwaites based his text on the Junius transcript, and it does not provide independent testimony to the readings of the manuscript before the fire.[31] He seems to have followed Junius's heading in entitling his copy of the transcript *Fragmentum Historiæ Judith*, and Wanley, noting both Junius and Thwaites, used the same phrase, slightly expanded, in his brief description of the poem in Hickes's *Thesaurus*.[32] Thereafter, the term 'fragment' formed part

---

n.6, incorrectly states that 'the irregular pointing of *Judith* ... is on the whole accurately copied by Junius': Junius's punctuation of the text is extensive, where that of the MS is sparse (merely sixteen points in all), but he also fails to register the MS punctuation at the end of folio 203r (verse 40b), 203v (60b), and (67b), and 208r (268a).

[30] The work, its contents and reception are discussed by Adams (1917), 79–80, 119, Bennett (1938), 69–75, and Murphy (1980–1), 154–7. For Thwaites's doubt about whether to include *Jud* in the *Heptateuchus*, see his letter to Hickes (Bod. Lib. MS Eng. hist. c.6, f.118).

[31] See the same letter to Hickes (Bod. Lib. MS Eng. hist. c.6, f.118) for his statement that he has seen Junius's copy; his misattribution of *Jud* there to MS Otho B XI confirms that he cannot have used Vitellius A XV. Sweet, 136, fails to mention the Junius transcript and incorrectly states that, because of the damage to the manuscript, 'in places we must rely on the readings in Edward Thwaites's *Heptateuchus (&c.), Historiæ Judith Fragmentum* (1698)'. Timmer, 1–2, quotes Madan to the effect that Thwaites followed Junius, but misleadingly remarks that 'Junius's transcript is on the whole more correct than Thwaites' edition, but neither shows much care in reproducing the þ and ð of the manuscript accurately'. Thwaites generally copies Junius carefully (even following his added punctuation, though he pays no particular attention to Junius's use of *þ* and ð) and so preserves all of his non-trivial departures from the forms of the manuscript. In addition, he introduces errors of his own at 59 *somme* (MS *womme*), 98 *ganam* (MS *genam*), 108 *eornost* (MS *eornoste*), 213 *bedeahte* (MS *beðeahte*), 239 *heofod-* (MS *heafod-*).

[32] II, 219: 'Fragmentum Poeticum Hist. Judithæ & Holofernis, Saxonice ante Conquæst. scriptum. Quod descripsit cl. Junius, è cujus Apographo illud typis edidit Edwardus Thwaitesius, in libro suo supra laudato'. For Hickes's discussion of the supposed influence of the Danish scalds and of Norse mythology on *Jud*—the earliest critical discussion of the poem and, indeed, of O.E. poetry—see *Thesaurus*, I, part I, chapter XXI, pp.101–34. In this section, Hickes quotes

of the title in the nineteenth century, though it has since been known simply as *Judith*.[33] Thorpe's edition, in his *Analecta Anglo-Saxonica*, was the first to be based upon the manuscript, with supplementary readings from Thwaites. Cook's detailed single-text edition likewise did not make use of the transcript. However, both the main editors of this century—Dobbie and Timmer—supplement the manuscript with readings from Junius. Although the poem has rather frequently appeared in anthologies, it has not been re-edited since 1953.

## 3 Language

### *Spelling and Standardisation*

The consequence of Bible translation into the vernacular is the greatly increased literary and cultural status of that vernacular.[34] A linguistic corollary of heightened status is the standardisation of linguistic forms. Standardisation is also particularly associated with late WS manuscripts produced after the Benedictine reform from the 960s onwards. The orthography of the poem does indeed display very considerable regularity and, in one important respect, this goes beyond the degree of standardisation usually associated with late WS texts. In general, each word has a single spelling, but the following are the areas where some irregularities are discernible:[35]

(i) Before nasals, West Germanic *a* is represented by <*a*> and <*o*>; <*o*> is preferred before <*m*> (e.g. *somod* 4x), but there is more variation before <*n*>. Parallel forms are: *camp* 200, *comp-* 332; *hand* 198, *hond* 130; *land-* 226, *lond-* 314; *gemang* 225,

liberally from the text of the poem, following Thwaites, but introduces many errors of his own.

[33] Note the heading *Aus dem Fragment von Judith* in Grimm (1812), 43, Leo's description of the poem as *Fragment eines angelsächsischen Heldengedichts*, Thorpe's title, *Judith: a Fragment*, and the titles of the editions of Nilsson and Cook. Ettmüller was the first to use the shorter title in 1850.

[34] On this, see Shepherd (1969). Bede's story of Cædmon shows that translation of parts of the Bible was undertaken from quite soon after the conversion of the Anglo-Saxons. The legend of divine inspiration may have sanctioned the use of the vernacular in such works.

[35] Excluding *-l/ -ll* (e.g. *gefeol(l)*, *-ful(l)*), *-g/-h* (*burg-/burh-*), and *maðm/madm*.

*gemong* 193, 303; (gen. pl.) *manna* 235, *monna* 52, 181;[36] *rand-* 188, *rond-* 11, 20; *þancol-* 172, *-þoncol* 105, 131, 145, 330, 341; *þanonne* 132, *ðonan* 118.

Cook's comprehensive list of these spellings gives a total of 27 <*a*> spellings (5 before <*m*>) to 34 <*o*> spellings (12 before <*m*>),[37] a distribution dissimilar to that found in *Beowulf*.[38] Spellings with <*o*> are preferred in early WS texts, but <*a*> predominates in late WS ones.

(ii) Before *l* + consonant, Primitive O.E. *æ* is spelled <*æ*> and <*a*> alongside the normal late WS <*ea*>; variation within the same word occurs only with *ealdor(-)*, 'prince' (<*ea*> 6x, <*a*> 1x if the incomplete erasure of initial *b-* in l.32 is accepted as an erasure). The following is a complete list of the <*æ*> and <*a*> spellings, with complete, or disproportionate, use in verse indicated by the symbols †, (†), as in the glossary:

(a) <*æ*>: † *ælf-* 14, † *bælc* 267. See below on phonology for discussion.

(b) <*a*>: *aldor*, 'prince', 32(?), (†) *aldor*, 'age', 120, 347 (in the poetic phrases *awa to aldre* and *to widan aldre*), (†) *alwalda* 84, † *baldor* 9, 49, 338, *wald* 206 (in the formula *wulf in walde*), *waldend* 5, 61. Unbroken and retracted *a* is a characteristic feature of Anglian, but one which is found not infrequently in early WS; *ea* is the norm in late WS prose.

All other instances show the expected <*ea*> form, and, here, non-poetic lexemes predominate (including *beald*, *eald*, *eal(l)*, *healf*, *gewealdan*, *weal(l)*). The correspondence between <*a*> spellings and poetic register (together with the reverse correspondence between <*ea*> spellings and non-poetic register) is evidence that poets, irrespective of their dialect, admitted a certain Anglian colouring in their compositions, and this accordingly precludes

---

[36] There is otherwise an orthographic distinction between *manna*, 'man' and *mon*, 'man', 'one'.

[37] Cook, xliii.

[38] See Klaeber (1950), lxxxix, n.1: Scribe A prefers <*a*>, whilst B has a stronger preference for <o> in his section of *Beo* (especially in ll.2200–3182) than he has in *Jud*. A sound change underlies the variation, but the mixing of spellings in a single text shows orthographic confusion; see Hamer (1967), §13.

interpretation of such spellings as indicators of the poem's original dialect.[39]

(iii) With the exception of *gȳt*, 2x, <*i*> represents the monophthongisation of *ie* from palatal diphthongisation of *e* (*-gifa* 279, *-gifan* 88, *gifeðe* 157, *gifu* 2, *scild(-)* 204, 304), whilst <*y*> generally represents the monophthongisation of *ie* from i-mutation of *ea* and *eo/io* (*byldan* 268, *fyllan* 194, *fyrd-* 220, *gyrnan* 346, *gyst-* 40, *hyrde* 60, *scyppend* 78, *-wyrðe* 153, *yldesta* 10, 242, *-yrfe* 339, *yrre* 225; *dȳre* 318, *dȳrsian* 299, *hȳhsta* 308,[40] *hȳran* 24, 160, *nȳd* 277, *scȳne* 316, *stȳran* 60, *-sȳfre* 76, *þȳstre* 34, *þȳstru* 118, *ȳcan* 183, *-ȳwan* 174; exceptions are mainly after palatals: *cirman* 270, *cirran* 311, *girwan* 9, *-scīne* 14, but note also *bīgan* 267, *nīwian* 98), except that <*i*> consistently represents the monophthongisation of *ie*, from i-mutation of *ea*, before palatals, (*mihte(n)*, *-on* 6x, *(-)mihtig* 5x, *niht* 3x). In simpler terms, with the seven exceptions of *gȳt* (2x), *gyrnan*, *gyst*, *scyppend*, *scȳne*, and *nīwian*, the reflexes of early WS *ie* are spelled <*i*> in the vicinity of palatals (25x), and <*y*> elsewhere (22x, including *fyrst* 324[41]). Scribe B does not make this distinction in his section of *Beowulf* and it was probably, therefore, a feature of his exemplar.[42] <*i*> also represents the product of palatal umlaut of *e* or *eo*: *(ge)riht* 97, 202. There is little evidence of the change of *y* (from i-mutation of *u*) to *i* before

---

[39] Three words in the list of <*a*> spellings are not poetic words. On *aldor*, 'prince', note Stanley (1969), 59: 'The spellings of the word **aldor**, 'lord' ... confirm that Anglian dialect peculiarities were regarded by West Saxon scribes as proper for verse'. On *waldend*, see Lutz (1984), 62: 'later Anglo-Saxon scribes who wrote Standard Late West Saxon followed two different spelling conventions for the agent noun *w(e)aldend*, one for poetry and one for prose'; the <*a*> spelling is poetic, and the word is associated, in Lutz's view, with the many poetic words for 'ruler'.

[40] Beside *hēhsta*, 3x.

[41] On *fyrst*, see Campbell, §299(a).

[42] Cameron, *et al.* (1981), 41–2, section A 4.2, for example, list 13 instances of <*i*> and 16 of <*y*> (including two of *gȳt*) for the reflex of *ie* from palatal diphthongisation of *e* in this section of *Beo*. All figures for the spellings of the two scribes in *Beo* are taken from Cameron, *et. al.* (1981). Gradon (1962), especially at 66–7 and 68–72, shows that this type of orthographic consistency is found in a number of Ælfrician MSS: 'a carefully written manuscript of the late tenth century, nearly contemporary with its original, will probably show *i* for Late Old English *y* [etymological *y* and early WS *ie*] before palatals but *y* in other positions' (at 72).

palatals (only *hige(-)*, 3x, beside *dryht-*, 1x, *dryhten*, 8x, *hyht(-)*, 2x). On the other hand, there is considerable orthographic variation in the representation of *i*. In late WS, in the vicinity of labials, it frequently becomes *y* (*anbyht-* 38, *bysmer-* 100, *lyfdon* 296, *-lyfigende* 180, 315, *nymðe* 52, *symbel* 44, *symel* 15; *swȳðe* 88, 182), but there are also <*y*> spellings for *i* in other positions, especially in words of normally low natural stress (*hyne* 6x, *hyre* 12x, *hyt* 174 beside *hit* 130, *hyra* 8x, *syndon* 195, *syððan* 4x, *þyder* 129, *þysne* 90, *þyssa* 187, *ðysse* 66, *ys* 6x; only *genyðerian* 113, has high stress). <*i*> for *ȳ* occurs in the proper name *Assyrias* (232, 309, beside <*y*> in 218, 265).

(iv) Scribe B sometimes uses the inverted spelling *swyrd* presumably for *swurd* from *sweord* (in *Judith*, 4x, *sweord* 5x; in *Beowulf*, 4x, *sweord* 19x)[43] mainly when the noun is in a non-alliterating position. This spelling does not occur elsewhere in O.E. poetry, and it is absent from the part of *Beowulf* written by Scribe A.[44]

(v) As well as *hyt* 174, *hit* 130 (*hyt* 9x, *hit* 5x in Scribe B's part of *Beowulf*, but always *hit* in Scribe A's), there are variant spellings of other third person pronoun forms (variation in *Beowulf* is given in brackets): acc. sing. fem. *hi* 2x, *hie* 2x (no forms attested); nom. pl. *hi* 7x, *hie* 17x (*hi* 6x, *hie* 9x, *hy* 4x; A *hi* 3x, *hie* 44x, *hig* 2x, *hy* 3x); gen. pl. *heora* 2x, *hyra* 8x (*hiora* 2x, *hyra* 3x; A *heora* 4x, *hiera* 1x, *hiora* 1x, *hira* 3x, *hyra* 5x).

(vi) A degree of centralisation of vowels in unstressed final syllables is attested by the following irregularities: in nouns and adjectives, <*an*> and <*on*> for dat. pl. *-um* (*hornbogan* 222, *yldestan* 242, *laðestan* 314; *toðon* 272); in verbs, <*on*> for inf. *-an* (*forlæton* 150, *tobredon* 247), <*an*> and <*en*> for pret. pl. indic. *-on* (*onettan* 139, *dynedan* 204, *w[i]stan* 207, *gewitan* 290; *mihten* 24n., 136, and note the MS correction *gebrohton* 54, with superscript <*o*> above underdotted <*e*>), <*an*> for pres. pl. subj. *-en* (*fysan* 189), and one possible instance of <*on*> for pret. pl. subj. *-en* (*wæron* 31n.). The larger group of verb spellings shows a rate of

[43] See Campbell, §324.

[44] Scribe A, however, uses *swyrd* once in *Christopher*, Rypins (1924), 75, l.17.

occurrence in *Judith* approximately the same as that for Scribe B's part of *Beowulf* but double that of Scribe A's.[45]

(vii) Centralisation is also evident in some unstressed, medial syllables. In nouns, there is variation of *-u-/-o-* and of final *-u/-o* in combination (*beaduwe* 175, *beadowe* 213; *medu-* 26, *medo-* 3x). Class II weak verbs show variation in the pret. indic. which seems patterned, with sing. *-ode* (3x, but *-ede* in *dynede* 23) and pl. *-eden* (6x); *-od(-)* is regular in the past participle (12x, apart from *genyðerad* 113).

These inconsistencies are few and in (ii), (iii) and perhaps (vii), register, phonology and morphology respectively reveal under-lying orthographic regularities. Because in (iv), (v) and (vi) the practice of Scribe B is the same (or similar) in both the texts that he copied whilst that of Scribe A in *Beowulf* is different, and because irregularity in the spelling of the vowels of those unstressed syllables in (vi) is common in late WS, these variations may have been introduced by Scribe B (though the centralised forms of the class II weak preterites in (vii) differ from those in B's part of *Beowulf* where *-o-* predominates in both sing. and pl.). Only *swyrd*, however, is an unusual spelling.

Certain invariable spellings in the poem are in the main characteristic of late WS. Figures for both scribes' spellings in *Beowulf* are given for comparison. Because <*io*> spellings are absent from both *Judith* and *Christopher*, some have suggested that these two texts were together in a previous collection before being copied for the *Beowulf* manuscript,[46] and so figures for that prose text (here abbreviated *C*) are also given:

(i) *(be)com(on)* 4x (A 17x, *(-)cwom(-)* 11x, B 4x, *(-)cwom(-)* 13x; *C* 2x, *(-)cwom(-)* 0x).

(ii) *dryhten* 8x (A 10x, <*i*> 15x, B 22x, <*i*> 1x; *C* 4x, <*i*> 6x).

(iii) *het* 5x (A 7x, *heht* 5x, B 6x, *heht* 2x; *C* 13x, *heht* 0x).

(iv) *hyne* 6x (A <*y*> 6x, <*i*> 40x, B <*y*> 24x, <*i*> 3x; *C* <*y*> 11x, <*i*> 0x).

---

[45] Cameron *et al.* (1981), 58–62, count 27 examples of vowel variation in verb inflexions in Scribe B's part of *Beo* and 13 in that of Scribe A.

[46] Sisam (1953), 67–8, Lucas (1990), 473–4.

(v) <*io*> 0x (A 11x, B 115x; *C* 0x).[47]

(vi) <*e*> between *sc-* and a following back vowel 5x (A 7x, without <*e*> 55x, B 26x, without <*e*> 7x; *C* 0x, without <*e*> 4x).

(vii) *sylf* 4x (A 1x, *self* 17x, B 16x, *seolfa* 1x; *C sylf* 4x).

(viii) *þam* 32x (A 10x, *þæm* 38x, B 43x, *þæm* 0x; *C* 15x, *þæm* 1x).

(ix) *þys(-)* 3x (A 6x, <*ı*> 8x, B 1x, <*ı*> 4x; *C* 7x, <*ı*> 4x).

(x) *ys* 6x (A 0x, <*ı*> 20x, B 4x, <*ı*> 11x; *C* 6x, <*ı*> 1x).

The spellings *dryhten* and *sc* with glide *e* appear to be characteristic of Scribe B. *Hyne*, *sylf* and *þam* are typical spellings of *Judith*, the second part of *Beowulf* and *Christopher*, and of these, the use of *hyne* is the most noteworthy, being a much less frequent spelling in late WS than *hine*. Apart from these, and the well known absence of <*io*>, *Judith* and *Christopher* also share the forms *com*, *het* and *ys*, but these are common late forms, and it is the presence alongside these of earlier spellings in *Beowulf* which is significant. Overall, the list shows the general consistency of the orthography of *Judith* and *Christopher*, beside that of *Beowulf*.

Finally, in the use of <*ð*> and <*þ*>, the orthography displays a remarkable regularity. <*ð*> is used, without exception, word finally (64x, including 12x at the end of the first element of compounds) and word medially (103x, including 7x after prefixes);[48] in combination, excluding the abbreviation *oðþ*, <*-ðð-*> is regular (11x, except for *oðþrong* 185, and the error *Iudithðe* 40). <*þ*> occurs at the beginning of the second element of compounds (7x, except for *searoðoncol* 145),[49] and predominates at the beginning of stressed words (38x; <*ð-*> 12x, of which only three, in 86a, 129a and 164a, are verse initial). However, in word-initial positions that are also verse-initial, there are very few exceptions to the use of <*þ*> (77x, <*ð*> only at 21b, 86a, 129a, 164a, 238b, 239a) and regular verse-initial spellings with thorn

[47] The figures are taken from Lucas (1990), 474. On the varying use of <*io*> in *Beo* and *Jud*, see also ten Brink (1888), chapter 4, Rypins (1924), xiv–xxix, and Hulbert (1928).

[48] <*th*> is used in the foreign proper names *Judith* and *Bethulia*.

[49] In O.E. manuscripts, the elements of compounds are written separately, so, from a *scribal* point of view, the beginning of the second element could be regarded as the beginning of a separate word. The scribes also frequently, but not regularly, separate prefixes from their stems (e.g. *oð þrong* 185).

are found in the preposition *þurh* (6x), the forms of the demonstrative that begin with <*þ*-> (21x, <*ð*-> only at 238b, 239a), the clause-initial relative particle *þe* (13x, with *ðe* in verse non-initial position in 346a), the clause-initial conjunctions *þa*, *þær*, *þe*, *þeah*, *þenden* and *þonne* (8x), and the adverbs *þa* and *þær* when clause initial (14x, with one exception in 21b). Conversely, <*ðe*> appears in combination with *þæs*, *þa* and *ærðon* (7x), the adverbs *ða*, *ðær* and *ðeah* are spelled with eth when verse and clause non-initial (37x, with one exception in 280b), and <*ð*> predominates in the relevant demonstrative forms that occur in the dip (54x, <*þ*-> 19x). Both lexical and metrical principles, then, seem to lie behind the use of thorn and eth, with the former marking initial positions and the latter non-initial positions, significant variation being confined to the word-initial, but verse non-initial position where these two principles come into conflict. The few exceptions in other positions may be scribal errors, or disruption of a systematic orthography by a scribe subsequent to the one who imposed it. Although these principles are similar to those used by Scribe B in *Beowulf* and Scribe A in *Christopher*—both being averse to non-initial use of thorn (there are about a dozen examples of medial and one of final *þ* in *Beowulf* 1939f.,[50] and eight medial and two final uses of *þ* in *Christopher*)—neither shows the remarkable consistency of *Judith* in this regard, and Scribe B in *Beowulf* is not systematic in the avoidance of verse-initial eth. If this system is the work of Scribe B, then he was more particularly careful in applying it to *Judith*; if a previous copier was responsible then a relatively short process of transmission between the manuscript which first contained this systematic orthography and the existing manuscript is likely (for the system would have been effaced by a scribe who used <*þ*> and <*ð*> indifferently).[51] In either case, such regularity

[50] The figures are from Davidson (1890), 43, who also notes that Scribe A in *Beo* uses medial <*þ*> and <*ð*> indifferently, as, indeed, he does in *Wonders*.

[51] The coincidence of compulsory, or quasi-compulsory, word non-initial <*ð*> in both texts copied by B beside the indifference of A in his part of *Beo* must mean that *either* B introduced this system where A merely followed his exemplar, *or* that it was in B's exemplar of both texts and was disrupted by A in his part of *Beo*. The latter is suggested by the evidence that B was the more responsive of the two to the orthographic features of his exemplar (e.g. in his use of <*io*> and other archaic spellings in *Beo* not found in A), the former by the unlikeliness of

demonstrates a surprising degree of respect for the copying of vernacular poetry in a manuscript not associated with Winchester (the centre of late WS standardisation).[52]

## *Phonology and Dialect*

The great majority of phonological forms in the poem are late WS. The spellings which traditional philology would suggest represent sounds not of this dialect are as follows (in chronological order, with restricted poetic use indicated):

A: Stressed syllables

(i) Germanic *ǣ* appears as *ē* (general in non-WS; 28x in *Beowulf*, 19x in B): † *mece* 78, 104, *þegon* 19. Campbell notes that *mece* is the usual spelling in the poetry and that 'this is held to be due to its being an Angl. word not normally used by WS speakers'.[53] *Þicgan* is not a poetic word, but its strong preterite form occurs in poetry (10x with *ē*, only 1x with *ǣ*) and non-WS prose, whilst the weak form, *þigde/-on*, is common in WS prose but occurs only once in poetry. Dobbie views *þegon* here as the result of 'close imitation of the older poetic formulas'.[54]

(ii) *æ* is retracted to *a* before *l* + consonant (an Anglian feature; 52x in *Beowulf*, 10x in B): 10x; see above for the frequent use of these spellings in poetry, irrespective of dialect. <*a*> is found even in late WS poetry like *The Battle of Maldon*.

(iii) *i* is unbroken before *r* + consonant (regular in Anglian): † *fira* 24, 33 (with subsequent loss of *h* and compensatory

---

such an unusual systematic use of these letters being evident in both the poems he chose to copy despite the fact that in other respects their orthography seems to have been quite different (e.g. the complete absence of archaic spellings from *Jud*). Perhaps B was a passive scribe in some respects, but actively changed his exemplar in others.

[52] But note that WS provides at least one other example of a standard orthographic system not of the Winchester school: see Gretsch (1994), 59–77, esp. 75–7, on the spelling of the *Fonthill Letter*. Ker, xxxi, notes that though <*þ*> and <*ð*> were for long used indifferently, 'in s. xi the general rule was that **þ** should be written at the beginning of a word and **ð** medially and finally'; its strict observation in *Jud* and the metrical aspect of the rule are, however, remarkable.

[53] §128, n.2.

[54] Dobbie, lxv.

lengthening). Anglian spelling is consistent even in WS verse like *The Metres of Boethius* (4x).

(iv) ǣ is found after palatal *sc*-: pret. pl. *scǣron* 304 (no examples in *Beowulf* 1939f.), either with (Kentish and Mercian) absence of palatal diphthongisation, or <æ> for *ēa* (by the influence on WS of Mercian spelling[55]), or <æ> for *ē* (with late WS smoothing of *ēa*),[56] which occurs sporadically in late O.E. MSS.[57]

(v) *æ* appears as *æ* before *l* + consonant + *i*: † *ælf*- 14, † *bælc* 267 (4x in *Beowulf*, all in B).[58] In both, *ea* by breaking should subsequently have been subject to i-mutation giving *ie* and then *y* in late WS, but *æ* represents the Anglian i-mutation of retracted *a*.[59] Campbell notes, however, that 'the name-element *Ælf*- was not given WS form (cf. *ielf* elf)',[60] perhaps suggesting to poet or scribe that <*ælf*-> was the proper spelling of the word as a compound element. *Bælc* occurs elsewhere only in *Genesis A* 54 *bælc forbigde*, the same phrase as in *Judith* 267a, which may be a poetic formula.[61]

(vi) the i-mutation of *ēa* appears as *ē* (regular in non-WS; 14x in *Beowulf*, 11x in B): *behð* 174;[62] but Campbell states that

---

[55] Campbell, §185, cites some early WS exceptions to this sound change which 'are, no doubt, to be attributed to the influence of Merc. spelling'.

[56] But *ēa* was not first smoothed to ǣ and then raised to *ē*, because original ǣ is not affected (Campbell, §314, n.1). It is generally assumed that *ēa* of whatever origin had become ǣ in Anglian and WS by the early part of the eleventh century (see Wright (1928), §63), but this is doubted by Bliss (1949–50), 85–6.

[57] See Schlemilch (1914), 5, 18.

[58] In *ælmihtig* the underlying form of the first element did not have *l* + consonant (cf. Gothic *ala*-) and <*æl*-> is the normal WS spelling.

[59] See Fulk (1992), 284.

[60] §200.1, n.4.

[61] Tolkien (1981), 42, suggests that the non-WS form *bælc* with *æ* before *lc* 'has been preserved because a scribe could not transpose it', but if *Jud* was so transcribed, other stems with *æ* + *l* + consonant + *i* (e.g. *gebyldan*, *yldesta*) were correctly transposed.

[62] Timmer, 3, incorrectly regards *ē* here as late WS smoothing of *ēa*, but fem. abstract nouns in *-iðo* regularly undergo i-mutation; see Wright (1914), §§371–2 and 613, and Holthausen, 22, *bīecð*. The spelling <*h*> for palatalised *c* in the combination *cð* after a front vowel caused by i-mutation cannot be explained if *ēa* (with a back second element) remained before a velar *c* causing smoothing (see Campbell, §§428, 483).

'spellings of Angl. type often penetrate WS texts'.[63] It should also be noted that the word is unique.

(vii) back mutation of *æ* is not restricted to positions where the intervening consonant is a liquid or a labial (a feature of Anglian and Kentish; 59x in *Beowulf*, 21x in B, 19 of which are in the following two lexemes): † *beado(-)* 3x, † *heaðo-* 179, 212. Timmer says that these 'should be seen as traditional words, appearing in WSax from the early Anglian poetry'; Campbell, on the other hand, regards them as 'quite a feature of the WS transcripts of OE poems', but later notes vowel parasiting in *beaduwe* as 'especially WS'.[64]

(viii) *ea* is smoothed to *æ*, with subsequent raising to *e* before *r* + back consonant (a Mercian feature; 1x in *Beowulf*, *hergum* 3072): † *sterced-* 55, 227 (cf. *stærced- Andreas* 1233, *Elene* 38). Timmer too conveniently interprets these forms as failure of breaking and confusion of <*æ*> and <*e*>; Fulk, on the other hand, sees *sterced-* as an Anglian form unfamiliar to a WS scribe, rather than a poeticism.[65]

(ix) *eo* is smoothed to *e* before *r* + back consonant (regular in Anglian): † *(-)ferhð(-)* 8x. The smoothed form is regular in poetry, including *The Metres of Boethius* (5x) and *The Death of Edgar* (1x), whilst the unsmoothed form occurs only once.

(x) *ǣ*, the i-mutation of *ā*, appears as *ē* (not found in *Beowulf* 1939f.): (†) *gesne* 112, 279. This may be either Kentish raising of *ǣ*, or Anglian raising of *ǣ* before a following dental.[66] The general absence of Kentish features makes the former unlikely.

**B**: Unstressed syllables

(i) *seceð* 96 is an uncontracted form of the third pers. sing. pres. indic. not corroborated by the metre (the verse is hypermetric if *seceð* is not syncopated, but normal if it is; the a-

---

[63] Campbell §200.

[64] Timmer, 4, and Campbell, §§207, 365, respectively. Mutation of *e* is confined in the poem to positions before liquids and labials (note *medo* 4x, *metod* 2x, beside mutated forms in *Beo* 1939f.), except for *sweotol* where *eo* and *u* are the normal WS forms (see Campbell, §218).

[65] Timmer, 5, and (also with criticism of Timmer) Fulk (1992), 300–1.

[66] See Campbell, §288 and 292, respectively. But the spelling <*geasne*>, found 4x in the poetry, shows that the word is difficult.

verse is an isolated normal verse in a hypermetric cluster and so the b-verse may also be normal).[67] Though uncontracted forms were formerly considered by some to be Anglian, they are regular in all poetry, and were probably 'associated in the South with the language of verse'.[68]

(ii) *hafað* 197 is Anglian (beside WS *hæfð*), but usual in verse, including *The Metres of Boethius* (10x).

Of these features, **A** (i), (ii), (iii), (vii), (ix), and **B** (i), and (ii) have no value as indicators of the poem's original dialect because the examples are common poeticisms attested in poetry known not to be Anglian. Five words remain as possible remnants of an underlying non-WS original, all of which are consonant with that original being Mercian: *scǣron*, *bælc*, *bēhð*, *sterced-*, and *gēsne*, but of these only *scǣron* is a common word, with the others being poetic, or mainly poetic, and (except for the difficult word *gēsne*) rare or (in the case of *bēhð*) *hapax legomenon*. As we cannot certainly distinguish poetic features from Anglian ones,[69] there is no means of knowing whether these forms should be interpreted in terms of dialect or register, for the features of an Anglian poem transcribed into WS would look very similar to a WS poem using conventional poetic linguistic forms strongly coloured by an earlier Anglian tradition.[70] A normalising WS copier transcribing the dialect might be expected to have had difficulties in regularising the spelling of rare or unique words, but we have no means of knowing whether *bælc*, *bēhð* and *sterced-* were indeed rare at the time, and there is, in any case, an obvious danger in resting an argument on rare words which might have had a different phonological history from common ones. All we can conclude from an analysis of the phonology is that the poem is either WS in origin or that it has been so thoroughly West-Saxonised in its process of transmission that its original dialect cannot be determined with any certainty, except that that dialect is

[67] See C96a.

[68] Sisam (1953), 124; see also Tupper (1912), 84–5.

[69] The poetic *beaduwe* with 'Anglian' back mutation and 'WS' vowel parasiting provides an instructive warning.

[70] See below, Date (vii), on syllabic *-ig* as a possible WS feature confirmed by the metre.

likelier than not to have been Mercian.[71] If such a process of West-Saxonisation took place, it has been effected more rigorously than is the case with other supposedly Anglian poems preserved in WS manuscripts, but the orthographic standardisation detailed above would inevitably have effaced the original dialect if that was not WS. This task, if it took place, was probably not undertaken by Scribe B, for he does not regularise the forms of *Beowulf* to the same degree.

### *Vocabulary and Dialect*

No aspect of the poem's language has been studied with a view to establishing its dialect more exhaustively or less conclusively than its vocabulary. Here there is room only for a brief review. Both an Anglian and a WS home for the poem have been argued on the basis of lexis. Wenisch lists the following words of the poem as Anglian, or generally thought of as Anglian (with numbers of occurrence, restricted use in verse, and incidence in poetic phrasing noted; those in bold are unstressed in the dip[72]):
*acweðan* (3x, all in the formula *7 ꝥ word acwæð*), (†) *aldor*, 'eternity' (2x, in the formulas *awa to aldre*, *to widan aldre*[73]), *beðeccan* 213, *eaðmedu* 170, *gefeon* 205, *gefrignan* (2x, once unstressed), *gystærn* 40, ***in*** (10x for *on*), *morðor* (2x, cf. *Andreas* 1170b *morþres brytta*), *nænig* 51, ***nymðe*** 52, *ræfnan* 11, *recene* 188, † *sælan* 114, *symbel*, 'feast', 15, (†) ***þenden*** 66, (†) *þrag* 237 (in the formula *ealle þrage*), *þreat* (2x, once in the formula

[71] But see Campbell, §§19–22, and Hogg, 4, n.3: the terms for O.E. dialects are imprecise and forms in the texts reflect scriptorium traditions as well as the spoken forms of particular geographical areas. We do not know which scriptorium produced the *Beo* manuscript (see Cameron, *et. al.* (1981), 36–7, but note Stanley's remarks about its provincialisms, (1981), 210), nor which first produced *Jud* (despite Timmer, 5, who incorrectly states as fact that it was written in the language of the Worcester scriptorium).

[72] Readings not confirmed by the metre are less significant in this regard: see Sisam (1953), 121–2 and Stanley (1995, for 1994), 12–13. In addition, *acweðan*, *beðeccan*, *gefeon*, *nænig*, and *þrag*, though stressed, are not confirmed by alliteration (that lexemes might vary quite freely in such positions is seen in *Soul I* and *II* ll. 2, 19, 20, 33, 51, 105, 114). To these might be added *gystærn* (beside the WS *gysthus*).

[73] On the fossilised morphology of this formula, see C347a.

*gumena ðreate*), *unlæd* 102, *unlyfigende* (2x), *wæccan* 142 (cf. *Beowulf* 1268a *wæccendne wer*), and (†) *worn* 163.[74]

Five of these are poetic, or mainly poetic, in occurrence, four are formulaic (and a further two may be); in addition, ten are attested in the WS poem *The Metres of Boethius*,[75] and fourteen in the small corpus of poetry accepted by Wenisch as WS or Southern,[76] so that, in the case of *Judith*, we cannot tell whether the use of these words shows that the poet was Anglian, or a Southerner using the proper 'Anglian' vocabulary of verse. Furthermore, of the ten found in the Northumbrian version of Luke's Gospel and accordingly examined by Wenisch (*acweðan*, *gefeon*, *gefrignan*, *gystærn*, *morðor*, *nænig*, *recene*, *symbel*, *þreat*, *wæccan*), only the infrequent *gystærn* is not found at all in either early or late WS prose, so that, with these, we do not know whether their use in *Judith* represents Anglian use or rare WS use.[77] Of the remaining five which do not occur in Southern verse and are not dealt with by Wenisch—*eaðmedu*, *nymðe*, *ræfnan*, *unlæd*, *unlyfigende*—three can also be attested in WS prose,[78] leaving only *gystærn*, *ræfnan* and *unlyfigende* as words which possibly indicate an underlying Anglian dialect. These facts, then—frequent poetic use, non-Anglian poetic use and occasional WS prose use—fundamentally damage this lexical test of dialect.

---

[74] See Wenisch (1982), 291–2, and n.90, 91 for references.

[75] ***beðeccan***, ***gefrignan***, ***in***, ***morðor***, ***nænig***, ***recene***, ***þenden***, ***þrag***, ***þreat***, and *worn*, mainly at points where the underlying prose is different. *In* is not straightforwardly Anglian: *on* progressively displaced *in* in the South (see Miller (1890–8), xxxiii–xliv, and note Pope (1967–8), 23, n.3).

[76] ***acweðan***, ***aldor***, ***beðeccan***, ***gefeon***, ***gefrignan***, ***in***, ***morðor***, ***nænig***, ***recene***, ***sælan***, ***þenden***, ***þrag***, ***þreat***, ***worn***, in *Mald*, *CEdg*, *DEdw*, *GenB*, and *JDay I*.

[77] See Wenisch (1979), 100–2, 137–43, 156–60, 169, 184 9, 189–205, 208–11, 230–2, 242–6, and 247–8, respectively. Stanley (1995, for 1994) 13–19, on Wenisch's remarks on the meaning of *þreat* in Ælfric, shows how he sometimes uses special pleading to discount inconvenient WS occurrence. The absence of some of these words from late prose, almost all of which is WS, may be a matter of date rather than dialect.

[78] *eaðmedu*: Bately (1986), 42, l.16; *nymðe*: Yerkes (1984), O.E. page 48, ll.5–6, with the form *nemþe* (and see p.xxxvi: this is a text with 'Winchester' vocabulary); *unlæd*: Carnicelli (1969), 97, l.14, and Gretsch (1994), 99, section 10, l.2.

The following items have been adduced as evidence of a Southern or WS origin[79] (with restricted use in prose indicated by ¶;[80] the word in bold is unstressed in the dip[81]):
¶ *beæftan* 112, ¶ *beheafdian* 289, ¶ ***binnan*** 64, ¶ *hopian* 117, ¶ *ofdune* 290, ¶ *onufan* 252 (and also the form *ēow* 188, rather than *ēowic*).
These words, however, prove to be as problematic as the last group as markers of dialect. With the exception of *ēow*, all occur with disproportionate frequency in prose, and none, as we might accordingly expect, is found in a formula. Prosaic register is, perhaps, confirmed by the fact that Wenisch finds limited occurrence of all but *hopian* and *onufan* in Anglian prose.[82] *Ofdune*, indeed, occurs commonly in non-Southern texts, and is only WS if the poem is late.[83] Their appearance in *Judith*, therefore, may show (probably late) dilution of the standard poetic register, rather than WS origin.[84] But, in any case, sporadic Anglian use compromises their definition as Southern in just the way that occasional WS use of 'Anglian' words makes their dialect character equivocal.[85] *Hopian* may be a West-Saxonism,

---

[79] See Tupper (1912), 88, Stanley (1971), 390, (1981), 198, and (1989), 340.

[80] As defined by Stanley (1971), 385–8.

[81] See n.72, above. In addition, *beæftan* and *ofdune* do not alliterate (though there is extra ornamental alliteration in 112).

[82] (1982), 283–4 (and for occasional non-WS use of other words which are predominantly WS in occurrence). On Anglian use of *onufan*, see Fulk (1992), 336, n.147.

[83] See Meroney (1945), 379, '*ofdune* originated in the north and spreading southward met less resistance in the Saxon area' displacing *niðer* (which is normal in verse).

[84] Other words in the poem which occur with disproportionate frequency in prose are: *arod*, *ærðonðe*, *bolla*, *fætels*, *forceorfan*, *guðfana*, *gyrnan*, *herereaf*, *herpað*, *genyðerian*, *oferdrencan*, *onwriðan*, *geswutelian*, *træf*, *þeowen*, *ðinen*. None is in a formula (but cf. 43b *to træfe þam hean* and *Beo* 919b *to sele þam hean*); none displays non-WS phonology.

[85] Although Fulk (1992), 323, regards the use of *ēow* rather than *ēowic* in 188b as 'the only very good metrical evidence of a Southern origin' for *Jud* (presumably because the disyllabic form would produce anacrusis in a type where it is forbidden in *Beo*), note that *The Vespasian Psalter* has *eowic* beside the shorter form, not instead of it (Kuhn (1965), 264, cites *eowic* 4x and *eow* 2x). In any case, such anacrusis does occur, although rarely, outside *Beo* (see verse 258b, and see Metre (5)).

as Stanley thinks,[86] but Fulk, citing early Middle English use in Anglian texts, follows Dietrich in seeing it as a late addition to the common stock of O.E. vocabulary, which seems as likely as that it is a WS word which spread in currency.[87] At the least, it must be admitted that, just as Anglian vocabulary is difficult to disambiguate from poetic register, so WS vocabulary cannot readily be distinguished from late usage. Finally, verses like *gesne beæftan* and *þ ge recene eow*, which appear to combine Anglian and WS features, show, if this is the truth of the matter, that some Anglo-Saxon readers, irrespective of their own dialect, tolerated even the immediate juxtaposition of features from different dialects; if so, texts with mixed dialect features might not be imperfect transcribings of poems from one dialect to another, but texts which were produced in that form.

## 4 Prosody

### *Alliteration*

The poet follows the normal rules about alliterative quality, with the following qualifications:

(i) Velar and palatal *g* alliterate, but the poem offers some difficulty in this regard.[88] If the poet pronounced the name of his heroine with an initial [j], then a number of lines with this sound alliterate with the velar (13, 123, 256, 333), but none contains another alliterating palatal.[89] Two lines , however, lack alliteration if the different sounds do not alliterate: 9 (*girwan: gumena*) and

---

[86] (1981), 198.

[87] Fulk (1992), 335, n.147, Dietrich (1853), 214–22 and *MED hōpen*. Wenisch (1982), 295–8, speculates that *hopian* is a substitution for *hycgan*.

[88] See Appendix I, Alliteration, section A, for details.

[89] The proper name *Judith* did not, so far as we know, become an English personal name in this period (see Searle, 321–2). The poet may, however, have been familiar with the names of Judith, daughter of Charles the Bald and wife of Æthelwulf of Wessex, and Judith, wife of Louis I. Non-English pronunciation (with greater alliterative licence) cannot therefore be ruled out. Ælfric, however, allows the name to alliterate with vowels: see Assmann (1889), 108, l.209; 110, l.274; 111, l.299; 115, l.418. See, further, Hutcheson (1995), 16 and n.59.

238 (*ongeaton: grame*).[90] On the other hand, two verses show alliterative abnormality if they do:

2a gifena in ðys ginnan grunde
149b hyre togeanes gan

The first has triple alliteration in a hypermetric a-verse requiring only double alliteration. Such alliteration is rare, but not unknown, in this metrical context in the rest of the corpus,[91] and is a further illustration of the extra alliterative patterning in the poem.[92] The second, however, violates the central rule that the b-verse must have alliteration only on its first stave. Cook corrects by transposing the verses of the line, but, as it also violates Kuhn's Law of Particles, with an unstressed, yet displaced, sentence particle—*hyre*—which is not corrected by the transposition, the problem goes deeper and the verse may be corrupt.[93] Though the evidence of the poem seems, on balance, to confirm its adherence to established practice, the rareness of the two sounds in alliteration by comparison with the frequency of their alliteration apart (excluding lines containing the proper name, velar alliterates with palatal in only two lines, but velar with velar in fifteen, and palatal with palatal in two),[94] and the fact that all six lines with three stresses alliterating do so only on the velar or the palatal, but not the two together (velar: 22, 32, 224, 305, 328, palatal: 2) - where alliteration of the two might have eased the poet's task, and would, in any case, have been statistically more likely, may mean that the poet was reluctant to use this phonetic licence freely.

---

[90] Verse 279a contains a self-alliterating cpd., *goldgifan*, that is not required by the metre. Timmer, 8, gives l.22 as a further example, but *gyte-* is a deverbal noun from *guton*, the pl. pret. of *gēotan*, 'to pour', with i-mutation of *u* (see Lass and Anderson (1975), 234). Ll.112 and 279 likewise have forms (*gǣst*, *gēsne*) with velars before front vowels produced by i-mutation, and this sound change post-dated the completion of the process of palatalisation before front vowels (see Campbell, §170, but note the difficult spelling *geasne*).

[91] See C2a.

[92] See Appendix I, Alliteration, section B.

[93] As perhaps is 279b *gæstes gesne* which has double alliteration on the velar.

[94] The same figures for *Beo*, ll.1–350 are 21, 10 and 1, respectively, and show that the *Beo* poet frequently used this traditional phonetic licence.

(ii) Consonant cluster alliteration: with the exception of l.55, the poet observes the rule that *sc*- and *st*- may only alliterate with themselves.[95] In addition, however, other clusters alliterate only with themselves on fifteen occasions, which is more frequent than is usual.[96] Although it might be expected that such alliteration would occasionally occur by accident, other explanations seem likelier in the circumstances. In ll.23, 29, 83, 164,[97] it is found in combination with rhyme, or other alliterative effects, and ought, accordingly, to be understood as a minor type of rhetorical ornamentation.[98] Five cases show alliteration on *h*- clusters, and, with the exception of l.23 which also has rhyme, the other four may show weakening of the aspirate before a consonant, rather than cluster alliteration:

37 hringum[99] gehrodene. Hie hraðe[100] fremedon
205 hlude[101] hlummon. Þæs se hlanca gefeah
214 hwealfum lindum, þa ðe hwile ær
282 hreoh on mode, ond his hrægl somod

Though there are two lines in which an *h*- cluster alliterates with *h*- and a vowel (251, 289), there are no examples of different *h*-clusters alliterating as happens generally elsewhere in the

---

95 See C55 for suggested emendations. Elsewhere in the poetry, *sterced*- alliterates normally. For *sn-:st*- alliteration, cf. *Capt* 7. Initial *sp*- does not occur in *Jud* in positions requiring alliteration.

96 See the list in Appendix I, Alliteration, Section B (1). There are also nine lines in which two of three alliterating positions show the same cluster. *Beo*, ll.1–350, by contrast, has only two lines of such cluster alliteration—99 and 334—and only three (102, 121, 277) with two of three positions alliterating on the same cluster.

97 On 23 and 29, see pp.66–7; on 164, pp.84-5; on 83, see below.

98 Cluster alliteration is certainly used as ornamentation in *Rim*, where it is very frequent.

99 Cf. *Mald* 161: *reaf and hringas, and gerenod swurd*, where the metrical type in the a-verse usually requires double alliteration.

100 *Raðe* is a by-form of *hraðe*; see Klaeber (1950), 277, section 4.g, and Scragg (1981), 83–4.

101 *Hlude* occurs frequently in the few lines of O.E. poetry which alliterate on *hl*-: *And* 1360, *Rim* 28, *Rid* 33.3, *PPs* 73.14.2, 123.4.2, *CPEp* 20, *Metrical Charm* 4.3. But see, also, C205.

poetry,[102] and one line which almost certainly shows loss of the aspirate:

249 wer[ig]ferhðe hwearfum þringan.[103]

All the remaining examples are of alliteration on *s-* clusters. Line 247 alliterates on *sl-*; and no other words beginning with *sl-* alliterate in the poem. Lines.125 and 199 have alliteration on *sn-*, and l.55, though plainly irregular in its b-verse, has double alliteration on *sn-* in the a-verse. There are no other words beginning with *sn-* in the poem. Four lines (80, 106, 240, 321) have alliteration only on *sw-*.[104] A similar tightening of the rules with regard to *s-* clusters (in addition to *sc-*, *sp-*, *st-*) is apparent in *The Battle of Maldon*.[105] Such high regard for alliterative rules in late poetry (if *Judith* is late) is surprising given the loosening of the rules associated with much late verse.

Various types of alliterative supererogation occur quite frequently both within and across lines. Though some instances of these may be chance, others are fairly clearly ornamental.[106] Lines 83–6a are a case in point:

"Ic ðe, frymða god, ond frofre gæst,
bearn alwaldan, biddan wylle
miltse þinre me þearfendre,
ðrynesse ðrym."

---

[102] Except in *Mald*; see Scragg (1981), 77–8.

[103] See n.170 and C249b. Note also 313a *hræw* in a line with r- alliteration. On the implications for dating, see pp.45-6.

[104] Note also the alliteration in ll.30 and 337. As there are thirteen lines in which *sw-* alliterates with *s-* followed by a vowel, the alliteration of *sw-* is not governed in the same way as *sc-*, *sp-* and *st-*. But *sw-* is not found in *Jud* alliterating with other *s-* clusters.

[105] See Scragg (1981), 52, n.136. But the alliteration of *sl-:sw-* in *Brun* 4 suggests that that poem is normal.

[106] Some alliterative enjambement and continued alliteration may be by-products of the poet's general use of syntactic enjambement (e.g. C116–17, 206–7, 280–1; ll.66–7 *on ðysse worulde/ wunode*, may be a further instance). On the use of ornamental alliteration in O.E. verse and prose, see Orchard (1995).

Judith's speech is a formal plea for divine aid, and its first sentence contains a solemn invocation to the Trinity.[107] Its alliterations go well beyond the normal requirements: there is cluster alliteration in l.83, and in verse 86a, crossed alliteration in ll.83 and 85, and, possibly, in 84 (*-walda:wylle*), and alliterative enjambement in ll.85–6.[108] There is also inflectional rhyme in l.85. The density of these devices suggests artifice, and their use appears to be appropriate to the formality of the context, effecting a degree of stylistic heightening.

## *Metre*

Appendix II contains a scansion of the poem using the principles of Sievers and Bliss, together with the relevant tables showing the distribution of the metrical types. The following analysis deals only with the main points of departure from the pattern found in *Beowulf*. The metre of other poems (especially that of known late poems) is referred to where relevant. Other remarks may be found in the Commentary.

(i) Single alliteration occurs in the a-verse in metrical types with compulsory, or quasi-compulsory, double alliteration in the following instances:

| | | |
|---|---|---|
| Normal Type 1A1 | 282a | hreoh on mode |
| Type 1A2 | 331a | Eal þæt ða ðeodguman |
| Type 1A*1 | 76a | ealdre benæman |
| | 112a | gesne beæftan |
| | 166a | ealde ge geonge |
| | 231a | ecgum gecoste |
| | 256a | Iudith seo æðele |
| Type 2A3a(ii) | 29a | dryhtguman sine |
| Hypermetric Type 2A1(1D1) | 9a | girwan up swæsendo |

Although the five examples of type 1A*1 without double alliteration constitute a larger proportion than is displayed by

[107] See below, pp.74-5, on the genre of the speech as *lorica*.

[108] Crossed alliteration also occurs in combination with alliterative enjambement in ll.137–8, 155–6, 214–15, 235–6, 310–11.

*Beowulf*, exceptions do occur in both 1A1 and 1A*1 in that poem, and some of the exceptional verses in *Judith* find parallels there.[109] Transverse alliteration in l.331 may compensate for the lack of double alliteration.[110] Verse 282a has a prepositional phrase following the first stress, a metrical-syntactic pattern which demands double alliteration in *Beowulf.*[111] Verses 9a and 29a are more serious breaches, being, in the former case, the only example in the corpus, and, in the latter case, an extremely rare example, of their respective types with single alliteration, and 9a is one of only five heavy hypermetric a-verses in the corpus without double alliteration.[112] 9a is also the a-verse of one of the two lines in the poem which unambiguously demonstrate the alliteration of velar and palatal *g*-, although these two facts may not be connected. Rhyme in l.29 may perhaps compensate for the lack of double alliteration in its a-verse (compare *The Battle of Maldon* 271, *Widsith* 115a).

(ii) Double alliteration occurs in the a-verse in both examples of type d4, where only single alliteration occurs in the same type in *Beowulf*:

240a þæt him swyrdgeswing
264a hyra fyrngeflitu

[109] Cf. 76a with *Beo* 680a, 166a with *Beo* 72a. In 256a, the licence is perhaps linked to the use of the proper name.

[110] Hutcheson (1995), 34–5, n.128, maintains that *eal* is invariably stressed in verifiably late O.E. poetry. The poet, however, is inconsistent in his handling of this word. If *eal* is an unstressed proclitic, then verses 331a and 341b violate Kuhn's Law of Clause Openings, having an initial dip without a sentence particle; but if it is a sentence particle then 16b violates Kuhn's Law of Particles, with *eal* displaced but unstressed. For the possibility that *eal* in 331a is a particle with ornamental alliteration, see Dunning and Bliss (1969), 77–8.

[111] See Kendall (1991), 118–19, and Hutcheson (1995), 112. The rule is otherwise followed in *Jud*, with the possible exception of 306a (see C306a). Substitution of *on hreðre* (cf. 94a) would correct the alliteration. Similar emendations appear to be required on four occasions in *Beo* (965a, 1073b, 2298b, 3056a). For discussion of the possibility of scribal substitution of non-alliterating synonyms, see Lucas (1988), 148–9 and n.32.

[112] According to Bliss, 129–30, 132; and 126, respectively. See C9a, and on 29a, Hutcheson (1995), 23, n.89, and 186, and below, (4), on the breach of Kaluza's Law.

Bliss treats such alliteration within compounds in light verses as accidental, and it may be so here, for self-alliterating compounds do not occur in the other sub-types of light d (with the probable exception of 279a *his goldgifan*).[113]

(iii) Two verses of heavy type occur in the b-verse, instead of in the a-verse to which they are confined in *Beowulf*:

| | | |
|---|---|---|
| Type 1A*3 | 312b | wælscel oninnan |
| Type 1D5 | 211b | sang hildeleoð. |

In addition, there is one b-verse of heavy type which is confined to the a-verse in *Beowulf* when its second primary stress is resolved:

| | | |
|---|---|---|
| Type 2A3a(i) | 244b | færspel bodedon. |

The second element of *wælscel* in 312b, though its sense is obscure, is presumably meaningful and so carries secondary stress. In 211b, the verb alliterates and so must be stressed, even though this entails a nominal compound appearing without alliteration. None of these verses can be corrected in any simple way.[114] 211b marks a major departure from the metrical rules of *Beowulf*, rarely to be found even in late verse.

(iv) Though the number of examples is not large, there is a single exception to Kaluza's law. By this law, 'long' inflectional endings (either those that end in a consonant, or a vowel which etymologically had circumflex intonation, or a non-inflectional final syllable) prohibit resolution, whilst 'short' ones (all the rest) allow it.[115] Where resolution is metrically necessary, then, only

[113] See Bliss, 67; Hoover (1985), 71–4, however, regards it as functional. Because the cpd. in 279a alliterates with itself, the double alliteration of the b-verse cannot be corrected by reversal of the two verses.

[114] Hutcheson (1995), 188, following Binz (1906),130, emends 312b to *wæl feol on innan* but the sense of this clause is not transparent. See further C312b, and note also C275b. 244b may be an example of a rare type, rather than an unmetrical one: cf. *And* 370b, 1262b, where cpds. are also followed by weak prets..

[115] For further definition, and full analyses of the operation of the law in O.E. poetry, see Fulk (1992), 153–68 and Hutcheson (1995), 78–96. Bliss, 27–35, deals with its use in *Beo*.

'short' endings may be used, but, conversely, where resolution is forbidden, 'long' endings must be used. The relevant metrical types are 2A3a, with necessary resolution in the position of secondary stress, and 1D3, 2A1b and 2A3b, where it is forbidden in the final stressed position:

| | | | |
|---|---|---|---|
| Type 2A3a | 22a | goldwine gumena | (short vocalic *-e*) |
| | 29a | dryhtguman sine | (consonantal *-an*) |
| Type 1D3 | 71a | weras winsade | (long vocalic *-e*) |
| | 163a | weras wif somod | (consonantal *-od*) |
| | 224a | grame guðfrecan | (consonantal *-an*) |
| Type 2Alb | 190a | arfæst cyning | (consonantal *-ing*) |
| Type 2A3b | 47a | fleohnet fæger | (consonantal *-er*) |
| | 128a | blachleor ides | (consonantal *-es*) |

The consonantal ending in *dryhtguman* is exceptional, for it ought to preclude resolution, but seemingly does not. *Beowulf* does not provide a single example of a 'long' ending in this position in type 2A3a.[116] As 29a is anomalous in its metrical grammar, its alliteration and its use of rhyme, it is, accordingly, either corrupt, or the poet has sacrificed some of the normal rules to achieve rhyme.

(v) Anacrusis occurs in three verses:

| | | |
|---|---|---|
| Type 1A*1 | 176b | to eallum þam folce |
| | 196a | gedemed to deaðe |
| Type 2A1 | 258b | aweccan dorste |

As in *Beowulf*, anacrusis is used in the a-verse with double alliteration. Verse 258b shows anacrusis with the two breath groups of equal length, where it is forbidden in *Beowulf*. The verse may be regularised by emending to *weccan*, but irregular anacrusis in type 2A1 does occur very occasionally in other poems (e.g. *The Phoenix* 17a, 372b, though not in *The Battle of Brunanburh* or *The Battle of Maldon*).

[116] Fulk (1992), 159–61, finds ten exceptions in the rest of the poetry. The distinction between long and short endings is observed too in *Jud* in the only example of type C with a resolved second stress, 157b *ond tir gifeðe*, where this stress must be followed by a short ending.

(vi) Vowel parasites before *-l*, *-r*, *-m*, *-n* may be ignored in the scansion of *cumbol-* (243b, 259b), *-feðera* (210b), and *fæsten-* (162a), but not in certain other verses.[117] Fulk argues that parasiting accounts analogically for one of the three metrical remainders that the poem presents:

> But it is also probable that parasiting in verses like *wintergeworpum* licensed a new metrical type, since *heafodgerimes* (*Judith* 308b) is the only verse of its type in the test group of poems.[118]

Alternatively, *hēafodrīmes*, with omission of the prefix *ge-*, would scan normally as 2*A*1, but, as the compound is unique, the metrical abnormality is, perhaps, better left untouched.

(vii) The relative proportion of verses belonging to each of the five main types is significantly different from that found in *Beowulf.* Types C, D and E together comprise 26.2% of the total number of normal verses in *Beowulf* (C: 8.6%, D: 9.0%, E: 8.6%, respectively),[119] but only 14.6% of the normal verses of *Judith* (C: 4.6%, D: 6.6%, E: 3.4%, respectively). Verses with secondary stress in addition to two full stresses comprise 15.0% of non-hypermetric verses in *Beowulf*, but only 9.8% of such verses in *Judith*, and heavy verses (with three stressed elements) are particularly uncommon (only 112b, 129b, 163a, 210a). On the other hand, there is a marked increase in type d (that type of light verse with a single main stress and a syllable carrying secondary or tertiary stress), with 16.0% of verses in *Judith* belonging to this type, but only 10.9% in *Beowulf.* The change mainly results from the *Judith* poet's preference for allowing nominal or adjectival compounds to stand as the only stressed element of the verse, where the *Beowulf* poet prefers to combine them with another stressed element. Although this shift involves no change to the normal metrical rules, it does contribute to a sense of a different

[117] 49b, 155a, 156b, 257a, as listed by Fulk (1992), 82. On 156b, see Hutcheson (1995), 51–2. Examples of parasiting in cpds. in *Jud* are given in Terasawa (1994), 117–18, and for discussion, see Hutcheson (1995), 130–1.

[118] Fulk (1992), 81; see also Hutcheson (1995), 185. The other two remainders, 265b and 275b, are dealt with in the Commentary.

[119] Using the figures in Bliss, Table I, Appendix C, 122–3.

rhythm in *Judith* from that of *Beowulf.*[120] Neither *The Battle of Brunanburh* nor *The Battle of Maldon* shows an increase in type d, though the latter shows fewer heavy verses than *Judith.*[121]

(viii) Bliss demonstrates that the poet of *Beowulf* avoids combining type A with itself, preferring to include one verse of this type with a different type, perhaps so that 'the norm shall not be obscured by the variations'.[122] It is commoner in *Judith*, with 24 lines showing repetition across the two verses.[123] The increase is connected with the feminine and inflectional rhymes (in ll.23, 29, 115, 304, and, possibly, 202). The poet's practice does, however, accord with that of the *Beowulf* poet in combining different, rather than identical, sub-types of A.[124] Only four lines (115, 164, 190, 213) are exceptions to this. A similar increase in A combined with A is found in both *The Battle of Brunanburh* and *The Battle of Maldon.*

(ix) According to Bliss, there are only 23 hypermetric verses in the whole of *Beowulf* (0.4%),[125] but it is extremely frequent in *Judith*, with 136 verses of this type (19.5%). This is the most obvious and important difference between the two poems. Expanded lines are, however, common in *Daniel*, *The Dream of the Rood*, *Guthlac A*, and *Maxims I.*[126] With the exception of l.132, which forms a singleton expanded line, all, as is usual, occur in clusters, and some, like ll.54–68 and 337–49, are among the most extended in the corpus. To some extent, as in *The Dream of the Rood*, there is an alignment of the hypermetric verse with parts of the structure. The beginning and end of the poem (as we have it) are both long clusters of expanded lines with a number of

---

[120] There appears to be considerable variation across the poetic corpus in these respects. *GuthB*, for example, shows four times as many heavy verses as *GuthA*; see Roberts (1971), 114. Heavy verses are less frequent in late verse, comprising, for example, only about 8% of the verses of *Mald*: see Griffith (1985), 96 and 276.

[121] For discussion of the possible connection between lateness of date and diminishing use of heavy verses, see Cable (1981).

[122] Bliss, 137.

[123] Ll.23, 26, 29, 70, 74, 101, 114, 115, 129, 164, 167, 190, 202, 213, 267, 296, 304, 306(?), 312, 316, 317, 327, 328, 331(?).

[124] The rule is outlined by Suzuki (1994).

[125] Bliss, 162.

[126] See Bliss, 162–8.

verbal echoes which also link them.[127] This may represent a rhetorical use of metre, but there are no such echoes between the remaining clusters. The first half of the poem up to the beheading scene is densely packed with long clusters (2–12, 16–21, 30–4, 54–68, 88–99), whilst the remainder of the poem, excluding its hypermetric conclusion, contains only seven expanded lines (132, 272–3, 287–90). There does not appear to be any further structuring of them in the first section.[128] The battle scenes are devoid of hypermetric verse (apart from the statement in 289b–90 that the Assyrians threw away their weapons) perhaps because the poet was concerned not to slow down the pace of the narrative by the use of a more leisurely metrical form.

Almost all the hypermetric verses of the poem are standard in type. Bliss discovered that a number of poems—*Beowulf*, *Guthlac B*, and *The Seafarer*—show only heavy hypermetric types in the a-verse, and light ones in the b-verse.[129] With the exception of three light a-verses, the hypermetric verses of *Judith* conform to this model:

| | | |
|---|---|---|
| Type a(1D) | 345a | to ðam ælmihtigan |
| Type a(2A) | 90a | geheawan þysne morðres bryttan |
| | 349a | ond swegles dreamas. |

The first is often emended to *a to ðam ælmihtigan* so that it accurately echoes verse 7a.[130] Verse 90a contains an initial stressed element, the infinitive *geheawan*, which ought to be stressed and alliterate as well. If it is stressed, the verse is the only one in the poem with postponed alliteration. If it is not stressed, its position in the dip is nearly unique in the corpus, for it violates the rule of the metrical grammar which forbids the appearance of stressed elements in the dip.[131] It could be corrected by reversing the order of the verb and its auxiliary, *mote*, in the preceding

[127] On the echoes, see pp.92–3; note also Bartlett (1935), 68: 'expanded lines often occur ... heaped at the beginning or at the end of a long logical group'.

[128] See Bartlett (1935), 69: 'It has been impossible to find any controlling principle in the arrangement of most of the long lines of ... *Judith*'.

[129] Bliss, 96.

[130] See C345a.

[131] Cf., perhaps, *Mald* 39b *and niman frið æt us*.

verse.[132] The third example cannot readily be emended. The remaining a-verses are all heavy, and, accordingly, (with the exception of 9a) all have double alliteration.

The combination of different types across the expanded line gives it a metrical diversity analogous to that of the normal one, but there is a remarkable lack of diversity from line to line which is unparalleled in the passages of normal verse. Some 62 of the 68 hypermetric b-verses are of only two types, a(1A*) and a(2A), and 35 of the a-verses are also of two types, 1A*(2A) and 2A(2A).[133] Only two metrical segments—1A* and 2A—therefore form the basic stress pattern of nearly three-quarters of all of these verses. Hypermetric types with the segment 1A are surprisingly uncommon, given their frequency in the corpus, occurring in only seven a-verses and four b-verses. Conversely, the poet four times uses types incorporating the very rare segment 3A, which he does not use in normal verse, and which occurs only once in hypermetric verse outside this poem:

| | | |
|---|---|---|
| Type 1A*(3A) | 10a | ealle ða yldestan ðegnas |
| Type 3A(1A) | 34a | nealæhte niht seo þystre |
| | 98a | haligre hyht geniwod |
| Type 3A(2A) | 8a | winhatan wyrcean georne.[134] |

This evidence shows a slight tendency on the part of the poet to expand the average length of the hypermetric a-verse by the avoidance of a common short segment, and by the use of a long one apparently forbidden in *Beowulf*.[135]

This comparison with the metre of *Beowulf* supports the conclusion that the metrical and alliterative rules of the *Judith* poet are almost identical to those of the poem usually used to establish the norms of O.E. metre. Features (iv), (vii) and (viii) may indicate lateness of date, but there may be other

[132] See C90a.
[133] The details are given in Appendix II, Table III.
[134] *GuthA* 741a is type a(3A); the related segment 3A* occurs only once in type 3A*(2A), *ChristC* 1423a. The appearance of 3A in *Jud* may, perhaps, be connected with the apparent failure of Kaluza's Law in verse 29a *dryhtguman sine*: the consonantal inflection of the cpd. ought to inhibit resolution, but, if it is not resolved, the verse is type 3A3.
[135] See Bliss, 94–5.

explanations. Only nine verses are abnormal: 9a, 29a, 90a, 149b, 211b, 258b, 279b, 308b, 312b. Three—149b, 308b and 312b—are also abnormal or unique in some other respect, which may suggest corruption, and three, 90a, 258b, and 308b, could be regularised by simple emendations. Verses 29a, 90a, 149b, and 211b also violate rules of the metrical grammar, as well as alliterative or metrical rules, and it is in this important area that the rules governing this poem are significantly different from those which operate in *Beowulf*.

## *Metrical Grammar*

The metrical grammar differs from that of *Beowulf* in two significant respects: its rules of precedence, in particular as they affect finite verbs, are different, and there is a higher proportion of violations of Kuhn's Law of Particles.

(i) Precedence: finite verbs in the b-verse usually either occupy the second lift, or are unstressed in the initial dip. If they occupy the first lift and alliterate, they ought to have been displaced from their normal position in the verse-clause, but the word occupying the second lift should not bear more natural stress than the finite verb according to the hierarchy of stress in the parts of speech as outlined by Kuhn.[136] There are few exceptions to this rule in *Beowulf*, though it occasionally happens in other poems.[137] *Judith*, however, for its length, presents a significant number of examples. Alliterating finite verbs in the b-verse may be divided into clause initial and clause non-initial examples. The following list of them gives the syntactic groups in Bliss to which the finite verbs belong,[138] together with a scansion

[136] Kuhn (1933). A brief outline is given by Bliss, 6–7, and Kendall (1991), 15–17, though the latter differs from Kuhn in his treatment of infinitives as sentence particles.

[137] For examples of this rare licence, and discussion, see Stanley (1984), 214–15.

[138] The groups are defined at Bliss, 10; 1, 2, 3, 4, and 7 are the relevant ones here:
(1) The verb is preceded by a stressed element;
(2) The verb is in apposition to a verb in group (1) which immediately precedes it;
(3) The verb is the only particle before the first stressed element;
(4) The verb is the last particle before the first element;
(7) The verb forms a whole clause in itself.

and the part of speech occupying the second lift (if it is higher in the hierarchy of stress than the finite verb):

(a) Clause non-initial:

| | | | | |
|---|---|---|---|---|
| Group 1 | Type 1A*1 | 25 | styrmde ond gylede | |
| | | 26 | manode geneahhe[139] | |
| | | 29 | drencte mid wine | (noun) |
| | | 44 | reste on symbel | (adj.) |
| | | 72 | læddon to bedde | (noun) |
| | | 164 | þrungon ond urnon | |
| | Type 2A1 | 208 | þohton tilian | (inf.) |
| | Type 1D5 | 211 | sang hildeleoð | (noun, cpd.)[140] |
| | Type 1A*1 | 255 | wæron ætsomne | |
| | | 260 | hæfde geworden | (participle) |
| | | 325 | wægon ond læddon | |
| Group 4 | Type 3B1 | 27 | þæt hi gebærdon wel | |
| | | 153 | þæt ge ne þyrfen leng | |
| | | 183 | ac him ne uðe god | (noun) |
| | Type 2B1 | 209 | ac him fleah on last | (noun) |
| | | 291 | Him mon feaht on last | (noun) |

(b) Clause initial:

| | | | | |
|---|---|---|---|---|
| Group 2 | Type 1A*1 | 23 | hlynede ond dynede | |
| Group 3 | Type 2A1 | 204 | Dynedan scildas | (noun) |
| | | 207 | wistan begen | (noun) |
| | | 223 | Styrmdon hlude | |
| | | 253 | Mynton ealle | |
| | | 262 | fuhton þearle | |
| Group 7 | Type 1A1 | 296 | Flugon ða ðe lyfdon. | |

The exceptional verses are mainly of groups (1) and (3); those in group (4) are not particularly unusual: the phrase *him ... on last*, 'in their wake', shows the noun functioning almost as a preposition with the sense 'behind', 'after', and phrasing with the

[139] 26a *modig 7 medugal* may be construed with either the preceding or the following clause, so 26b could also be treated as clause initial.

[140] This verse belongs to group (1) because the verb is preceded by its sub.: see C209b, 211b.

same order as in 209b and 291b is found in other poems;[141] *unnan* takes precedence in the b-verse several times in *Beowulf*.[142] In group (1), the verb has been displaced from its normal position and therefore behaves as a stressed element. Such verbs are commonly verse-initial in the a-verse in *Beowulf* and may be followed there by a stressed element with a high alliterative requirement.[143] There are only five b-verses of this group in *Beowulf* and none of these is followed by such a word.[144] Yet *Judith* provides seven examples which depart from this rule, and give precedence to the finite verb over all types of stressed elements, even including a nominal compound, the highest member of the hierarchy.[145] They are a-verse metrical-grammatical types which have been displaced to the b-verse. In group (3), the verb is in its normal syntactic position, but, in all six cases, must be treated as a stressed element or these lines lack alliteration. There are eleven b-verses of this kind in *Beowulf*—proportionately, a much smaller rate of occurrence—but two are followed by nouns.[146] Two of the six in *Judith* likewise precede nouns, giving a total of nine exceptional verses. Of these nine only one can be paralleled elsewhere in the corpus, and then only in a late and poor text, *The Paris Psalter* 87.17.2b *wæron ætsomne*. The frequency with which alliterating finite verbs head the b-verse in *Judith* and are followed by nouns complicates the scansion of b-verses with finite verbs which are in the initial dip

---

[141] *Finn* 17b *hwearf him on laste*, *GenA* 138b *Him arn on last*.

[142] *Beo* 960b, 1225b, 2855b.

[143] Examples are given in Bliss, 10.

[144] Verses 105b, 2344b, 2663b, 2899b, 3055b.

[145] See Kendall (1991), 160–1; Carr (1939), 429–35, gives the few exceptions.

[146] See Bliss, 12–13. The two with following nouns are 1137b *fundode wrecca* and 2717b *seah on enta geweorc*. Conversely, a-verses with alliterating finite verbs of group (3) are proportionately rarer in *Jud* than in *Beo* (only 194, 202, 227, and possibly 31); 227, and possibly 31, are the only instances where the poet allows verb-sub. order with the verb alliterating and clause-initial in the a-verse. In addition, there are no a-verse examples in the poem of Bliss's group (5) in which the finite verb alliterates, as in *bugon þa to bence* (*Beo* 327a), and only two where it does not alliterate (176, 278). These facts are connected to the increase in enjambement. Finite verbs in the b-verse outnumber those in the a-verse by a ratio of more than four to one, and there are twelve cases in which a finite verb in the initial dip of the b-verse is followed by the adv. *þa* .

before an alliterating stressed element, but which alliterate in an apparently accidental way:

290 gewitan him werigferhðe
311 Cirdon cynerofe.

The first, if stressed, would break the rule that an initial alliterating and stressed finite verb in the b-verse must not be prefixed, so allowing an audience to assign it to the dip, but the second must have caused difficulty, especially given the relative infrequency of *c-* alliteration.

How is this alteration of the traditional grammar to be explained? Comparison only with *Beowulf* to some extent gives too narrow a picture of the tradition, for other poets differ in this respect from the model of *Beowulf*.[147] Campbell connects verbal licence with the form of the lay, but there is no reason to believe that *Judith* was influenced by this genre.[148] If the poem is late in date, the loosening of the rules which seems to have happened at that time may be responsible for the change, though *Judith* is not loose in most other respects.[149] Rather, its metrical-grammatical peculiarity is quite specific and, significantly, fits in with other aspects of the poet's style: in various ways the text makes greater and more varied use of verbs than is usual. The poet is particularly fond of verbal nouns from the present participle,[150] and he lends added energy to his verse by the deployment of series of verbs in ll.23–5 and 162–4.[151] The quite frequent use of

---

[147] See Donoghue (1987), 166, 168, and his Appendix I, 127–77, and Grinda (1984), who note more prominent use of alliterating finites in *Met* and *PPs*. Unlike these texts, however, *Jud* is metrically normal.

[148] Campbell (1962), 16–17; Stanley (1984), 213–15, is sceptical of this view as it applies to *Beo*, and Donoghue (1987), 100–1, doubts its wider applicability. *Jud* does not share some of the features that Campbell regards as characteristic of lay form, e.g. the frequent use of obsolescent words; nor is its narrative compressed, as is usual in lay.

[149] But different late poems display different kinds of departures from tradition. The defects of *Mald* are mainly alliterative rather than metrical-grammatical: only 127b and 128b there show the finite verb stressed ahead of a word with a high alliterative requirement.

[150] These are listed in C5a which also includes nouns in *-nd* (on the distinction, see Campbell, §633).

[151] See pp.66–7 and 84–5.

verse-end rhyme highlights verbs more than the alliterative system does (e.g. ll.63, 115, 304). In the narration of the battles, the poet favours long sequences of short clauses, which necessarily involves the use of more verbs than a narrative with longer clauses and more variation. The heightened precedence given to finite verbs is, then, another means by which he injects vigour into his narrative. That the motivation for the change was stylistic rather than linguistic is also suggested by their remarkable clustering in ll.204b–12a, for no less than five b-verses in this section illustrate this feature: 204, 207–9 and 211. Yet the scene is the highly traditional one of the beasts of battle. In diction and imagery, these lines are almost entirely conventional,[152] but their syntax is completely new.[153] It is hard to resist the conclusion here that this is a tactical relaxation of the rules by the poet to give fresh life to an ancient formula, rather than an incompetent realisation of established grammatical rules. The effect of this rhetorical manoeuvre marks out the narrative of the poem from the norms of O.E. poetic narrative, and establishes the relative modernity of the poet:

> We may contrast our general impression of stasis based on high nominal density and relative paucity of verbs in Old English verse with our general impression of movement and action based on the greater and more varied use made of verbs by many Middle English and Modern English poets.[154]

(ii) Kuhn's Laws: there are only two violations (one uncertain) of Kuhn's Law of Clause Openings,[155] but six of his more important Law of Particles ('Sentence particles are grouped in the first dip of the clause. The first dip precedes either the first or the

---

[152] See Griffith (1993), 186–90.

[153] Contrast, e.g., *Brun* 60–5, which shares much of the vocabulary, but whose metrical grammar is normal: no violations of the normal rules of precedence are to be found in any other instance of the scene.

[154] Stanley (1994), 152.

[155] Verse 162a and 341b (if *ealles* is proclitic). See C162, and n.110. Both could readily be corrected by the insertion of *and* at the head of the verse, but the poet may be responsible rather than a scribe.

second stressed word in the clause').[156] In their normal position, sentence particles are not stressed, but displacement from the first dip produces stress. The violations of this rule fall into two distinct groups:

(a) A clause non-initial auxiliary verb is displaced, but remains unstressed:

| | |
|---|---|
| 49b–50a | þæt se bealofulla/ *mihte* wlitan þurh |
| 220b–21a | Hie ða fromlice/ *leton* forð fleogan |
| 269b–70a | Hi ða somod ealle/ *ongunnon* cohhetan |

(b) A third person pronoun is displaced, but remains unstressed:

| | |
|---|---|
| 52b ff. | nymðe se modiga hwæne/ ... *him* þe near hete/ ... gegangan |
| 147b ff. | ond ða lungre het/ gleawhydig wif gumena sumne/ ... *hyre* togeanes gan |
| 169b–70 | ond ða ofostlice/ *hie* mid eaðmedum in forleton. |

In the first group, the removal of the auxiliary to the initial dip leaves the reduced verse in each case metrically defective, with only three syllables, rather than the minimum of four. In the second, such emendation would not create metrical difficulty, but in the first two instances the initial dip is so far before the offending particle, whilst it is so closely connected to the following stressed element ('the nearer to him', 'towards her') that it could not be removed to the dip without the creation of major syntactic disjunction. Only in the last case may the aberration readily be corrected (by placing *hie* in the initial dip). If the other two are corrupt (and the alliteration of 149b surely is), the corruption is too deep to correct, and, given their syntactic similarity, it may not be scribal. The syntactic similarities of the first group, together with the lack of obvious corrections, also may suggest that these verses are original. If so, it may not be a coincidence that these breaches also involve finite verbs.[157]

---

[156] The translation is from Kendall (1991), 17–18.

[157] Most other aspects of the metrical grammar are normal and do not require comment, but see n.110 and n.146. On the treatment of light verses of type a as clause initial, see C158a. On alliteration in prepositional phrases after the first stress of the verse, see n.111. On the scansion of *unsyfra*, see C76b. There is one

## *Enjambement*

O.E. poetry varies widely in the use of enjambement. Traditionally, these variations have been seen as evidence for the dating of the poems, with the end-stopped style generally viewed as early, and the run-on style as late.[158] But late O.E. poetry—if *Judith* is late (see below)—shows both styles. *The Battle of Maldon* is predominantly end-stopped, but *Judith* displays the run-on style at its most developed, with some 90 medial pauses as against nearly 20 final stops.[159] Some have interpreted this as a defect of style: 'the verses give the effect of a never ending flow, but this continuous effect is gained at a heavy structural cost'.[160] The clarity of the narrative, despite Malone's view, is not clouded by the overlapping of syntactic and alliterative units. The end-stopped fitts clearly separate the main sections of the narrative. The speeches all either begin at the beginning or end at the end of a line, or both. The occasions on which poetic formulas from the b-verse of one line cross over into the a-verse of the next could also have helped an Anglo-Saxon to grasp the flow of the syntax.[161] Furthermore, sentences in *Judith* are not as long as in many O.E. narrative poems, and are noticeably short in the battle scenes, so the plurilinear unit is never a paragraph. Finally, variation is much more frequently introduced in the a-verse than in the b-verse, and, as Lehmann has noticed, a consequence of

---

exception to 'Bliss's Rule' by which metrically monosyllabic auxiliaries are confined to the first half-line of the clause (see Bliss (1981), 160–1, and Donoghue (1987), 9–10): *mæge* in 330a occurs in the second half-line of the clause, perhaps because the poet wished to avoid excess alliteration in 329, or because a scribe altered a preterite *mihte*.

[158] See, especially, Heusler (1956), 254–65.

[159] For statistics and discussion, see Griffith (1985), 115–28. Similar figures for *Jud* are given by Tatlock (1923), 7, and Phillpotts (1929), 173.

[160] Malone (1943), 204. The opinion is repeated by Leslie (1968), 77. Others regard excessive end-stopping as a defect, and the avoidance of enjambement can lead to the use of padding to complete a line; on this, see respectively Lapidge (1979), 217, on Aldhelm's Latin verse ('The fact that nine out of ten lines in Aldhelm are end-stopped suggests that Aldhelm was able to think in terms of only one hexameter at a time'), and Tatlock (1923), 7, on formulas as padding in Laȝamon.

[161] On this, see Nicholson (1963), 287–92.

this is the appearance of passages in which the b-verse contains the burden of the narrative, whilst the a-verse is appositional or supplementary:

Wiggend sæton,
weras wæccende wearde heoldon
in ðam fæstenne, swa ðam folce ær
geomormodum Iudith bebead,
searoðoncol mægð, þa heo on sið gewat,
ides ellenrof. (141b–6a).

Taken to extremes such a style would narrow the function of the initial verse to that of space-filler, but the *Judith* poet modulates the syntax.[162] It remains, however, a structure immanent enough to guide the reader through much of the enjambement, for, on some 40 or so occasions, part or all of an a-verse that is linked syntactically to its preceding b-verse simply amplifies or varies some or all of the content of that preceding verse.[163]

## 5 Date

The question of the poem's date of composition is inseparable from that of its dialect: if it is WS, it is likely to be late (i.e. late ninth or tenth century); if it is Anglian, it may be earlier, but it is impossible to say how much earlier. Furthermore, some evidence for the dialect may have chronological implications, or, indeed, be evidence for the date rather than the dialect. Fanciful and speciously specific dates have been given by different editors (Cook offers 856, Timmer narrows it to 'round about 930, but before 937'),[164] but there is no historical information to support their hypotheses. The following linguistic and prosodic features

[162] See Lehmann (1956), 150; he does not note, however, that there are a few sections in which the a-verse bears the burden of the narrative (e.g. 236–40), and others in which both verses carry the narrative forward (e.g. 67b–77a).

[163] The relevant a-verses are: (where an epithet amplifies a preceding pron.) 5, 11, 20, 31, 38, 66, 146; (where an epithet varies a preceding name or epithet) 17, 21, 22, 39, 58, 60, 72, 93, 124, 128, 142, 145, 155, 178, 187, 190, 207, 262; (with variation not involving epithets) 37, 94, 163, 164, 182, 205, 213, 214, 222, 246, 267, 280, 289, 304, 343, 344.

[164] Cook, xxiv–xxxiv, Timmer, 10.

(see the above sections, where relevant, for details) point to a relatively late date rather than an early one, but at best we can only date the poem to a century:

(i) the absence of early WS forms, of archaic spellings (if not removed by a modernising scribe), and the use of <*i*> for late O.E. *y* before palatals (if this was a feature of the original text).[165]

(ii) *hopian* 117 (rather than *hycgan*). The word is first recorded in Alfred (in the phrase *hopian to*), and in the poetry is attested only in *The Metres of Boethius* (in the same phrase) and in *Judith* (not in this phrase). Absence of earlier usage does not prove that *Judith* must be late, and 'late' in this context means only 'probably not much earlier than late ninth century'.

(iii) *ofdune* 290. The form seems to be northern in origin and spread southwards replacing *nyðer*, though concurrence of the two in the works of both Alfred and Ælfric shows that 'the idiom was unsettled in West Saxon'.[166] The dominance of *nyðer* in the verse suggests either WS scribal interference, or the prosaic register of *ofdune*. If the poem is southern, this usage suggests that it is also late.

(iv) the alliteration of palatal and velar *g*. The poem provides mixed evidence: two lines certainly demonstrate it, but verse 149b then shows double alliteration. Bliss shows how *The Battle of Brunanburh* alliterates palatal and velar, but *The Battle of Maldon* does not, concluding that 'the two varieties of *g* had ceased to alliterate in the course of the tenth century', which might suggest, in a simplistic chronology, a date between the two.[167] The poem does seem to mark a stage in the process of the cessation of this type of alliteration, but it is unwise to posit a steady chronological decline not affected by the conservatism of a poet or the genre of his composition.

(v) the preponderance of cluster alliteration which involves initial *h-* and the alliteration of *hw-* and *w-* in l.249. These may indicate composition at a time during the process of the falling

---

[165] See Klaeber (1950), lxxi, for the three distinctly early WS forms in Scribe B's part of *Beo*, and n.42, above, for the possible dating implications of <*i*> for *y* before palatals.

[166] See Meroney (1945), 378–9.

[167] The quotation is from p.102; the argument is to be found in chapter 16. See Amos (1980), 100–2, for further discussion.

together of *hl-* and *l-*, *hr-* and *r-*, and *hw-* and *w-*. In the case of *hr->r-*, the process appears to have been completed 'by the middle of the eleventh century ... whereas *hn-*, *hl-*, and *hw-* were still distinguishable from *n-*, *l-*, and *w-*'.[168] On the other hand, the matter is complicated by the known or possible existence of by-forms (*rađe*, *wearf*),[169] and by the fact that *hw-/w-* alliteration is not unknown in poetry that is certainly early.[170]

(vi) the unusual frequency of rhyme (see Appendix I).[171] End rhyme is more frequent in *The Battle of Maldon* and the Chronicle poems of irregular alliteration and metre (*The Death of Alfred* 1036 and *The Death of King William* 1087), perhaps because of the influence of popular poetry,[172] but it is absent from Chronicle poems that are regular (and from O.E. poetry in general). *Judith*, however, shows quite frequent rhyme but regular metre, and so cannot be grouped with these late texts. There appear to be stylistic reasons for the rhymes.

(vii) syllabic *-ig-* which cannot be ignored in the metre in *medowērig* 229a, 245a. Some 21 verses in the poetry display this feature,[173] 14 in *The Metres of Boethius* and one in *The Battle of Maldon*. Amos rightly points out, however, that these are both WS poems as well as late ones, and so *-ig* may be an indicator of dialect rather than (or as well as) of date.[174] There is one example in a poem thought to be early (*Exodus* 50a).[175]

---

[168] Goossens (1969), 75; for further discussion see Suzuki (1996), 305–7. Pope (1967–8), 129 and n.1, shows that in Ælfric 'the gradually weakening aspiration of *h* before certain consonants ... has gone far enough to involve most if not all words beginning with *hr* or *hl*, and it may sometimes, though very rarely, extend to *hw*'.

[169] See n.99 and C249b, respectively.

[170] See *LRid* 11 and C249b. Though this poem is Northumbrian, the development of *hw-* > *w-* appears to have taken place first in the South (but in the other clusters first in the North—see Luick (1964), §704). Alliterative licence rather than phonetic accuracy may be the explanation. It follows that this is evidence of uncertain significance, and that, unless a text is localisable, it cannot be dated accurately by this criterion. See, also, Foster (1892), 27 and Amos (1980), 94–5.

[171] On this as a dating criterion for *Jud*, see Foster (1892), 28–33, and, for criticism of this view, Amos (1980), 92–4.

[172] See Campbell (1938), 33, and Sklar (1975).

[173] For two slightly different lists, see Sievers (1885), 461 and Fulk (1992), 194–5. Further discussion may be found in Hutcheson (1995), 64–5.

[174] (1980), 28.

[175] On this, see Fulk (1992), 195–6.

Features (i), (v) and (vii) have only little value as indicators of date, and (vi) none at all, but (ii), (iii) and (iv) have some significance and are consistent with the poem being late ninth or tenth century in date, but the tentativeness of this conclusion must be admitted.

## 6 Treatment of the Source

The main source of the poem is chapters 12.10 to 16.1 of the biblical *Book of Judith*, which the Anglo-Saxons, following Jerome, regarded as canonical.[176] For two reasons, it is impossible to be sure which text, or texts, of the biblical story were known to the poet. First, although it is very unlikely that he knew the Septuagint,[177] he might still have had access to more than one Latin version of the Old Testament. Many Latin Bibles of the earlier Middle Ages appear to have been heterogeneous mixtures of readings from the Vulgate and the Old Latin version(s),[178] and some Anglo-Saxons are known to have used both, or to have known readings from both.[179] Some Old Latin influence is

[176] On Ælfric's acceptance of the canonicity of Judith, see Stanley (1985), 439. See, also, Marsden (1995), 450–1, on its shifting position in the canon.

[177] A-S knowledge of Greek may, however, have been underestimated; see Bodden (1986). For possible influence of the Septuagint (or an OL version) on the O.E. *Daniel*, see Hofer (1889), Farrell (1974), 69 and Remley (1996), 231–333. As the OL Bible generally follows the Greek of the Septuagint closely, it is difficult to distinguish knowledge of the one from that of the other.

[178] There are both accidental and conscious mixings of the two. On the former, see Glunz (1933), 13: 'The forms of the Vulgate text [which Irish, Anglo-Saxon, and Frankish monks] propagated seem to be mere chance products of the copying of the originals, whether these contained the Vulgate or a pre-Jeromian text'. Gregory the Great, however, offers a programmatic mixture: 'I shall expound the new translation; but whenever it is necessary for the justification of my exposition, I adopt the old translation in between the new one as testimony; for the Apostolic See, which I, by the will of God, am holding, uses both translations, and so shall also the work of my study be supported by both' (quoted from Glunz, (1933), 17, and see PL 75, 516). The opinion of the founder of the A-S church may have justified the continued use of OL texts by that church.

[179] Bede used the Vulgate and more than one OL version in his commentaries on the Acts; see Laistner (1937). Nichols (1964) shows that Ælfric's apparent deviations from the Vulgate in his translation of Genesis represent 'close translations of Old Latin readings' (at 11). See also Marsden (1994), and (1995), 53: 'The vernacular prose translations of parts of the Old Testament made in the

apparent in other vernacular O.E. poems which are based on parts of the Old Testament.[180] Not all recensions of the Old Latin have survived.[181] Furthermore, following the school of Alcuin, copies of the Vulgate also incorporated material from patristic literature.[182] Secondly, the poet's method of abbreviating and generalising the source prevents its readings from being determined with any precision.[183] However, the text that he knew undoubtedly resembled the Vulgate; for example, the graphic scene in ll.267b–72a of the poem in which the Assyrians stand around their leader's tent, coughing in order to wake him, is based on chapter 14, verse 9, of the Vulgate:

> And they that were in the tent came, and made a noise before the door of the chamber to awake him:

---

later Anglo-Saxon period ... are demonstrably based on good Vulgate texts but also present anomalies which indicate Old Latin contamination'.

180 See Doane (1978), 59–60, Remley (1988), and Lucas (1994), 53.

181 Laistner, (1937), 47, notes that Bede used an OL recension which 'differed substantially from any now extant'. Cross and Livingstone, (1974), 996, point out that 'the MSS of the Old Latin differ greatly among themselves, and it was largely the desire to remedy the inconveniences arising out of such differences that led Jerome (who asserted that there were almost as many different texts as MSS.) to undertake his Vulgate'. The difficult question of whether these differences represent different translations of the Greek, or different recensions of a single translation, is discussed by Kennedy, in Hastings (1900), III, 48–9.

182 See Glunz, (1933), 72–148. Such additions rarely altered the literal sense, being intended to clarify it by reference to patristic interpretation, so uniting text and commentary. There are also 'Christological amplifications' in the OL translation of the OT, see Kedar (1988), 311.

183 Note Marsden, (1995), 442: 'As far as the identification of specific Vulgate textual traditions is concerned, the Old Testament poems provide little firm evidence. Indeed, I have found none in either *Exodus* ... or *Judith*.' There are only two surviving complete pre-Conquest A-S Bibles: the Codex Amiatinus which cannot have been known to the poet as it was in Italy from an early date, and the 'Royal' Bible, London BL, Royal 1. E. VII + VIII, which is a Vulgate text. For Royal's few variant Vulgate readings in Judith, see Marsden, (1995), 371–2; for its very few OL readings, see Marsden (1994), 236–7. Surviving incomplete A-S Bibles of ninth-century date or earlier are listed by Brown (1989), 41–2 (none contains Judith). Some Judith readings are preserved in the Leiden glossary: see Hessels (1906), 19–20.

> endeavouring by art to break his rest, that Holofernes might awake, not by their calling him, but by their noise.[184]

But verses 9 and 10 of this chapter do not appear in the Old Latin version, which here follows the Greek more closely.[185] On the other hand, the poem provides a little evidence that he might have known a few Old Latin readings.[186] When Judith prepares herself for Holofernes' party, the Vulgate records that she 'dressed herself out with her garments', but the Old Latin, again following the Greek more closely, adds that she put on 'all her woman's attire'; the O.E. poet, at the analogous point in his changed narrative, does not mention her clothes but does describe her as 'laden with rings and decked with ornaments'.[187] When Judith gives the head of Holofernes to her maid, the Vulgate states that she told her to place it in her bag, but the Old Latin adds that this bag contained their food, and the poet makes the same remark in the same place.[188] The poet could have introduced these details here by reference to earlier parts of the Vulgate (e.g. the ornaments in 10.3), or from his own imagination, but the coincidence of his account and the Old Latin text(s) at these two

---

[184] See Appendix III for the Latin of the Vulgate; translations of the Vulgate are from the Douay version, Catholic Truth Society (1956).

[185] See Sabatier (1751), 784. The added scene in the Vulgate probably derives from Jerome's mysterious lost 'Chaldee' text of Judith, which appears to have been quite different from the Greek (see Charles (1913), 243–4).

[186] Relevant sections of Sabatier's text (based on five OL MSS) are given in Appendix III. The OL readings referred to, or given, in n.185 and n.187–9 are also, with the exceptions of 13.2 *soporati* and 14.14 *luctu*, confirmed by two OL MSS not used by Sabatier, Bodleian MS Auctar. E., infra 1–2 (microfilm Sf. W. 251) and Munich MS 6239 (see Belsheim (1893), 51–74). Auctar. E., infra 1–2, 'the Auct. Bible', is a mid-twelfth-century English Bible and gives both the OL *and* the Vulgate versions of Judith (see Oakeshott (1981), 30). Munich MS 6239 is said to be the oldest type of OL text and is somewhat briefer than that found in Sabatier (see Kennedy, in Hastings (1900), 60). The eleven extant OL MSS of Judith are often regarded as stemming from one original: see Kennedy, in Hastings (1900), 51 and 60, and Charles (1913), 243, but note also Bogaert (1970). The OL Bible is being edited at the Vetus Latina Institut in Beuron, but Judith has not yet been published.

[187] Cf. V 12.15 '*Et surrexit, et ornavit se vestimento suo*', OL 12.15 '*Et surgens, ornavit se vestibus, et omni muliebri ornatu*', and *Jud* 34b–7a.

[188] Cf. V 13.11 '*et iussit ut mitteret illud in peram suam*', OL 13.11 '*et misit illud in peram escarum suarum*', and *Jud* 127–9.

points is suggestive.[189] However, the Vulgate and the Old Latin resemble each other much more than either of them resembles the poem, and so, where the poet uses, or omits, material which is common to both the Vulgate and the Old Latin, or where his adaptation inhibits the exact determination of the source reading, the following discussion refers simply to the 'source', without prejudice to the question of whether he knew the one, or the other, or both, at any of these particular points. Unless otherwise stated, however, quotations and their translations are taken from the Vulgate.

The content of the source in all versions falls into two sections: a historical introduction, and the story of Judith. Its first three chapters deal with the vengeance of Nabuchodonosor (undertaken by his general Holofernes) on the various nations which decline to take part in his war with the Medes. With the refusal of the Jews to submit to Holofernes in the fourth chapter, the geographical focus of the narrative narrows to the Assyrian camp and the besieged Jewish city of Bethulia, and the broad panorama of peoples and places is replaced by an interest in individuals: Achior the Ammonite, officer of Holofernes, who advises his leader to leave the Israelites alone, and who is banished to Bethulia for his pains; Ozias, the ruler of Bethulia, who is persuaded by his people to surrender within five days following the exhaustion of their water supply; and the wise and beautiful widow Judith who is finally introduced in chapter eight. Hearing of the decision of Ozias, she convinces the chief men of the city that she herself can effect their deliverance. Taking with her only her single maidservant and her food, she travels to the Assyrian camp, and in an audience with Holofernes mendaciously persuades him that the Israelites have been abandoned by their God, and simultaneously ensnares him with her beauty. On the fourth day after her arrival, Holofernes holds a banquet for his servants to which he invites her. Her presence at the event excites him to such a degree that he drinks far more than usual, and, after the guests have departed, he lies in a senseless stupor on his bed. The heroine seizes her opportunity, beheads him with two strokes

[189] There are other echoes of OL readings: 30b *on swiman lagon*, 13.2 *soporati*; 111a *forð on ða flore*, 13.10 *à toro* [Munich: *de toro in terra*]; 281b *ongan his feax teran*, 14.14 *luctu*. See also n.196 and n.237–9.

of his own sword and escapes back to Bethulia with the head. She displays this trophy to the joyful citizens, and Achior is so overcome that he converts to Judaism. Roused by an Israelite sortie, the Assyrians unsuccessfully attempt by a general disturbance to wake their leader. When Bagao, his personal servant, enters his tent and finds him assassinated, the Assyrians flee in panic, pursued by the Israelites, who sack their camp and give the belongings of Holofernes to Judith. Joachim, the high priest, visits her from Jerusalem, and all bless her. The final chapter contains a hymn of praise by Judith, and closes by relating that she offered Holofernes' weaponry to God, and remained a chaste widow until the end of her days at the age of 105. The whole is a work of historical fiction which illustrates God's special relationship with the Israelites, showing that his power may manifest itself even through the hands of a woman.

The O.E. poem is a fragment: it begins in mid-sentence at the point where Holofernes is about to hold his party, and it is not known how much of the opening is lost.[190] The end of the surviving text is almost certainly the end of the poem, although it does not deal directly with the final chapter of the source. Enough survives, however, for the poet's approach to Bible translation to be apparent. His work is not a mechanical translation of Scripture in the manner of *The Paris Psalter*, nor a close paraphrase of it as may be found in *Genesis A*; instead, somewhat in the fashion of the poet of *Exodus*, the poet concentrates on the key dramatic event and makes consistent changes to the source which show that he has his own coherent interpretation of it. Unlike the *Exodus* poet, he avoids explicit reference to allegorical interpretations from patristic commentary, choosing instead to handle the book as a simple exemplum of the triumph of Christian faith over the power of evil. Campbell is in the main correct to state that 'the story as a whole is told to minimize the unique and to emphasize the typical',[191] although the poem is not entirely devoid of the unique, as the treatment of the canopy illustrates. Simplification, reduction and rearrangement are the hallmarks of the poet's

[190] See pp.3–4.
[191] Campbell (1971), 155.

method, and the following are the principal results of his application of them:

(i) The list of characters is much diminished. Bagao, who conveys Holofernes' invitation to Judith (12.12), who closes the chamber door after the party (13.1), who discovers his master's headless corpse and the disappearance of Judith (14.13, 15), and who, in a state of some distress, announces the catastrophic news to the Assyrians (14.14, 16), is reduced to anonymity and his part confined to the discovery of the body and the announcement (ll.275–90). Ozias, prince of the people of Israel, who blesses Judith on her triumphant return (13.23), and who summons men from all the cities of Israel to help press home the victory over the Assyrians (15.5–6), and Joachim, the high priest of Jerusalem, who honours her victory by visiting her (15.9), are both omitted, despite the fact that they are figures of social prominence whose actions, slight though they are in the narrative, give public recognition to the triumph of the heroine. With the exceptions of the added, unnamed warrior (148b *gumena sumne*) who is ordered by Judith to escort her into the city, and her maid, who is not named in either the source or the poem, the Israelites are treated *en masse*. The part of the maid is more limited: in the source, Judith bids her to wait outside the tent of Holofernes and keep watch (13.5), but this action is not mentioned by the poet, and it is Judith, not the maid, who places the head in their food bag (ll.125–32, compare 13.11). Even Achior, the most important character in the book after Judith and Holofernes, and an example of the type of the sympathetic Gentile, is eliminated by the poet, though he is an exile, and this theme greatly appealed to O.E. poets. This last change is particularly important, for Achior appears in both parts of the *Book of Judith*: chapters five and six are largely given over to the story of his advice to Holofernes and subsequent exile to Bethulia, and he reappears in chapters thirteen and fourteen, wherein, upon seeing the head of Holofernes, he swoons, gives reverence to Judith, and converts to Judaism. Achior's rite of passage illustrates the reversal of fortune that is one of the book's main themes. This sub-plot binds together the two parts of the source, and the poet's radical excision of it and its key figure demonstrates, as Woolf has shown,[192] that the treatment of the first section of the source in the lost opening to the poem must have been highly selective, and was in all probability very brief, for it would not have made sense to include Achior in the one part, only to exclude him from the other. The poet's generalising method, if applied to this highly detailed first section, must necessarily have led to its substantial truncation. The first chapter, for example, shows a sustained interest in proper names, many of them exotic:

> 1.5–6: Nabuchodonosor king of the Assyrians ... fought against Arphaxad and overcame him, in the great plain which is called Ragua, about the Euphrates, and the Tigris, and the Jadason: in the plain of Erioch the king of the Elicians.

By contrast, Bethulia is the only place name, and Judith and Holofernes the only personal names in the whole of the O.E. poem.[193]

(ii) The two remaining characters are flattened and placed in stark moral opposition. Although they are not complex or rounded figures in the source, they are stripped bare by the poet of whatever slight indications of character interest that they possessed. Holofernes is not an attractive person in the source. He is characterised by great fury (e.g. 5.2), violent passion (e.g. 6.1), and immoderate indulgence (see 12.20). His courtesy and hospitality to Judith (12.5–6, 17) are doubtless motivated by his 'burning with the desire of her' (12.16), although, beyond this observation, his intentions towards her are not made explicit, but his words to her—even if we choose to disbelieve their apparently friendly tone—suggest a character who is at least recognisable as human, and a voice which affects the role of host:

[192] Woolf (1986), 123.

[193] By this method, the poet also avoids the technical difficulties involved in the accommodation of foreign names with unusual sound or stress patterns to the alliterative and metrical structures of the native poetic form. O.E. poems with Latin sources tend to restrict the borrowing of proper names.

> 12.17: Drink now, and sit down and be merry; for thou hast found favour before me.

His invitation to Judith, as it is relayed to Vagao, is not a simple summons to attend his supper, but one which acknowledges her free will:

> 12.10: Go, and persuade that Hebrew woman, to consent of her own accord to dwell with me.

These are Holofernes' only speeches in the section of the source covered by the poem, and both are cut out by the poet, so eliding the disjunction there is there between the politeness of his actual words and the baseness of his presumed intentions. Conversely, in the poem, Holofernes does not speak directly at all, but the immorality of his intentions is clear. His orders are related by the narrator (e.g. 9, 32, 34), as are his invitation and exhortation to his warriors (8–10, 26–7), and we are told by the narrator that Judith is simply commanded to be fetched, with no concern expressed for her wishes in the matter (34–6). And the more dominant moralising voice of the narrator in the poem makes the nature of Holofernes' intentions unambiguously corrupt (though not explicitly sexual):

> þohte ða beorhtan idese
> mid widle ond mid womme besmitan. Ne wolde þæt wuldres dema
> geðafian, þrymmes hyrde (58b–60a).

These remarks have no direct counterpart in Scripture, but the poet has here taken and adapted the words that Judith speaks later to the Bethulians (13.20 'And the Lord hath not suffered me his handmaid to be defiled: but hath brought me back to you without pollution of sin') and placed them in the mouth of the narrator before the intended action to which they refer.

In the Bible, Holofernes is the general of Nabuchodonosor's armies, he is wealthy and enormously powerful, but he is not the king, and the point of his mission is to show that 'there is no God but Nabuchodonosor' (6.2). Scripture presents a marked opposition between Holofernes and Judith, but this is secondary to that between Nabuchodonosor and God. Although the fragmentary nature of the poem prevents certainty on this point, it seems that the poet has conflated the general and his king: he gives the former epithets which are more appropriate to the latter (12a *folces ræswan*, 21a *eorla dryhten*, 22a *goldwine gumena*, etc., and one, 66a *ðeoden gumena*, which is also used of God in l.91); he omits the sole reference to the king in the part of the source covered by the poem, in Bagao's speech of lamentation (14.16 'One Hebrew woman hath made confusion in the house of king Nabuchodonosor'); he has Judith refer to Holofernes vaguely as a 'heathen warrior' (179a *hæðenes heaðorinces*), where, in the source, she more correctly and technically titles him 'the general of the army of the Assyrians' (13.19). Had the poet retained the subordinate position of Holofernes—as Ælfric does[194]—he would not have been free to figure him as the embodiment of evil. Consequently, the relation between the principal characters in the poem is different from that in the source: where the source gives two contrasting pairs, the poem brings Holofernes into contraposition with both God and Judith. The poet appears to have sacrificed the symmetrical balance of the source in order to blacken irredeemably the characterisation of Holofernes: by so much as he is placed in antithetical position to the divinity, by so much is he satanised.[195]

The Old Testament characterisation of Judith largely precedes the point at which the poem picks up the story, but certain changes in the main action, in the narrator's comments, and in her speeches, indicate the style of her transformation. Chapters eight to twelve depict her as a rich and beautiful widow, extremely orthodox, of good repute, holy, even wise, articulate, courageous, and quite prepared to use her beauty to save Bethulia and to lie in the service of God. The moral interest of her character lies in the discordance between her religiosity and her mendacity, between her holiness and her murderousness; and the social interest in the reversal of normal gender roles—the enemy is slain, as Scripture reiterates, through the hand of a woman. She is the female form of

[194] He is referred to as *ealdormann* by Ælfric; see Crawford (1969), 48, l.774. For comparison of *Jud* with Ælfric's version, see Pringle (1975) and Magennis (1995a). On Ælfric's interpretation of the story, see also Clayton (1994).

[195] Further on this, see section 8.

that perversity, the devout assassin, but her potential psychological complexity is not explored in the source. She is an extreme figure, simply presented, though she may provoke a complex response. She appears, for example, at her most pious and lachrymose just before she beheads him:

> 13.6: And Judith stood before the bed praying with tears; and the motion of her lips in silence.[196]

This incongruous juxtaposition of sentimental emotion and homicidal intention is disturbing. The O.E. poet, however, exaggerates the simplicity of her depiction, and minimises some features he may have found troubling. He once mentions that she is beautiful, even as beautiful as an elf, *ælfscine*,[197] but he does not press the point, and his use of adjectives for her which mean 'bright' may indicate inner virtue rather than physical beauty.[198] He is not interested in her clothing, omitting the statement in 12.15 that she 'dressed herself out with her garments', though most of the details of her preparations precede chapter 12. He omits, too, the effect of her appearance on Holofernes: his heart was smitten and he was 'burning with the desire of her' (12.16). The compound *wundenlocc* twice describes her hair (ll.77, 103) and may refer to the statement in the source that it was 'curled' or 'braided' (10.3), but it is also used generally of the Israelites in l.325.[199] Lucas notes that it was the custom for Anglo-Saxon women to cover their hair, so that, whether *wunden* means 'curled' or 'curly', the significant point is that at least some of her hair is visible,[200] and this might have appeared daring enough to a Christian Anglo-Saxon audience. It remains a fact, nevertheless, that the poet scarcely mentions her physical appearance, and closes his poem without mentioning those parts of Judith's song in which she celebrates the seductive power of her looks:

---

[196] The OL states more simply: *Et stetit Judith ad caput ejus, et dixit in corde suo* (some OL MSS also omit *in corde suo*). In not referring to her tearfulness in the introduction to her speech, or to its interiority (see ll.80b–2), the poet may either be adapting the Vulgate, or following an OL reading.

[197] See C14. The precise meaning of this cpd. is uncertain.

[198] See C58.

[199] See C77 on this difficulty.

[200] Lucas (1992), 19–20.

> 16.10–11: She anointed her face with ointment, and bound up her locks with a crown: she took a new robe to deceive him. Her sandals ravished his eyes, her beauty made his soul her captive: with a sword she cut off his head.

Her words demonstrate her sexual knowingness and manipulativeness: she intentionally sets out to ensnare Holofernes with her beauty, thereby to cause his death. The O.E. poet, so far as we can tell, suppressed this aspect of her. That this lies behind the de-emphasising of her beauty, is strongly suggested by the single important change that he makes to the plot. In the original story, Judith accepts Holofernes' invitation to his party, and her presence throughout the entire event prompts him to become drunk:

> 12.20: And Holofernes was made merry on her occasion, and drank exceeding much wine, so much as he had never drunk in his life.

But the poet leaves out his invitation, her acceptance, her dressing, her entrance, his desire for her, their conversation, her eating and drinking, and the cause of his excessive drinking (i.e. from the second part of 12.10 to the first part of 12.20), and, in the poem, the riotous party has ended, and Holofernes' officers are unconscious before he orders her to be fetched. So famous is the story of Judith that any significant change to it must have been powerfully motivated, and the motivation seems to have been a desire to avoid any complicity on her part in the drunkenness and in the awakening of his lust for her.[201] The effect is to create a contrast, not evident in the source, between his terrifying wickedness and her fearful innocence. The Bible shows a woman who is able to manipulate men, who is cool under pressure, and in control of the situation. The poem presents a less invulnerable heroine: the narrator adds the remark that she needed God to rescue her from the 'greatest terror' (3–4); she seems concerned

[201] On the authority for this change, see pp.79–80 and n.274.

lest Holofernes should wake from his stupor (76b–7a);[202] her speech immediately before the murder centralises her emotional state (86–94) in a fashion quite different from the tone of the source. Her courage and her ability to act like a man are divinely inspired (94b–5a), and are referred to by the poet only after her prayer has been answered.[203] The heroine of the source is resourceful enough at the outset to request that she be allowed to leave the Assyrian camp by night to pray (12.5) in order, in reality, to establish a means of escape after the assassination:

> 13.12: And they two went out according to their custom, as it were to prayer. And they passed the camp ...

The poet, however, cuts out the element of deceit and says merely that Judith and her maid went on until they came out of that host (132b–5), without any explanation of how they managed this unchallenged, though the implication of the change from the limited guest list of the party in the source (to which only the servants are invited) to the larger gathering of the poem which all the senior thanes attend, together with the added emphasis on their unconsciousness (28–33a, compare Vulgate 13.2),[204] is that too many of the Assyrians were too drunk for any of them to notice or care about their departure. The poet, then, downplays the sexuality and sexual power of the heroine, and removes those devious aspects of her behaviour which a Christian reader might find immoral.[205]

(iii) The poet ignores concrete details in his source which are extraneous to the central story, or remodels others which did not fit in with his particular moral interpretation of it. Some drop out as a result of his removal of certain characters, like, for example, Achior's blessing of Judith 'by thy God in every tabernacle of Jacob' (13.14), and his circumcision following conversion (14.6),

---

[202] This concern is noted by Olsen (1982), 290.

[203] See below, pp.68–70.

[204] But see n.189: an OL reading may underlie this emphasis.

[205] Similar opinions about the poet's transformation of the protagonist are to be found in Magennis (1983), 333–4, Lucas (1992), and Belanoff (1993), 247–53. On the general lack of concern with, or discomfort with, sexual themes in O.E. literature, see Magennis (1995b), 1–27 (on *Jud* at 12–13).

though an Anglo-Saxon author might, in any case, have omitted this.[206] Others seem merely irrelevant to his purposes: the source mentions various parts of Holofernes' tent—its chamber doors (13.1), the pillars around his bed which hold up the canopy (13.10), and to one of which his sword is tied (13.8), and the curtain which separates its private part from the rest (14.13–14)—but the poet edits them all out. The canopy is the single descriptive detail of the tent that the poet retains, and his treatment of it forms an important exception to his reductive technique. In chapter 10.19 of the source—some way before 12.10, where the narrative of the poem begins—Judith sees Holofernes in his tent 'sitting under a canopy, which was woven of purple and gold, with emeralds and precious stones', and, in the same scene, he sees her and is 'caught by his eyes' (10.17); after she has beheaded him, she takes it down from the pillars (13.10) and returns home to display it to the Bethulians along with the head (13.19) as a sign of her victory. The poet interpolates his original description of it as—what has been called—a sort of 'two-way mirror', through which Holofernes can spy on his men whilst they cannot see him, at the moment in his new treatment of the visit of Judith when she is brought to his bed after the party (i.e. between ll.41b–6a where she is brought to his tent, and 54b–5a where she is taken to bed).

Both the revision and the new position of the description call for comment. The movement of the canopy from chapter 10 to the treatment of chapter 13 might suggest that the poet's eye was caught by an interesting detail from a part of the source preceding the beginning of his treatment of it, for it is not mentioned as if it had already been introduced in an earlier part of his poem, and, at first glance, it reads as a digression from the main theme of the narrative in this section (in a poem which does not elsewhere digress) ostensibly showing the distrust Holofernes has of his men. But the poet's rearrangement of the source and his departure from his normal method, which is otherwise consistent, suggest another meaning that is implied only. By his positioning of it at

[206] Cf. Ælfric's remark on this custom: 'Nu secge we betwux þisum þæt nan Cristen man ne mot nu swa don', (Crawford (1969), 127).

the very moment when Judith enters Holofernes' bed,[207] but before Holofernes enters the tent, and by his apparent invention of the idea that it could not be seen through from the outside, the poet protects the heroine from any lustful gaze of Holofernes before he collapses unconscious on the bed: she is hidden from him and momentarily placed in a kind of purdah by the same net he uses to hide himself from his men. Where the source shows Judith almost flaunting herself before the Assyrian general (12.15 'And she arose and dressed herself out with her garments: and going in she stood before his face'), the O.E. poet cuts out this verse, and, by a complete reversal, veils her from any impure look. Just as he introduces physical space between Judith and the riotous party, he inserts a physical screen between her and her enemy in the time of her greatest need. In this version, the lust of Holofernes is not stimulated in the slightest by Judith, but arises entirely from his innate evil. The poet's new reading of the characters leads to a new function for the canopy. After this scene, it is not mentioned again. This Judith takes and displays the head alone. Perhaps the poet did not wish his heroine to be thought of as a thief, but he was, more probably, disturbed by her statement in the source when she triumphantly displays the object and cries 'behold his canopy, wherein he lay in his drunkenness' (13.19), and so disassociated her from direct contact with an object contaminated by Holofernes' intemperance.[208] The canopy shows that the treatment of concrete detail in the poem is subordinated to its moral design.[209]

(iv) The poem contains other examples of the reordering of the source. In particular, some material from the last chapter of the book, which is dominated by the song of Judith and whose substance does not form the end of the poem, has shaped certain

[207] Note that the syntax of 54b indicates *completed* action, the result of the process of bringing her to his bed. See further C54b.

[208] Similarly, though the Vulgate states that she kills Holofernes with his own sword, the poem does not mention that it is his, and where the Vulgate has her roll away his headless body (13.10), the poem substitutes the head rolling away as a consequence of the second blow. There is less physical contact in the poem between Holofernes, or Holofernes' things, and the heroine. Only the statement in 13.9 where she takes him by the hair in order the more readily to slay him is kept (98b–103a).

[209] Further on the canopy, see pp.78–9.

other sections of it. In 15.14, the spoils of Holofernes' goods are given by the Bethulians to Judith:

> But all those things that were proved to be the peculiar goods of Holofernes they gave to Judith in gold, and silver, and garments and precious stones, and all household stuff.

The Old Latin adds to the list his tent and bed. The poem, however, gives a somewhat different version in ll.334–41: along with his treasure and unspecified private property (339b *sundoryrfes*), they give her his sword, helmet and mailcoat. This list has been changed by reference to 16.23, in which Judith offers up 'as an anathema of oblivion all the arms of Holofernes, which the people gave her', and the alteration is motivated by the accommodation of the story to the heroic mode of O.E. poetry, where swords and helmets are common, but tents and beds are not. In 16.20–1, Judith sings of the vengeance that the Lord will take on any nation that rises up against the Israelites:

> In the day of judgment he will visit them: for he will give fire, and worms into their flesh, that they may burn, and may feel for ever.

Hell, in the sense of Gehenna, the place of retribution for evil deeds, is rarely mentioned in the Old Testament, but it is manifest in her words here, and recurs in the description of the place to which Holofernes' soul is condemned in ll.112–20. His spirit, likewise, suffers eternally (114b *syððan æfre*, 120 *awa to aldre, butan ende forð*) in a place of fire (116b *in helle bryne*) where there are worms which bind him (115a *wyrmum bewunden*, 119a *wyrmsele*). This reorganisation has been caused by the poet's Christianisation of the source. The impact of these two traditions—vernacular poetry and Christian doctrine on the poet's interpretation of his Scriptural source merits separate treatment.

## 7 *Judith* and Old English Poetic Tradition

The accommodation of the source to the conventions of O.E. poetry essentially means that the poet's interpretation is dressed up in heroic fashion. The characteristic ideas and themes of the poetry are not, however, arbitrarily tagged on, but are carefully disposed in such a manner as to bring out the moral message. The opposition between Judith and Holofernes, and the conflict between the Hebrews and the Assyrians, represent successive moral oppositions of good and evil, but they are also imaged by the poet as contrasts of the heroic and the anti-heroic. Whilst this assimilation to the native poetic tradition works simply with the presentation of the Hebrew army and the battle, the interpretation of the protagonist as hero and the inversion of convention to establish Holofernes as anti-hero are more complex.

The victory of the Hebrews over the Assyrians is viewed by the poet as the manifestation of their spiritual ascendancy, so the fight displays the most obvious amplification of the source with a straightforward adaptation to the conventions of O.E. poetic battle narrative. Indeed, those parts of the second half of the poem where the focus shifts to the war between the followers find only the briefest literal authority in Scripture: the scene of the Hebrews' approach to battle (ll.199–220a) is an elaboration of the brief statement in chapter 14.7 that 'every man took his arms and they went out with a great noise and shouting', and the battle which ensues in ll.220b–41a is a complete invention by the poet, being an imminent rather than an actual event in the source (14.12). The return to battle narrative and the flight of the Assyrians in ll.290b–314a is a markedly different rendition of chapter 15.1–6 (with, for example, Ozias' summoning of the Israelite army omitted), and the spoiling of the Assyrian camp in ll.314b–42a shows changes from the parallel scene in 15.7–8 and 15.13–14 with an expansion of its heroic potential. Close analogues to almost all of what has been added can, however, be found in other O.E. poems, and other O.E. poets insert battle scenes into their compositions with little or no precedent in their sources.[210] The following are the most prominent motifs in the scenes of the approach to battle and the battle itself which are traditional: bearing of banners (201b), noise of shields (204b–5a), beasts of battle (205b–12a, 295–6a), an initial shower of arrows and spears (220b–3a, 224b–5a), warriors' rage (223b–4a, 225b, 305b–6a), unsheathing of swords (229b–31a), ceaseless pursuit of the fleeing enemy (236–7, 298b–300a), an interruption by the narrator in the first person (246b), splitting of the shield-wall (302–5a), and the small number of foes who return home alive (311b–12a).[211] Some of the parallels to these themes in other poems also show remarkable verbal similarities with their expression here. For example, the passage in which the Hebrews draw their swords closely echoes the phrasing and word order of its analogue in *Genesis A*:

Mundum brugdon
scealcas of sceaðum scirmæled swyrd,
ecgum gecoste (229b–31a)

Handum brugdon
hæleð of scæðum hringmæled sweord,
ecgum dihtig (*Genesis A* 1991b–3a).

Apart from the substitution of synonyms (*mund:hand*, *scealc: hæleð*), and some slight variation (*scir-:hring-*, *gecoste:dihtig*), these lines are identical. The poet of *Judith* is unlikely to have been influenced by *Genesis A*; such a supposition would lead to the conclusion that he was influenced to much the same degree by most of the poetry. Rather, the narration of battle is central to

[210] Note the added battle in *GenA* 1960–2095, the much expanded one in *El* 18–56a, 94b–143, and the interpretation of the flight across the Red Sea as a battle in *Ex*. The depiction of the flight of the Assyrians as a battle is not, however, unique, cf. the illustration of this scene in the Winchester Bible (Oakeshott (1981), facing 19).

[211] Cf. the following passages in the surviving poetic corpus which most closely resemble these motifs in *Jud*: advance with banners, *Ex* 342b–3a; noise of shields, *El* 50b; beasts of battle, *Brun* 60–5a; shower of arrows, *El* 116–20; warriors' rage, *Mald* 295–6a; unsheathing of swords, *GenA* 1991b–3a; the pursuit, *El* 138–40a; narrator's intervention, *GenA* 2060a; splitting of shield-wall, *Brun* 5b–6a; few return home, *El* 142b–3.

heroic poetry, and therefore highly traditional in its expression.[212] The poet's choice of familiar heroic theme to express the spiritual ascendence of the Hebrews naturally involved its articulation in familiar language.

In the Greek original, the heroine's lying is the frequent cause of dramatic irony: when she speaks of her lord, Holofernes and the Assyrians take her to refer, as she intends, to Holofernes, but the reader knows that, in fact, she refers to God.[213] Most of this is removed from the Vulgate;[214] but the O.E. version is reinvested with ironic meaning. Having stripped away the mendacity of the protagonist, the poet cannot place ironic words in her mouth. Instead, the utterances of the narrator and the structuring by the poet, rather than the speeches of the heroine, are responsible for the new doubleness of meaning. But the purpose of the irony remains similar to that of the Greek original: to belittle Holofernes and the Assyrians. The narrator of *Judith*, like certain other narrators of O.E. poems, but unlike the narrator of the Vulgate account, injects dramatic irony into the narration.[215] We know, for example, that Holofernes and his officers are doomed:

hie þæt fæge þegon,
rofe rondwiggende, þeah ðæs se rica ne wende,
egesful eorla dryhten (19b–21a).

We know that God will not allow him to rape Judith (59b–61a), that he is soon to die (63b–65a), that the Assyrians will not succeed in their attempt to wake their lord (274b) and are defeated (265b–7a, 272b). As the narrator tells us, however, they know none of this, and the close juxtaposition of our knowledge and their ignorance makes them appear ridiculous. Placed

---

[212] Heinemann (1970), 83, regards the added battle scenes in *Jud* as unusual in the O.E. corpus because the poet 'quite obviously sympathizes with the offensive army. [O.E.] poets usually ... support the defensive army'. But the Bethulians have hitherto been in the defensive position, besieged in Bethulia, and are now taking vengeance.

[213] See Charles (1913), 260–1, chapter 11.6, 11.16, 12.4, etc.; and for discussion of the ironic use of 'my lord', see Dancy (1972), 110.

[214] See, however, C66a.

[215] Cf. *Beo* 180–8, 734–6a, 1233b–5, 2341–4, and *Mald* 89–90. The irony in these poems, however, functions to different effect.

immediately after the narrator's comment that Holofernes did not know that those who drank were doomed (19b–21a) is the scene of his riotous drunkenness (21b–7); inserted between the narrator's remarks on the imminent defeat of the Assyrians (265b–7a, 272b) is the scene of their noisy attempt to wake Holofernes and alert him to the battle. Such ironic juxtaposition leads in these instances to comic effect. The poet also uses heroic conventions ironically: the relationship between Holofernes and his men is a parody of the usual one between the leader of men and his followers in O.E. poetry.[216] He has retainers (10a *ðegnas*, 38a *anbyhtscealcas*), and they are brave warriors (17a *bealde byrnwiggende*, 20a *rofe rondwiggende*). He is their gold-friend (22a *goldwine gumena*), and is frequently referred to in the opening scene by epithets which label his role as lord of men (9b *se gumena baldor*, 21a *eorla dryhten*, 39a *byrnwigena brego*, etc.). He exhorts his retainers (26a *manode*) and commands his warriors (32b, 34b, *het*), and they are always prompt to do his bidding (10b *ofstum miclum*, 37b *hraðe*, 41b *fromlice*, 55a *snude*). That this picture is, however, to be read ironically is not left in doubt. The narrator makes it abundantly clear that Holofernes is a perversion of the heroic chieftain. He is the evil one (28a *se inwidda*, 48b *se bealofulla*), terrifying (4b *þæs hehstan brogan*, 21a *egesful*) and steeped in violence (34b *niða geblonden*). Heroic language for him is used alongside such remarks with pointed inappropriateness: he is *egesful eorla dryhten*, 'the terrible lord of noble men', *swiðmod sinces brytta*, 'the arrogant giver of treasure' (30a), *se bealofulla ... wigena baldor*, 'the wicked prince of warriors' (48b–9b). That the benevolent relation between lord and men invoked by the epithets *goldwine gumena* and *sinces brytta* is inapplicable to this lord and these men is the most obvious meaning of the description of the canopy as a 'two-way mirror' behind which Holofernes may spy on his men, though hidden from them. He does not trust them and they do his bidding out of fear, not respect. There is also an incongruous

[216] Stanley states that 'there is no parody in Old English literature', but allows that 'moments of *literary* awareness of incongruities or moral or social insufficiencies may lead to touches of parody in works that are not parodies as a whole', and accepts that there is irony at the Assyrians' expense in *Jud*: see Stanley (1988), 3 and 69, and (1994), 165, respectively.

relationship between language and action. He exhorts his men to drink deep at the banquet, not to stiffen their resolve in battle.[217] His retainers are described as stout-hearted (55b *stercedferhðe*) shield-warriors (42a *lindwiggende*), but they are here leading a woman to bed, not marching to war. A change from the source, and structural contrast sharpen this irony: the solitary Bagao who leads Judith to Holofernes' tent is replaced by an armed band, and the Hebrews' speedy advance to battle (200b, 212b *stopon*) in retrospect makes the Assyrian 'advance' on Judith's guest-house and their 'retreat' from Holofernes' tent appear absurd (39b, 69b *stopon*).[218] Style—and in particular rhyme—is also a vehicle for the poet's irony. As Stanley has noticed, 'in the phrase *slegefæge hæleð* ... the rhyming adjective, merrily as it seems, proclaim[s] the heroes' end';[219] rhyme is used for exactly the same purpose to announce the end of Holofernes in 61b–63:

Gewat ða se deofulcunda ...
bealofull his beddes neosan, þær he sceolde his blæd forleosan

and sound effects likewise accompany Holofernes' storming drunkenness and his retainers' enforced drinking:

Ða wearð Holofernus
goldwine gumena, on gytesalum:
hloh ond hlydde, hlynede ond dynede,
þæt mihten fira bearn feorran gehyran
hu se stiðmoda styrmde ond gylede ...
Swa se inwidda ofer ealne dæg
dryhtguman sine drencte mid wine (21b–5, 28–9).

The remarkable accumulation of assonant, and nearly tautological verbs, the rhyme both within and across verses, and the consonant cluster alliteration all exaggerate the noisiness. Stylistic excess

---

[217] Contrast the use of *manian*, 'to urge (to do what ought to be done)', in l.26 with *Mald* 228, 231. Holofernes thinks it proper to urge his men to become drunk, but the poet takes a different view.
[218] Further discussion of such ironic parallels and contrasts may be found in Pringle (1975), 93–4, and Tyler (1992), 16–19.
[219] Stanley (1994), 165.

mimics excessive behaviour. This scene of feasting is a travesty of the heroic banquet in the hall,[220] the debauched prelude to an intended rape, not the joyful celebration of victory in battle, and aural stylistic devices are so distinctive a feature of it as to suggest self-conscious artifice by the poet.[221] This ironic and comic overturning of heroic conventions is the special achievement of the poem, and it is carefully controlled by the poet. *Judith* as a whole is *not* a parody of the heroic; rather characters with moral authority are invested with heroic, or quasi-heroic stature, whilst those without it are caricatured as heroic imposters.

In some ways, the Scriptural Judith is an unpromising figure for heroic reinterpretation. Although she is the main and most active single figure in the source, and although her beheading of her foe is a violent act done with a weapon, which might readily be construed heroically,[222] she is nonetheless a woman (where the typical Germanic hero is male), and one who uses her sexuality, not a sword, as her main weapon. If it is important for the Germanic hero to possess great physical strength, like Beowulf does, then no attribute in the source qualifies her for this role. Indeed, her relative physical weakness is crucial to the story, for its main point is the illustration of the overwhelming power of the divinity which may wreak vengeance on his enemies even through the hand of a woman. The central figure may only be given her own strength by compromising this message. Neither can she easily be seen as the Germanic chieftain with a comitatus; she is not the ruler of the Israelites, nor even prince of the Bethulians, she does not lead them into battle, and she does not have a group of loyal followers, but only a solitary unnamed

---

[220] On the banquet scene, see Magennis (1983).

[221] The style of the passage is so mannered, and so unusual in O.E. poetry in its rhyme and accumulation of verbs, as to suggest the manipulation of classical rhetorical devices: the expansive richness may be seen as *copia*, the single sub. with many verbs as a fine example of *diazeugma*, the combination of sounds for loudness and mimetic effect as illustrative of both *cacemphaton* and *onomatopoeia*. On the propensity for internal end rhyme, however, in O.E. metrical patterns of Type A in which both stresses are resolved (as in 23b), see Hutcheson (1995), 177 and 180.

[222] A precedent is found in Prudentius' *Psychomachia*, Thomson (1969), I, 282–3, where Chastity, after her bloody battle with Lust, cites the example of Judith and refers to her as *aspera Iudith ... caelitus audax* ('unyielding Judith ... heavenly brave').

maid. For these reasons it would be surprising if the poem gave us a full-blown picture of Judith as hero, and, as has already been shown, the poet in some ways downplays the powerfulness of the Judith of the source as part of his Christianisation of her. Her speech immediately before she beheads Holofernes, for example, is dramatically placed at the moment when the audience of the poem may have expected a heroic *beot*, but the content of this speech could not be further from a vaunting promise to do or die. She says that she is sad (87b *geomor*), and disturbed by grief (88a *mid sorgum gedrefed*), she asks for divine protection (90b–91a); she is humble, not boastful, and sounds in some ways more like the passive martyr than the conquering hero. Her speech to the Bethulians before they march out to battle is given at the moment when we might expect a general to exhort the troops. She stiffens their resolve by showing them the head of Holofernes, she mentions all the proper weaponry (191–4), and she shrewdly proclaims that the Assyrians are doomed because the Hebrews have God on their side. But her address is a curious mixture of request (187b *biddan wylle*) and command (191b *berað*); it is not introduced by a verb suggestive of heroic speech like *maþelian* ('to make a speech'), or *manian* ('to exhort'), but by the more colourless *sprecan* ('to say'); and it is referred to later as *lar* (333b), 'teaching', which smacks more of religious instruction than heroic exhortation.

Nevertheless, from the point at which her prayer is answered and God inspires her with courage (95a *mid elne onbryrde*), the poet does heroise Judith to a certain extent.[223] After this moment, heroism has divine sanction and does not compromise, but confirm, the point of the story: because of her faith, God strengthens her with qualities of the male hero.[224] In the source, all bless her because she has acted manfully (15.11) and the poet now expands upon this. Heroic courage, *ellen*, not previously

[223] Opinions vary on the degree from the position of Lucas (1992), 26, who argues that she is 'not a fully heroic figure', to that of Godden (1991), 222, who states that 'in the representation of Judith ... there seems to be a full-hearted acceptance of heroic values'.

[224] The O.E. poetic tradition may not be solely responsible for the heroising of Judith: see n.222. Kaske (1982), 13–29, sees heroism in *Jud*, as in *Beo*, as a synthesis of Germanic and Christian ideals.

mentioned, is now ascribed to her on three occasions: 133b *ellenþriste* (together with her maid), 146a *ellenrof*, and, most crucially, in the instant of her triumph when, with the second blow, she lops off the head:

> Sloh ða eornoste
> ides ellenrof oðre siðe
> þone hæðenan hund (108b–10a).

The adjective *ellenrof* is applied elsewhere in the poetry exclusively to men.[225] Where *ides ælfscinu* (14a) has no masculine parallel, the phrase *ides ellenrof* is the female equivalent of masculine epithets like *eorl ellenrof*, *beorn ellenrof*, and *wiga ellenrof*.[226] Likewise, the quality of being *modig*, 'courageous', is generally a male one, but is applied to Judith in the unique epithet *mægð modigre* (334a) which may be compared with the male *modig mon*,[227] and *modig maguþegn*.[228] The heroine and her maid are described as *collenferhðe* (134b), 'bold, elated', and are the only women to be so labelled in the surviving poetry.[229] These terms masculinise and heroise Judith by the redirecting of gendered language. Carr, noting the 'very few terms referring to women' in West Germanic poetry, observed that *Judith* is no exception in this respect 'where Holofernes is described by 28 compounds and Judith by only 12'.[230] The poet, it seems, did not inherit a word-hoard of ready-fashioned epithets for a female hero, for none of the phrases used of Judith in the poem is repeated in its entirety in the rest of the corpus.[231] That the closest parallels to several are epithets for men suggests, rather, that the

---

[225] Seventeen times of men, including Adam (*GenA* 1119), Abraham (*GenA* 1782, 1844), Andrew (*And* 1392), Beowulf (*Beo* 340), and Waldere (*WaldB* 11), but not of women.
[226] See *Beo* 3063, *GenA* 1119, and *WaldB* 11, respectively.
[227] See *Jul* 513, *Mald* 147.
[228] See *And* 1140, 1515, *Beo* 2757, *Men* 82.
[229] Elsewhere on twelve occasions all of men, including Beowulf (*Beo* 1806), Wiglaf (*Beo* 2785), and Andrew (*And* 538, 1578).
[230] Carr (1939), 443–4.
[231] Except, perhaps, for 58b *ða beortan idese*: cf. *GenA* 1728a *wlitebeorht ides*.

poet adapted and transferred language appropriate for the male hero.[232]

The poet's incomplete idealisation of her as heroine is therefore the product partly of the message of the source and partly of the nature of the tradition in which he was composing. Overall, the use of heroic language for individuals shows a balance between its ironic application to Holofernes, an anti-hero, and its re-gendered use of Judith, a quasi-hero.

## 8 *Judith* and Christian Tradition

The Germanic ideal of womanhood was of woman as an embodiment of wisdom and prophecy rather than a martial ideal of her as an Amazon, and if Judith cannot completely be converted into the latter, she may readily be interpreted as the former.[233] Given the value of wisdom to the Anglo-Saxons, it is not surprising that the poet chose to draw out this element.[234] Wisdom, however, may take the form of the faith of the Christian saint as well as the prescience of the Germanic woman; it is 'the common denominator between religious and heroic ideals',[235] and because the wisdom of the heroine of *Judith* fits into a specific Christian tradition of interpreting her in this fashion, it is dealt with here. In a general sense, Judith belongs to a line of wise women of the Old Testament,[236] but the Vulgate gives little direct authority for this view of her. Her wisdom is marvelled at by

[232] In addition to *ides ellenrof*, note 74a *þeowen þrymful* and *Rid* 3.67a *þrymful þeow*; 145a *searoðoncol mægð* and *ChristA* 220a *secg searoþoncol*, *Rid* 40.97a *secgas searoþoncle*; 148a *gleawhydig wif* and *GenA* 2257a *wishidig wer*. See also C132a.

[233] Robinson (1993b), 155–63, outlines this Germanic ideal, and deals with Judith at 159–60. For further discussion, see Belanoff (1989). Other female heroes in O.E. poetry show wisdom: Cynewulf heightens this aspect of both Juliana and Elene (see respectively Calder (1981), 81–2, and Hill (1971)).

[234] For discussion of the nature and uses of wisdom in O.E. poetry, see Shippey (1972), 53–79, and (1976), 1–47.

[235] Locherbie-Cameron (1988), 75. On wisdom as a key component of classical, Christian and Germanic heroism, see Curtius (1953), 167–82, and Kaske (1963), 270–3; and with particular reference to its expression in *Jud*, Kaske (1982) and Mushabac (1973).

[236] Cf. Rebecca, Abigail, Debora and Esther, and note the link between female fortitude and wisdom in Proverbs 31.10–31.

Holofernes and his men (11.18 *mirabantur sapientiam eius*), but this is the Vulgate's sole reference to this quality, and as an Assyrian opinion, it need not count for much. Her plan may be taken to be a wise one, and we may infer this trait from her words, but the narrator does not make it explicit. The Old Latin version, however, gives it greater prominence.[237] Its narrator, adding to the Septuagint, includes in the opening description of her the statement that she was 'wise of heart, with a good mind' (8.7 *prudens corde, et bona in sensu*), and Ozias expands upon this, saying that:

> no one can withstand your words, because your wisdom has not just been revealed today, but from the beginning of your days all the people have known of your understanding.[238]

And Judith answers him: 'Listen to me, and I will do a wise thing'.[239]

Kaske has outlined the influence of such remarks upon the interpretations of patristic writers.[240] Fulgentius quotes the Old

---

[237] OL 11.18–19 refers twice to her wisdom: '*et mirati sunt in specie et in sapientia ejus, et dixerunt: Non est talis mulier, à cacumine montium usque ad summum terræ, in vultu, et sapientia sermonum*'.

[238] OL 8.28: '*non est qui resistat verbis tuis: quoniam non ex hodierno sapientia tua manifestata est, sed ab initio dierum tuorum scit omnis populus prudentiam tuam*'. Ozias's remarks are found in the Septuagint, but are abbreviated in the Vulgate, with the reference to her wisdom omitted.

[239] OL 8.30: '*Audite me, et faciam rem prudentem*'. The comment of Locherbie-Cameron (1988), 71, that this motif 'comes not from the source but from the poet', is misleading.

[240] Kaske (1982), 18–21. The following are the main medieval discussions of, or significant references to, the *Book of Judith* which pre-date the O.E. poem: Ambrose, *Liber de elia et jejunio* 9 (PL 14, col.707–8), *De officiis ministrorum* 3.13 (PL 16, col.169), *Liber de viduis* 7 (PL 16, col.245–7); Jerome, *Epistola 22, ad Eustochium* 21 (PL 22, col.408), *Epistola* 54, *ad Furiam* 16 (PL 22, col.559), *Epistola* 79, *ad Salvinam* 11 (PL 22, col.732), *Apologia adversus libros Rufini* 18 (PL 23, col.412), *Praefatio in librum Judith* (PL 29, col.37–40); pseudo-Augustine, *Sermones de Judith* 48–9 (PL 39, col.1839–41); Isidore, *Allegoriæ quædam sacræ scripturæ* (PL 83, col.116), *De ortu et obitu patrum* (PL 83, col.148); Rabanus Maurus, *Expositio in librum Judith* (PL 109, col.539–92); Fulgentius, *Epistola 2 ad Gallam viduam* 29–30 (Fraipont (1968), CCSL 91, 207–8); Prudentius, *Psychomachia*, Thomson (1969), I, 282–3; Dracontius, *De*

Latin text of 8.7; Jerome defends Judith's use of wise lying words, and Ambrose, too, remarks upon the wisdom of her deception; a pseudo-Augustinian homily states that she consoled her people by her wisdom.[241] Alcuin's pupil, Rabanus Maurus, the author of the first full commentary on the *Book of Judith*, highlights the effect of her wisdom and beauty on the Assyrians,[242] and in the dedicatory epistle to the Empress Judith compares her prudence to the virtue of her biblical forerunner.[243] Not all expositions of the book, however, refer to this characteristic, and no other text beside the O.E. poem makes such abundant reference to it.[244] The interpretations of Judith as a type of the Church and as a example of chastity are commoner,[245] though a relationship exists between her wisdom and the figuring of her as the Church.[246] Kaske is, accordingly, right to view this as a 'tradition of sorts' only, but yet one which would provide a 'natural enough suggestion' for the poet's amplification of this

---

*laudibus Dei* 3 (Vollmer (1905), MGH, Auctores antiquissimi, 14, 105); Aldhelm, *De virginitate prosa* 57 (Ehwald (1919), MGH, Auctores antiquissimi, 15, 316–17), *De virginitate carmen* (in the same volume, at 457); Milo of St. Amand, *De sobrietate* I, 16, 331–93 (Traube (1896), MGH, Poetae Latini aevi Carolini, 3, 625–7); *Versus de Iudit et Olofernum* (Strecker (1923), MGH, Poetae Latini aevi Carolini, 4.2, 459–62). Translations of a number of passages from these works may be found in Huppé (1970), 139–44.

241 See respectively *ad Gallam viduam*, Fraipont (1968), 207; *adversus libros Rufini*, PL 23, col.412; *de viduis* 7, PL 16, col.245; *Sermones de Judith*, PL 39, col.1839.

242 See the heading to chapter 11 of his *Expositio*, PL 109, col.568.

243 PL 109, col.540.

244 Kaske (1982), 267, n.20, lists those commentaries in which there is 'no emphasis' on her wisdom.

245 The text does not openly mention either allegorical interpretation, and chastity is not explicitly attributed to Judith, although the poet seems to have known something of exegesis, and his audience may have been predisposed to read the poem symbolically without clear guidance from the author. I deal here only with Christian meaning for which there is evidence in the terms, or structure, of the poem. Some critics regard the poem as more strongly marked by the allegories of medieval exegesis: see, e.g., Huppé (1970), 136–88, Campbell (1971), and Hermann (1976). For a review of such critical approaches to O.E. poems, see Rollinson (1973).

246 Because Ozias talks of the wisdom of her words, Rabanus sees her as expressing the teaching of clerics, *Expositio*, PL 109, col.559.

trait, which is alluded to more than any other.[247] Judith is *gleaw on geðonce* (13a), *ferhðgleawe* (41a), *ða snoteran idese* (55a), *þearle gemyndig* (74b), *seo snotere mægð* (125a), *searoðoncol mægð* (145a), *gleawhydig wif* (148a), *seo gleawe* (171a), and *gearoþoncolre* (341a).[248] That the phrasing of the epithets in ll.55a, 125a, 145a and 148a is unique to this poem does not support the thesis that the protagonist's wisdom is that of 'the typical Germanic wise-woman',[249] for typical ideas in traditional poetics come to be expressed in traditional language. On the other hand, the close association that the poet sees between her wisdom and her words almost certainly derives from the same connection made by the Old Latin, the Vulgate (to a lesser extent), and some of the commentators: her teaching is *gleawe* (333b) and this wisdom is effective, for we are told that everything that the Hebrews won they did so through this shrewd instruction; she is one of those who pray *mid ræde* (97a), and God grants her prayer for this reason; the adjectives *searoðoncol* (145a), *gleawhydig* (148a), and *gleawe* (171a) are placed immediately next to verbs of command (*bebead*, 144b, *het*, 147b, 171a) and come just

---

[247] Kaske (1982), 19. Of the Latin works mentioned above that comment on Judith and that are not by Anglo-Saxons, the following are known, or probably known, from A-S England (references are to Ogilvy (1967) by page, Gneuss (1981) by number, and Biggs, *et al.* (1990) by page): Ambrose, *De elia et jejunio* (Ogilvy, 61), *De officiis* (Ogilvy, 61, Gneuss, 543), *De viduis* (Ogilvy, 62, Gneuss, 203); Jerome, *Epistola 22* (Ogilvy, 174: 'A special favorite with Aldhelm, who uses it repeatedly in [*De Virginitate prosa*]', Gneuss, 229 and 264 are collections of Jerome's letters), *Adversus Rufinum* (Ogilvy, 181); Isidore *Allegoriae* (Ogilvy, 166, Gneuss, 578, 780), *De ortu et obitu patrum* (Ogilvy, 169, Gneuss, 578, 780); Rabanus Maurus, *Expositio in librum Judith* (Ogilvy, 234, Gneuss, 779); Prudentius, *Psychomachia* (Ogilvy, 231–2, Gneuss, 12, 38, 70, 191, 246, 285, 324, 537, 661, 852, Biggs, *et al.*, 153–4: 'Without doubt it was the best known of Prudentius' poems in Anglo-Saxon England'); Dracontius, *De laudibus Dei* (Biggs, *et al.*, 82–3); Milo of St. Amand, *De sobrietate* (Ogilvy, 205).

[248] She is not, however, described as *frod* (perhaps because of its association with age), or *wis*.

[249] Robinson (1993b), 160. *Gearoþoncol* is *hapax legomenon*; Judas in *El* is *gleaw in geþance* (806b) and *fyrhðgleaw* (880a), but Elene is not said to be either.

before her two speeches to the Bethulians (in ll.152b–8 and 177–98).[250]

However, little of the specific content of her speeches is taken directly from the source.[251] Though these may been recast in some ways according to vernacular poetic conventions,[252] Christian tradition underlies much of what is new. Hill has demonstrated the influence of the form of Celtic Christian prayer called the *lorica* on her cry for help in ll.83–94a.[253] An invocation to the Trinity in a moment of extreme peril is a defining feature of this form, but such invocations are comparatively rare in O.E. poetry, despite the fact that most of it is concerned with Christian theme.[254] Judith, however, alone and in her moment of gravest need, opens her speech with one:

> 'Ic ðe, frymða god,  ond frofre gæst,
> bearn alwaldan,  biddan wylle ... (83–4).

Though God the Father is not named as such,[255] and the order of the three persons is not the most normal one, there are three epithets, and the second and third unambiguously denote the Spirit and the Son,[256] and the narrator draws our attention to the nomenclature with the tautology that she 'named God by name' (80b–1a). The anachronism by which an Old Testament figure appeals to the Christian God proves to be merely superficial, for it

---

[250] Note also the close proximity of *gearoþoncolre* (342a) and *Iudith sægde* (342b). Ælfric in his homily on Judith also preserves the Assyrian wonder at her wise words; see Assmann (1889), 109, ll.242–3 ('*Hi ða wundrodon ... hire wislicra worda*'), and 110, ll.263–5 ('*his þegenas sædon, þæt swylc wimman nære on ealre eorðan ... swa wis on spræce*').

[251] But cf. 13.19 and ll.177–80 and 197b–8.

[252] See Shippey (1972), 122, 126, on her prayer as a speech of *þearf*, or 'need'. Her first speech to the Bethulians may be construed as the inverse of this: one celebrating the removal of need (especially ll.152b–4a).

[253] Hill (1981). Celtic examples of the form are more prolix and magical than Judith's prayer, so the influence is not complete. See Hughes (1970) for other types of Celtic Christian influence on early English prayer.

[254] Hill (1981), finds a total of eight.

[255] Note, however, Keiser (1919), 66: '*Fæder* is often used where God conceived as one or the first person is meant, though the term is also applied to Christ'.

[256] The unity of the three is shown, however, by the use of the sing. pron. *ðe*. On epithets for God in the poem, see Foster (1892), 68–70.

shows the insertion of exegetical interpretation of Judith's words into her own mouth, discussions of the Trinity sometimes including Judith's invocations in lists of Old Testament names for God which signify the nature of the Trinity as three in one.[257] To the Church Fathers, the Old Testament was a prefiguration of the New; exegesis, therefore, suggested to the poet the underlying spiritual truth of her appeal to God in the source, and, making this explicit, allowed him to model her speech as a conventional kind of prayer.

The Christianisation of Judith allows the voices of the Christian narrator and the heroine to echo each other. The narrator tells us that God would not allow Holofernes to carry out his intentions towards Judith (59b–60) and Judith tells the Hebrews that God would not allow Holofernes to persecute them any longer (183b–5a). Both affirm that God granted her victory (122–3, 185b–6a). The narrator states that the Assyrians are doomed (19b *hie þæt fæge þegon*), and so does she:

> ... fæge frumgaras. Fynd syndon eowere
> gedemed to deaðe (195–6a).

They seem to speak of the same God—both use the phrase *swegles ealdor* for him (88b, 124a)—and to possess the same knowledge, though his is merely historical, where hers shows a prescience that is divinely inspired. At the end of the poem, it is difficult, if not impossible, to separate their voices. The narrator informs us that Judith ascribed the glory of her victory to God:

> Ealles ðæs Iudith sægde
> wuldor weroda dryhtne (341b–2a)

and the poem concludes with just such an attribution of glory:

> Þæs sy ðam leofan dryhtne

---

[257] See the trinitarian amplification of the OL reading of Munich MS 6239 ('*Domine, Domine Deus*'), and note, e.g., Vigilius Thapsensis, *contra Varimadum*, Liber 1, *de Trinitate*, PL 62, col.354, (referring to Judith 9.17) and Benedictus I, *Epistola ad David*, PL 72, col.686, who both refer to her invocations in discussions of the Trinity.

wuldor to widan aldre ... (346b–7a)

The praising of God, or the ascription, is a conventional ending of the homiletic or devotional text, and rather commonly such ascriptions offer *wuldor*, 'glory', to the Creator.[258] As these lines are not formally introduced as speech, they are always treated as belonging to the Christian narrator, but the repetition of *wuldor* encourages their association with the voice of Judith, and, as the source ends with the canticle of Judith in which she sings the praises of the Lord, the end of the poem can readily be understood as an abbreviated and Christianised rendition of that song. *Judith*'s conclusion seems to show, then, the harmonising of two voices, and the blending of two ends, the canticle and the ascription.[259] Judith's wisdom supports the authority of the narrator's words, and the narrator affirms her Christian faith (e.g. 344b–5a); past and present, Old Testament and New Testament are brought together in this shared hymn of praise to the Creator.

For those who interpret Judith as *Ecclesia*, Holofernes represents the enemy of the Church, or Satan: Remigius of Auxerre and Rabanus Maurus, for example, both offer this signification.[260] The poet does not call Holofernes Satan, but, possibly following this tradition, he repeatedly selects diction for Holofernes and his men which characterises them as devilish. The Assyrians are called *ealdgeniðlan* (228b), *ealdfeondum* (315a), and *ealdhettende* (320b), 'the old enemy', which are calques of

---

[258] Note that Ælfric sometimes concludes hagiographic works in this fashion: e.g. *The Lives of the Saints* 31, St Martin, Skeat (1890 and 1900), II, 312, l.1493, '*Sy wuldor and lof þam wel-willendan scyppende*', and frequently uses the phrase *wuldor and lof* as a concluding formula.

[259] The ascription may have influenced the conclusions of other O.E. poems: see Campbell (1988), and note Gatch (1977), 62, '[*El*] concludes (lines 1228b–35) with a prayer, not unlike the usual homiletic ascription'.

[260] See respectively Remigius' gloss to the *Psychomachia*, Burnam (1910), 84–117, at 90, '*Significat enim aeclesiam, Olofernis vero Diabolum, quem modo veraciter aeclesia interficit*', and Rabanus, *Expositio*, PL 109, col.546, '*Holofernem hunc aut gentium principatum, qui persecutus est Ecclesiam Christi, aut ipsum etiam iniquorum omnium caput, et novissimum perditionis filium possumus intelligere*'. Ælfric gives the same allegorical reading in his homily on Judith; see C315a.

the common title of Satan as *hostis antiquus*.[261] They are Holofernes' *weagesiðas* (16b), 'comrades in misery/evil', and this rare compound appears twice in the Vercelli homilies of the followers of Satan.[262] Holofernes is explicitly called *se deofulcunda* (61b), 'the devilish one'. He is *se bealofulla* (48b, 100b, 248a), and *se inwidda* (28a), 'the evil one', which recall, as Hermann notes, the Scriptural labelling of Satan as *malus* and *malignus*.[263] Phrasing used of the devil in O.E. poetry is often to be found: he is *ðone wærlogan* (71b), 'the treacherous one', *þone atolan* (75a), 'the terrible one', *þysne morðres bryttan* (90a), 'this dispenser of great violence',[264] and the appearance of a demonstrative in all these strengthens the association with *the* devil. He is, accordingly, *swiðmod* (30a, 339a), 'arrogant' or 'too proud', for pride was the sin which was traditionally regarded as the cause of Satan's downfall.[265] When he is slain, his soul does not await the Day of Judgement, but immediately departs for his proper home, *ðam heolstran ham* (121a), hell, where he is destined to remain in perpetuity, without hope of change. Quite naturally, he is *nergende lað* (45b), 'abominable to the Saviour', and the poet contrasts him with God, Holofernes being *þæs hehstan brogan* (4b), where God is *þæs hehstan deman* (4a). Satan, in the conventional Christian view, strives to usurp God's lordship and falls as a result.[266] Because he presents Holofernes as devilish and merges him with Nabuchodonosor,[267] the poet may have felt that Holofernes had, like Satan and his king, tried to set himself up in rivalry to God,[268] as a kind of perverted mirror image of the divinity, and this may lie behind the use of the

[261] For parallels, see notes to these lines in the Commentary, and Hermann (1976), 9, n.14.
[262] See respectively homilies 9, Scragg (1992), 160, l.22 and 21, 355, l.94.
[263] Hermann (1976), 4, and see Matthew 13.19; I John 2.13, 14; 3.12.
[264] For occurrences of these terms elsewhere with this application, see notes to these lines in the Commentary, and Foster (1892), 72. Woolf (1953), 8, comments that 'all that [Satan] can dispense is evil, and he therefore becomes *morþres brytta*'.
[265] See Woolf (1953), 6–7. Nebuchadnezzar is *swiðmod* in *Dan.*
[266] For the treatment of this idea in *GenB*, see Doane (1991), 123–4.
[267] See pp.54–5.
[268] Note Vulgate 6.2: 'there is no God, but Nabuchodonosor', and cf. Satan's vaunt in *GenB* 283b: '*ic mæg wesan god swa he*'.

epithet *þearlmod ðeoden gumena* for both Holofernes (in 66a) and God (in 91a):

> Hæfde ða his ende gebidenne
> on eorðan unswæslicne, swylcne he ær æfter worhte,
> þearlmod ðeoden gumena, þenden he on ðysse worulde
> wunode under wolcna hrofe. Gefeol ða wine swa druncen
> se rice on his reste middan (64b–8a).

Holofernes, like Satan, achieves a miserable end, a catastrophic fall, which he does not expect because it is the opposite of what he has worked for, and it is at this moment, just before he falls onto his bed, doomed to fall further into hell, that the narrator ironically injects an epithet denoting high status properly applicable to God.[269] Likewise, the blackening of Holofernes as a devil-like figure may help to explain why the poet describes the canopy as shielding 'the evil one', who sits under it, from the sight of onlookers:

> fleohnet fæger ... þæt se bealofulla
> mihte wlitan þurh ... ond on hyne nænig
> monna cynnes (47a, 48a–9a, 51b–2a).

In *Genesis B*, Satan sets on his head a helmet of invisibility, *hæleðhelm* (444a).[270] In *The Whale*, he is described as 'covered by the helmet of invisibility', *heoloþhelme biþeaht* (45a), though *helm* here may have the extended sense of 'covering', for the prefix of the verb suggests the sense of complete surrounding.[271] Slightly differently, in *Juliana*, the devil says that he deprives

---

[269] Most of the epithets for Holofernes are variations on the idea 'lord of men' (9b, 12a, 21a, 22a, 32b, 39a, 49b, 254a, 338b), which is used of God only in 91a, though he is also described in 81b–2a as *nergend ealra woruldbuendra*, 'Saviour of all those dwelling in this world'. 61a *dugeða waldend*, and 342a *weroda dryhtne* probably refer to God as 'Lord of (the heavenly) Hosts', rather than of earthly ones. On the ironic voice of the narrator, see pp.64–7; it is Judith, whose voice is devoid of irony, who calls God *þearlmod þeoden gumena* in 91a. See also C66a.

[270] Further on the helmet of invisibility, see Doane (1991), 137, 277–8. In *Heliand* 5452, Pilate's wife is deceived by Satan who is hidden by a *heliðhelm*.

[271] See Squires (1988), 86.

men of their sight with a *misthelm* (470b), 'a covering of fog'. The poet of *Judith* introduces a realistic analogue of this magical covering—Holofernes is shrouded by the fly-net which prevents anyone from seeing him, just as the *hæleðhelm* prevents Satan from being seen,[272] but this net appears to be the product of artifice, rather than of magic, for it seems to be transparent at close quarters: no one could see through it, the poet tells us in 52b–4, unless Holofernes ordered someone to approach nearer.

For these changes to the central figures—the wisdom of Judith and the devilishness of Holofernes—the poet was probably indebted to exegetical tradition, but at no point does he explicitly allegorise them. Instead, he literalises whatever he may have taken from exegesis.[273] So, Judith is wise, but not a typification of wisdom, and Holofernes is devilish, but not simply a mask of Satan. In this tradition, too, may lie the authority for his major change to the plot. The original Judith drinks with Holofernes at his party, but consumes only that drink which her maid had prepared for her (12.19). The commentaries, accordingly, place great stress on Judith's total abstinence from alcoholic drink, seeing her as an example of temperance, and contrast this with the drunkenness of her enemy.[274] The poet, however, does not present her as a type of sobriety, but seems to have been sufficiently sensitive to this allegorical depiction of her to remove her from the intemperate situation in which the drinking takes place, and, through this new physical detachment, implies a heightened moral contrast. The poet's sense of the moral gulf between Judith and Holofernes has led him to suppress an inconvenient detail of the

---

[272] Woolf (1953), 3, states that the *hæleðhelm* has 'no origin in Christian history or legend'. The Christianisation of Holofernes as devilish, however, allows the poet to introduce the notion of a covering that confers invisibility, whatever its source.

[273] See Astell (1989); note also Shepherd (1966), 12, 'of all the surviving [O.E. poetic] treatments of the Bible, *Judith* is the one most empty of theological or typological implication'.

[274] See Ambrose, *de elia et jejunio*, PL 14, col.707, '*Denique bibebant vinum in ebrietate potentes, qui Holopherni principi militiæ regis Assyriorum se tradere gestiebant; sed non bibebat femina Judith*', Fulgentius, *ad Gallam viduam* 29, Fraipont (1968), 207, '*Ille pugnabat armis, ista ieiuniis; ille ebrietate, ista oratione*', and Astell (1989), 122–3. Some other details of the poem which may show patristic influence are dealt with in C47, C120 and C137.

source, and the commentaries furnished the justification for such editing. *Judith* does not incorporate their allegorical readings, but such exegesis seems silently to have shaped its narrative.

Patristic commentary, however, was not the only Christian inspiration for the poet's interpretation of his source. He was also influenced by the saint's life:

> The hagiographical form was the dominant narrative kind in the Old English period. Not only are the saints' lives more abundant in extant Old English literature than any other kind of story, but also many other narratives seem to have been influenced by them. Among the poetry, this can be seen in *Judith*, which, in its invention of the malignity and licentiousness of Holofernes and its stress on Judith's preservation of her chastity, shows unmistakably the influence of the life of the virgin martyr.[275]

*Judith* does not emphasise the heroine's preservation of her chastity and she is not martyred,[276] but it does indeed display some typical features of medieval hagiography. The ideology of the poem shows a simple opposition of the forces of good and evil, and this reflects the world of hagiography, in which the saint, the soldier of God, is threatened or assaulted by the devil or his servants, but finally triumphs over evil.The heroine is called *seo halige meowle* (56), *haligre* (98), *seo halige* (160), *ða halgan mægð* (260), and as O.E. *halig* means both 'holy' and 'saintly', her holiness may have been construed as saintliness.[277] She is also called blessed, *þa eadigan mægð* (35).[278] Though there is a more

[275] Woolf (1966), 64. For the view that the Anglo-Saxons may have regarded the biblical books of Judith and Daniel as Hebrew saints' lives, see Frank (1972), 220, n.39.

[276] Comparison of Judith with the virgin martyr is unfortunate in this respect because decapitation is a common fate of such a saint (e.g. Agnes, Juliana, Dorothea).

[277] Doubleday (1971), 438, states that her character is 'remade on the model of the saints' lives', but she is holy in the source (see 8.29 *mulier sancta*).

[278] Nelson (1990), 12, compares this epithet with its 'almost exact parallel' in *Jul* 352, *eadmægden*, but fails to note that this is an emendation of a corrupt verse. *Eadig* is used of both heroines (cf. *Jul* 105, 130, 627), but Judith is not called *mægden*.

direct source in exegesis for the added viciousness of Holofernes, Woolf is probably right to regard this as a movement towards a stock figure of hagiography, and to compare his transformation with Cynewulf's modification of the character of the consul Heliseus in *Juliana*: both are stripped of human interest, and are stereotyped as heathen and devilish persecutors of the heroine.[279] Hagiography here combines with exegesis to provide powerful motivation for the demonising of Holofernes. The conquest of evil is brought about in the saint's life by divine grace which is granted to the saint through purity of faith and devotion to God, and this is central to the exemplary purpose of the genre. The relationship between divine aid and the heroine's faith is, likewise, a powerful theme of *Judith* and connects together its beginning and end:

> Hyre ðæs fæder on roderum
> torhtmod tiðe gefremede, þe heo ahte trumne geleafan
> a to ðam ælmihtigan (5b–7a)

> Ealles ðæs Iudith sægde
> wuldor weroda dryhtne, þe hyre weorðmynde geaf,
> mærðe on moldan rice ... þæs ðe heo ahte soðne geleafan
> to ðam ælmihtigan (341b–5a).

*Geleafa*, 'faith', is always accompanied in Judith by an appropriate adjective—*trum* (6b), *soð* (89a, 344b), *riht* (97a)—which underlines the strength of the faith needed by the heroine and these phrases are not formulas of the poetry, but of homiletic and hagiographic O.E. prose.[280] The conventionality of the *vita* produced the frequent repetition of traditional clichés such as

[279] Woolf (1966), 44. Foster (1892), 72 compares names for both: 256 *galmod*, *Jul* 531, 598 *gealgmod*; 104 *feondsceaða*, 77 *womfull*, *Jul* 211 *womceaða*.

[280] *Soð* and *riht* commonly modify *geleafa* in such prose (e.g. Ælfric's St Eugenia, Skeat (1890), I, 32, l.132, 40, l.265, 50, l.426; and 30, l.98, respectively). *Trum* is less common in this context, but note Ælfric's Deposition of St Martin, Godden (1979), 292, l.166, and his homily on Judith, Assmann (1889), 107, l.165. On the mixing of poetic and non-poetic formulas in O.E. poetry, see Griffith (1988), 155–66.

these.[281] Even the comic touches of the poem—the absurdity of the added picture of Holofernes' drunken noisy party and the ridiculousness of the Assyrians' attempt to wake their dead leader—are a component part of the style of the saint's life, for evil, though terrifying, is finally exposed as folly.[282] Finally, the heroic aspects of the poem do not preclude the notion of hagiographic influence for the genre of the saint's life was traditionally blended with other genres:

> The persecutions of the Christians produced the *acta* and *passiones* of the martyrs. The *vitae* of the saints followed upon these. These new genres could be put into the system of forms of pagan literature. Thus, Biblical poems and saints' lives appear in the form of the Latin epic.[283]

*Judith*, likewise, is an amalgam of Christian saint's life and vernacular heroic form,[284] exemplary in purpose, and perhaps for a secular audience.[285]

## 9 Style and Structure

The discussion of O.E. poetic style is impeded by the fact that no work on vernacular poetics survives from the Anglo-Saxon period, even if any was written, and conclusions about the structure of a literary fragment must necessarily remain provisional. Some stylistic and structural features of *Judith*,

---

[281] See Levison (1910), 220: 'very many turns of phrase were repeated word for word again and again, and more than one *vita* is ... pieced together, like a mosaic, from fragments intended for the portraits of other saints'.

[282] Examples are given by Curtius (1953), 428, who remarks that 'comedy is also to be found in the *vita sancti* ... The pagans, the devils, the men of evil may behave as savagely as they will–they are the fools, and the saint reduces them *ad absurdum*, unmasks them, dupes them ... Sometimes it is the poet himself who laughs at the Devil'.

[283] Curtius (1953), 260.

[284] For discussion of the crossing of the saint's life with vernacular genres, see Auerbach (1965), 281–6, and note Woolf (1966), 40, who calls the *vita* 'part panegyric, part epic, part romance, part sermon'. For earlier views of the poem as Christian epic, see Herbison (1996), 348–54.

[285] Nelson (1990), 12–13, treats *Jud* as the 'story of a secular saint'; Shepherd (1966), 12, speculates that it was written as a 'Mirror for Princesses'.

however, are typical of O.E. poetry, although others appear to have been chosen to give clarity to the new reading of the story. The variation of familiar ideas is highly conventional, and this can be seen at its most developed in the battle scenes. The onset of fighting with the initial shower of arrows provides an example:

> Hie ða fromlice
> leton forð fleogan flana scuras,
> hildenædran of hornbogan,
> strælas stedehearde (220b–3a).

*Flan* and *stræl* are ordinary O.E. terms for 'arrow', and *hildenædre*, 'battle-adder', is a poetic compound and—probably—a traditional metaphor for the same idea; by their use, the object of the sentence is drawn out and varied. Along with the tautology is a measure of redundancy (220b *ða*, 221a *forð*, 222b *of hornbogan*, and 223a *stedehearde*, if this means 'firmly fixed' or 'very hard'). Without significant loss of the 'prose' sense, then, the sentence could be briefly translated as 'they swiftly fired arrows'. The leisureliness of the actual phrasing, though not as prolix as that of *Beowulf*, is an index of a high style, which was characterised by multiple poetic lexemes for common poetic ideas (e.g. the many poetic terms in the poem for warriors and their weapons). On the other hand, ideas which are unique to a particular poem often attract little or no variation (e.g the canopy, *fleohnet*; the maid's food bag, *fætels*; the tent of Holofernes, *træf*, and its inner chamber, *burgeteld*). The poets were predisposed by the nature of their poetic vocabulary to remove, or treat in abbreviated fashion, unfamiliar ideas from sources which they were casting into poetic form, and, conversely, to amplify those suited to their lexical resources. In this respect, in the battle scenes, the poet chose a style which suited his heroised vision of the story.[286]

[286] For other traditional stylistic features of *Jud*, see Foster (1892), 67f., especially 81–5. Perhaps the most important of these are pleonasm or superabundance (11–12 *comon feran*, 15b *sittan eodon*, 82b *word acwæð*), synecdoche, or the part standing for the whole (191b *berað linde forð*), euphemism, especially to express death (112b *gæst ellor hwearf*, 294b *hilde gesæged*), and incremental narrative progression (200b *stopon cynerofe*, 212b

Before the battle scenes, there are, however, passages which are very different in style:

> Genam ða þone hæðenan mannan
> fæste be feaxe sinum; teah hyne folmum wið hyre weard
> bysmerlice, ond þone bealofullan
> listum alede, laðne mannan,
> swa heo ðæs unlædan eaðost mihte
> wel gewealdan ... (98b–103a)

In these lines, and, to a slightly lesser extent, in the rest of this scene, there is almost no phrasing which may be called formulaic (only 101b may be found in other poetry[287]), almost no use of variation (with the exception of the same verse), and less poetic diction than may be found in the later battles (no nominal compounds, and only *sin* and *folm* are clearly poetic words). The key action of the poem, the beheading of Holofernes, is composed in a less conventional language than those later scenes. It appears less obviously heroic and less stereotyped, perhaps befitting a deed done by a woman only partly heroised by the poet. Unimpeded by apposition, however, the pace of the narrative appears to increase, and so, though lower in register, it does not lack vigour.

In addition, some sections of the poem which at first glance seem to be in the conventional style, in fact show the poet moving beyond the typical and creating unusual effects:[288]

> Here wæs on lustum;
> wið þæs fæstengeates folc onette,
> weras wif somod, wornum ond heapum,
> ðreatum ond ðrymmum þrungon ond urnon
> ongean ða þeodnes mægð þusendmælum,
> ealde ge geonge (161b–6a).

---

*Stopon heaðorincas*, 227a *stopon styrnmode*). Notable by their absence are those features which contribute to the looseness of much O.E. poetic narrative: the accumulation of synonyms, maxims, parenthetic statements, and digressive episodes (see Foster (1892), 86–7, for further details).

287 In the gen. pl. at *GenA* 2085a, *Ex* 57b, *Beo* 2672a.

288 The drinking scene provides another example.

The normal product of the accumulation of nouns of similar meaning is stasis, a slowing of the pace of the narrative, but here, as Stanley has remarked, there is 'a rare example of movement achieved less by verbs than by ... an unusually dense massing of *nomina* ... reflecting the tumultuous rushing of the joyful Israelites towards the victorious Judith'.[289] Though it would be logical to expect a greater accumulation of nouns to lead to a greater sense of stasis, Stanley's observation of the reverse effect here is accurate. The sense of urgent action is achieved by the rapid movement of the verse, by an unusual use of inflectional rhyme, or *homoeoptoton*, on the dative plural ending in 163b, 164a and 165b, and by the equally unusual combining of verses of identical length and metre in 163b, 164 and 166a.[290] Furthermore, the repetition of words for the central idea of 'crowd' in 163b–4a, and the variation of the closely associated notion of 'people' through the particularisations *weras*, *wif*, *ealde*, *geonge*, shows a new purpose for these commonplace aspects of the poetic style: they no longer function just as markers of a high style, but are also deployed mimetically. Stylistic inflation imitates the magnitude of the crowd.[291] No other O.E. poet is able to evoke scenes so powerfully and realistically as the *Judith* poet, but it is the style rather than the content of his descriptions which marks him out from the tradition. He is as little interested in the detailed description of people, places and objects as the other poets. His style is not more pictorial than theirs, but it is more aural: action is communicated powerfully by a stronger appeal to the ear than is usual. The scene of Holofernes' damnation illustrates this:

gæst ellor hwearf

[289] Stanley (1994), 152–3.

[290] The consonant cluster alliteration in 164 may also be ornamental. Cluster alliteration and rhyme also combine in ll.23, and 29. See Appendix I, Alliteration, section B, for lists of minor alliterative patterns, some of which may be ornamental. The rhetorical use of inflectional rhyme is rare, but not unknown in the rest of the corpus; cf. *Beo* 3171–2, 3181–2, and see Kendall (1991), 8–9, and n.21.

[291] As does the use of exaggeration (e.g. *þusendmælum*, 'in their thousands'; see also C161a on the unusual pl. form of the idiomatic phrase *on luste*).

under neowelne næs ond ðær genyðerad wæs,
susle gesæled syððan æfre,
wyrmum bewunden, witum gebunden,
hearde gehæfted in helle bryne
æfter hinsiðe. Ne ðearf he hopian no,
þystrum forðylmed, þæt he ðonan mote
of ðam wyrmsele, ac ðær wunian sceal
awa to ealdre butan ende forð
in ðam heolstran ham, hyhtwynna leas (112b–21).

The image of hell as dark and a place of torment filled with fire and serpents is commonplace. Less clichéd to us, but traditional in the medieval hellish picture, is its position beneath a cliff.[292] Much of the phrasing of these lines is also to be found elsewhere in the poetic corpus.[293] The style is, nonetheless, out of the ordinary, and its features are strikingly similar to those of ll.21b–5, and 161b–6a: there is rhyming of stem syllables (113 *næs: wæs*), of inflected syllables (on the dative plural *-um* in 115a, 115b, 118a, and on the *-ed* of weak past participles in 114a, 116a, 118a), and of both together (115 *bewunden: gebunden*); there are verses of identical length and metre in sequence or in close juxtaposition (114a, 115a, 115b, 116a, 118a), and these verses are, with the exception of 116a, identical in syntax. Rhyme is used for comic and imitative effect in the poem, and in this passage both are discernible. Although a scene of damnation can hardly be described as amusing, nevertheless the jingling tone suggests anything but concern for Holofernes' soul; indeed, we

[292] See C112b–21.

[293] Cf. the following verses: 112b and *Beo* 55b *fæder ellor hwearf*, 113a and *PPs* 106 25.2b *under neowulne grund*, 115b and *And* 580b *witum gebundene*, 116a and *Met* 25.49a *hearde gehæfted*, 118a and *El* 766a *þeostrum forþylmed*, 118b and *Met* 26.22b *þæt he þonan moste*, 119b and *Met* 11.56b *þe nu wunian sceal*, 120b and *JDay I* 306b *butan ende forð*, 121b and *Sat* 158b *hyhtwillan leas*. 114b *syððan æfre* and 120a *awa to aldre* are common. Brodeur (1968), 109, states that the poet's 'power of description and of evocation are, in the main, quite independent of the inherited wealth of formula', but the poet's style changes in this regard from scene to scene.

feel that the narrator relishes his terrifying doom.[294] Extreme actions in the poem—the drunken roaring of Holofernes, the ecstatic swarming of the Hebrews and the violent damning of Holofernes—are echoed by special and strong sound effects which, taken together, suggest an attempt by the poet to deploy, in specific locales, a mimetic style.[295]

The poem's style and structure help to express its central moral opposition: its rhetoric highlights figures which involve binary patterns, and antithesis, the conjoining of contrasting ideas, is the most dominant of these. Kaske notes how the poet carefully arranges his epithets for Judith and Holofernes in the early part of the text so that each of those 'characterizing Judith as wise is matched by a reference to Holofernes as powerful'.[296] In l.11, he is *ðam rican þeodne*, 'the powerful lord', and two lines later she is *gleaw on geðonce*, 'wise in thought'; in l.41, she is described as *ferhðgleawe*, 'wise at heart', and three lines afterwards he is called *se rica*, 'the powerful one'; in l.55, she is *ða snoteran idese*, 'that prudent lady', and in l.58, he is *burga ealdor*, 'ruler of cities'; he is again, and for the last time, termed *se rica* in l.68—ironically so in the context of his collapse, unconscious and helpless, onto his bed—and this contrasts with the description of Judith in l.74 as *þearle gemyndig*, 'very mindful'. By divine grace, she is granted the power—which he no longer possesses—to control his body, and this reversal leads to changed characterisation and a new antithesis: she is 'inspired with strength', *mid elne onbryrde* (95a), but he, in a very different vein, is now not a powerful lord, but merely 'that heathen man',

---

[294] This is also suggested by the repetitious adverbial tautology: *syððan æfre ... awa to aldre, butan ende forð*, 'for ever after ... for ever and ever, henceforth without end'.

[295] Mimesis may be apparent, too, in the narration of the battle. Fry (1967–8), 157–9, observes that before the onset of the battle 'only those trappings which can be seen from outside the ranks as the army advances, a line of shields with helmets and banners above it' are described, but as battle commences 'the listing of armaments then proceeds in decreasing capabilities of range: arrows, spears and swords' (159). However, a degree of mimesis is almost unavoidable in such narrative, and the battle description is in almost every respect highly traditional.

[296] Kaske (1982), 27.

*þone hæðenan mannan* (98b and compare 101b);[297] she is 'courageous', *ellenrof* (109a), and he is further belittled as 'that heathen dog', *þone hæðenan hund* (110a). Her elevation to the rank of hero goes hand in hand with his reduction to the level of the bestial. After his death, Holofernes is referred to in conjunction with Judith only once, in ll.253b–7a:

> Mynton ealle
> þæt se beorna brego  ond seo beorhte mægð
> in ðam wlitegan træfe  wæron ætsomne,
> Iudith seo æðele  ond se galmoda,
> egesfull ond afor.

The epithets in ll.254 and 256 show two antitheses organised into a chiastic pattern, and the ABBA structure of the chiasmus is clarified by the use of the demonstrative in each epithet (*se* ... *seo* ... *seo* ... *se*).[298] Antithesis also points up the opposition of Holofernes to God. In l.4, the alliteration is maintained by an unusual repetition of the same word (*hehstan*, perhaps in two different senses—'highest' and 'greatest'), [299] and this, together with the syntactic and rhythmical parallelism between the opposed epithets of the line, sharpens the religious opposition of the two.[300] In a speech filled with epithets (83–94), Judith refers frequently to God, but only once to her enemy, and she does so in a phrase which inverts the terms of one of her titles for God, *þysne morðres bryttan*, 'this dispenser of murder' (90a), where God is *torhtmod tires brytta*, 'the illustrious dispenser of honour' (93a). The double use of *þearlmod þeoden gumena* of Holofernes in 66a and of God in Judith's speech in l.91a may, by antithesis,

---

[297] Lucas (1992), 23, notes that the opposition is strengthened by the alliteration in l.98 on *halig* and *hæðen*. Cf. also the alliterating words in ll.7, 61, 256.

[298] For further discussion of chiasmus in the poem, see Hieatt (1980), 255. On the possible relation between chiasmus and plurilinear syntactic units with medial pauses in O.E. poetry, see Leslie (1968), 77, who uses this example. Two antitheses of epithets for Judith and Holofernes are also found in ll.56 and 58, but these are arranged in ABAB order.

[299] Word echo is pervasive in O.E. poetry, but usually involves repetition across lines rather than within the line.

[300] The contrast is noted by Huppé (1970), 158, and by Lucas (1992), 24. *Broga* either refers to Holofernes, or, as Huppé suggests, terror is here personified.

show the narrator in 66a ironising the perverted claim of the devilish to lordship.

A system of contrasting repetitions is seen in the pervasive use of compounds containing elements meaning 'mind' or 'spirit' (28 instances of 22 different compounds).[301] Though two are of doubtful sense,[302] and the use of irony disrupts the simplicity of the pattern,[303] in general the poet deploys complimentary but different forms for God, Judith and the maid, and pejorative ones for Holofernes.[304] All of the relevant compounds describing Judith denote her wisdom (41a *ferhðgleawe*, 145a *searoðoncol*, 148a *gleawhydig*, 341a *gearoþoncolre*);[305] the maid is also called wise but in different terms (131a *higeðoncolre*, 172b *þancolmode*); Judith and her maid together are brave and happy (134b *collenferhðe*, 140a *glædmode*); God is glorious (6a, 93a *torhtmod*). In stark contrast, Holofernes is fierce (25a *se stiðmoda*), arrogant (30a, 339a *swiðmod*), lustful (62a *galferhð*, 256b *se galmoda*), and hostile (105a *heteþoncolne*). Verse 30a *swiðmod sinces brytta* ('arrogant giver of treasure') and 93a *torhtmod tires brytta* ('glorious giver of honour') show that metrical repetition, word echo and formulaic variation may underline the contrast of sense. Various other uses of word echo and formulaic system reiterate these oppositions between Judith and Holofernes, and God and Holofernes.[306] Holofernes is the prince of men and cities, *se gumena aldor* (32b), and *burga*

---

[301] Tyler (1992), 17, compares this with their similar frequency in *Wan* and *Sea*, and concludes that (though *Jud* is not a contemplative poem) 'the high density ... points to design on the part of the poet'. See also Lucas (1992), 23.

[302] 233a, *niðhycgende* (where the ambiguity of sense leads to ambiguity of reference), and 269a, *sweorcendferhðe*.

[303] In addition to *þearlmod*, note *stercedferhðe* in 55b and 227b (with irony in the first).

[304] This contrast extends to the Hebrews and the Assyrians, as is noted by Tyler (1992), 17, but it is less marked than that between individuals. The Assyrians are weary (249a, 290b *werigferhðe*), whilst the Hebrews are stern (227a *styrnmode*), but both are sad (144a *geomormodum* of the Hebrews, 289b *hreowigmode* of the Assyrians), and no such cpds. are used of the Assyrians which have the pejorative force of those describing the viciousness of Holofernes.

[305] Only three other cpd. adjs. describe Judith: 14a *ælfscinu*, 77b, 103b *wundenlocc*, 109a, 146a *ellenrof*.

[306] On word echo in the poem, see Hieatt (1980), 254 and Pringle (1975), 92–3; on the question of the intentionality of such repetition, Tyler (1996).

*ealdor* (58a), but God is prince of heaven, *swegles ealdor* (88b, 124a),[307] and saviour of men, *nergend ealra woruldbuendra* (81b–2a). Judith is God's servant, *nergendes þeowen* (73b–4a), but Holofernes is hateful to him, *nergende lað* (45b). Holofernes becomes so drunk that he forgets his designs on Judith (68b *swa he nyste ræda nanne*); she, however, prays with a right mind (97a *mid ræde*). He is arrogant (26a *modig*, 52b *se modiga*), she is brave (334a *modigre*).[308] He is consigned to a dark home (121a *ðam heolstran ham*), she returns to her bright one (131b *ham*, 137 *þære wlitegan byrig weallas blican*).

Word echo is so pervasive that it becomes a structuring device, and whole passages are drawn together by multiple resemblances (repetitions are italicised):

*Wæs* ða *eft cumen*
leof *to* leodum, *ond ða* lungre *het*
*gleaw*hydig wif gumena sumne
of *ðære* ginnan *byrig* hyre togeanes gan,
ond hi *ofostlice in forlæton* (146b–50)

Æghwylcum wearð
men on *ðære* medo*byrig* mod areted,
syððan hie ongeaton þæt *wæs* Iudith *cumen*
*eft to* eðle, *ond ða ofostlice*
hie mid eaðmedum *in forleton*.
Þa seo *gleawe het* ... (168–71a).

In the second extract, we learn that the Bethulians learn that Judith has returned, which we learned in the first, and that they carry out the command we already know about. The language of the two passages is similar and, though it may seem unnecessarily

[307] This is a basic distinction between the epithets for God and Holofernes. Obviously, Holofernes cannot be called the lord of heaven, but God is, to the poet, the real lord of men, though he rarely terms him this (see n.269). God is also termed the ruler of heaven in l.5b *fæder on roderum*, and 80b *swegles weard*.

[308] These echoes involve other rhetorical devices such as *ploce*, the repetition of a word with a different sense, and *antistasis*, the repetition of a word in a contrary sense. For a discussion of the possible influence of classical rhetoric on the poem, see McPherson (1980), 109–40.

redundant to the modern reader, the effect is to emphasise the obedience of the Bethulians who quickly carry out her order and to draw together the two audiences, the readers and the Bethulians, for the language used of their realisation of her return matches that in which the narrator tells us. The Bethulians' joy, humility and obedience—the additional information of the second passage—are qualities which are, accordingly, supposed to be replicated in the poem's audience. As befits an exemplary mode, the style and structure work performatively, as the poet strives to enact in the reader the values which he shows his good characters displaying. This is the principle underlying the amplification of the role of the Hebrews and the new parallelism between Judith's triumph over Holofernes and their victory against the Assyrians: the attitude inspired in them by Judith is intended to inspire the audience of *Judith*.[309]

The death of Holofernes triggers the flight and defeat of the Assyrians, and serves as a lesson to the audience that evil defeats itself.[310] This, too, is brought home by the structured use of word echo, for a strong parallel exists between the second speech of Judith to the Bethulians and that of the unnamed servant of Holofernes to the Assyrians who respectively announce the death of Holofernes to their different audiences. Whilst Judith has the head displayed to the Bethulians, the second speaker laments that his lord lies beheaded (179b *heafod*, 290a *beheafdod*). Both open with *Her*, 'here', which occurs only at these two points, and also only in these two is the verb *getacnian*, 'to show', perhaps suggesting a generic relationship between them as public pronouncements of an important event. Both speakers conclude that the Assyrians are doomed (ll.195b–7a, 285a–9a). These two pairs of parallel passages show us how people in the poem learn about events which we already know about. If the narrator tells us of the Bethulians' happy discovery of the return of Judith (soon after he has told us of that event) in order to inspire a similar emotional response in us, then he tells us of the Assyrians'

309 Cf. Doane (1991), 113 on the dramatic style of *GenB*: 'as is the case with the much later miracle plays, the audience is a main player in the meaning of the biblically based action and is expected to complete and fulfill it in its own life'

310 See earlier pp.59–60: Holofernes' canopy, the means by which he spies unseen on his own men, finally appears to hide Judith.

unhappy discovery of the death of Holofernes (long after he has narrated that event to us, and some time after Judith has told the Bethulians) to show us the folly of those who remain ignorant until it is too late. The speech of the anonymous Assyrian is the moment when dramatic irony disappears from the poem: the Assyrians are the last to know the truth, but by then their fate is sealed. The structure of the poem reveals an interest in dramatic irony, and, as we might expect, this irony has a moral function.

As the second part reproduces the first, the poet not unnaturally links the end of the poem with the beginning of the main action, whether or not this was part of the beginning of the poem (repetitions are again italicised):

> *tweode*
> gifena in ðys ginnan *grunde* ... Hyre ðæs fæder on *roderum*
> torhtmod tiðe gefremede, *þe heo ahte* trumne *geleafan*
> a *to ðam ælmihtigan* (1b–2a, 5b–7a)

> þæs *ðe heo ahte* soðne *geleafan*
> *to ðam ælmihtigan.* Huru æt þam ende ne *tweode*
> þæs leanes ðe heo lange gyrnde. Þæs sy ðam leofan dryhtne
> wuldor to widan aldre, þe gesceop wind ond lyfte,
> *roderas* ond rume *grundas*, swylce eac reðe streamas
> ond swegles dreamas þurh his sylfes miltse (344b–9)

Some of these repetitions are of words or forms confined or nearly confined to these lines, and this makes the echo slightly louder: *tweogan* (ll.1, 345), *grund* (ll.2, 348), *ahte* (pret. 3 sg., ll.3, 6, 339, 344), *ælmihtig* (ll.7, 300, 345). Both are hypermetric sections (though not the only ones in the poem) and are similar in theme, dwelling on the connection between victory and true faith, though the end, unlike the beginning, moves on from earthly glory to heavenly (compare and contrast 2a *gifena in ðys ginnan grunde*, and 343a *mærðe on moldan rice*, 344a *sigorlean in swegles wuldre*).[311] Both also share a stylistic feature of particular

[311] Foster (1892), 81, commenting on the lack of long sentences in the poem, notes a syntactic similarity between the beginning and the end: 'The most complicated construction used gives a compound sentence with three clauses, each dependent on the preceding, (cf. ll.2–5: 342–346)'.

prominence: the frequency of epithets for God (especially in the a-verse, in 3a, 4a, 5a, 5b, 7a, and 342a, 345a, 346b) contrasts with a complete absence of epithets for Judith, who is not named at the start, and not named again after she ascribes the glory to God in l.341. She is referred to only by pronouns (especially in the b-verse, *heo* in 2b, 3b, 6b, 344b, 346a, *hie* 4b, *hyre* 5b, 342b). These two passages envelop that section of the main action which shows the active operation of divine grace and ultimately the pre-eminence of the divinity which puts even the heroine into secondary position. In the end, the poet places God above and beyond all; as he sees it, God is the true hero of the poem and the lord that all must serve, Judith and the Hebrews, the poet and the audience alike.[312]

[312] The echo has persuaded some that this opening must have been very close to the beginning of the poem, see Cook (1904), 21, note to 1b, and Doubleday (1971), 439. There is reason to doubt this (see pp.3–4). Doubleday's further argument that 'the second passage in part one likewise parallels the next-to-last passage in part two, and so on, until two contrasting passages, Judith's triumph in the city and her speech urging her people to battle are juxtaposed at the center of the poem' too schematically brings together scenes from the two halves.

# The Text

# Editorial Procedure

The text follows the spelling of the manuscript, except that apparent errors have been corrected. Abbreviations have been expanded without notice. The Tironian sign *7* has been expanded as *ond*, despite the text's mixture of <o> and <a> spellings before nasals, because this spelling is suggested by the erroneous use of the sign for the preposition *on* in l.332. Additions and emendations are given in the textual notes (below the text) and contain the forms in the manuscript together with the names of those who first suggested the correction. The superscript letters and words in the manuscript listed in these notes all appear to be in the same hand as that of the main text. Other discussion may be found in the commentary. Word-division and punctuation follow modern convention, not the divisions and points of the manuscript. Proper names have been capitalised. The paragraphing is editorial, although a new paragraph always begins after a section number, where there are large capitals in the manuscript. The section numbers have been placed on the right hand side of the page (as in the manuscript) and folio numbers have been added, together with (in round brackets) chapter and verse numbers from the Vulgate for convenience of reference to the source as given in Appendix III(a). On the left hand side, line numbers have been inserted. In the text, letters in round brackets indicate those which are now missing from the manuscript, or are illegible, but which can be supplied from the transcript made by Junius. Italicised letters mark those which are now only partly visible in the manuscript and whose reading is confirmed by the transcript. Readings of letters now covered by the mounting have been supplied from Malone.

# Judith

(t)*w*eode 202r
gifena in ðys ginnan gr(un)d(e). Heo ðær ða gearwe funde
mundbyr(d) æt ðam mæran þeodne, þa heo ahte mæste þearfe
hyldo þæs hehstan deman, þæt he hie wið þæs hehstan brogan
gefriðode, frymða waldend. Hyre ðæs fæder on roderum
torhtmod tiðe gefremede, þe heo ahte trumne geleafan
á to ðam ælmihtigan. Gefrægen ic ða Holofernus (12.10)
wínhatan wyrcean georne ond eallum wundrum þrymlic
girwan up swæsendo. To ðam het se gumena bal*d*or
ealle ða yldestan ðegnas; hie ðæt ofstum miclum
ræfndon, rondwiggende, comon to ðam rican þeodne
feran, folces ræswan. Þæt wæs þy feorðan dogore
þæs ðe Iudith hyne, gleaw on geðonce,
ides ælfscinu, ærest gesohte. X

Hie ða to ðam symle sittan eodon,
wlance to wíngedrince, ealle | *h*is weagesiðas, 202v
bealde byrnwiggen(de). Þær wæron bollan steape
boren æfter (b)encum gelome, swylce eac bunan ond orcas
fulle fletsittendum; hie þæt fæge þegon,
rofe rondwiggende, þeah ðæs se rica ne wende,
egesful eorla dryhten. Ða wearð Holofernus, (12.20)
goldwine gumena, on gytesalum:
hloh ond hlydde, hlynede ond dynede,
þæt mihten fira bearn feorran gehyran
hu se stiðmoda styrmde ond gylede,
modig ond medugal, manode geneahhe
bencsittende þæt hi gebærdon wel.
Swa se inwidda ofer ealne dæg
dryhtguman sine drencte mid wine, (13.2)
swiðmod sinces brytta, oðþæt hie on swiman lagon,
oferdrencte his duguðe ealle, swylce hie wæron deaðe geslegene,
agotene goda gehwylces. Swa het se gumena aldor

---

TEXTUAL NOTES

32 aldor] baldor *with* b *incompletely erased.*

fylgan fletsittendum, oðþæt fira bearnum (13.1)
nea|(l)æhte niht seo þystre. 203r
Het ða niða geblonden
þa eadigan mægð ofstum fetigan
to his bedreste, beagum gehlæste,
hringum gehrodene. Hie hraðe fremedon,
anbyhtscealcas, swa him heora ealdor bebead,
byrnwigena brego: bearhtme stopon
to ðam gysterne, þær hie Iudithðe
fundon ferhðgleawe, ond ða fromlice
lindwiggende lædan ongunnon
þa torhtan mægð to træfe þam hean,
þær se rica hyne reste on symbel
nihtes inne, nergende lað,
Holofernus. Þær wæs eallgylden (10.19)
fleohnet fæger ond ymbe þæs folctogan
bed ahongen, þæt se bealofulla
mihte wlitan þurh, wigena baldor,
on æghwylcne þe ðær inne cóm
hæleða bearna, ond on hyne nænig
monna cynnes, nymðe se modiga hwæne
niðe rofra him þe near hete
rinca to rune gegangan. Hie ða on reste gebrohton |
(sn)ude ða snoteran idese; eodon ða ste(rced)ferhðe 203v
hæleð heora hearran cyðan þæt wæs seo halige meowle
gebroht on hi*s* burgetelde. Þa wearð se brema on mode
bliðe, burga ealdor, þohte ða beorhtan idese (13.20?)
mid widle ond mid womme besmitan. Ne wolde þæt wuldres dem
geðafian, þrymmes hyrde, ac he him þæs ðinges gestyrde,
dryhten dugeða waldend. Gewat ða se deofulcunda,
galferhð, gumena ðreate,
bealofull his beddes neosan, þær he sceolde his blæd forleosa(n)
ædre binnan anre nihte. Hæfde ða his ende gebidenne
on eorðan unswæslicne, swylcne he ær æfter worhte,
þearlmod ðeoden gumena, þenden he on ðysse worulde
wunode under wolcna hrofe. Gefeol ða wine swa druncen

---

54 gebrohton] gebrohten *with* e *deleted by underdotting and* o *superscript.*

se rica on his reste middan, swa he nyste ræda nanne (13.4)
on gewitlocan. Wiggend stopon |
ut of ðam inne ofstum miclum, 204r
wera(s) winsade, þe ðone wærlogan,
laðne leodhatan, læddon to bedde
nehstan siðe.

Þa wæs nergendes
þeowen þrymful þearle gemyndig
hu heo þone atolan eaðost mihte
ealdre benæman ær se unsyfra,
womfull, onwoce. Genam ða wundenlocc (13.8)
scyppendes mægð scearpne mece,
scurum heardne, ond of sceaðe abræd
swiðran folme. Ongan ða swegles weard
be naman nemnan, nergend ealra
woruldbuendra, ond þæt word ácwæð: (13.7, 9)
"Ic ðe, frymða god, ond frofre gæst,
bearn alwaldan, biddan wylle
miltse þinre me þearfendre,
ðrynesse ðrym. Þearle ys me nu ða
heorte onhæted ond hige geomor,
swyðe mid sorgum gedrefed. Forgif me, swegles ealdor,
sigor ond soðne geleafan, þæt ic mid þys sweorde mote
geheawan þysne morðres bryttan. Geunne me minra ge|synta,
204v
þearlmod þeoden gumena: nah*t*(e) ic þinre næfre
miltse þon maran þearf(e). Gewrec nu, mihtig dryhten,
torhtmod tires brytta, þæt me ys þus torne on mode,
hate on hreðre minum."

Hi ða se hehsta dema
ædre mid elne onbryrde, swa he deð anra gehwylcne
herbuendra þe hyne him to helpe seceð
mid ræde ond mid rihte geleafan. Þa wearð hyre rume on mode,
haligre hyht geniwod. Genam ða þone hæðenan mannan (13.9)

---

85 þearfendre *Junius*] þearffendre *with* þearf *line-end and* fendre *line-initial.*
87 heorte onhæted *Thorpe*] heorte ys onhæted.
90 me] *superscript with mark of insertion.*

fæste be feaxe sinum; teah hyne folmum wið hyre weard
bysmerlice, ond þone bealofullan
listum alede, laðne mannan,
swa heo ðæs unlædan eaðost mihte
wel gewealdan. Sloh ða wundenlocc (13.10)
þone feondsceaðan fagum mece,
heteþoncolne, þæt heo healfne forcearf
þone sweoran him, þæt he on swiman læg,
druncen ond dolhwund. Næs ða dead þa gyt,
ealles orsawle. Sloh ða eornoste
ides ellenróf | (oð)re siðe 205r
þone hæðenan hund, þæt him þæt heafod wand
forð on ða flore. Læg se fula leap
gesne beæftan, gæst ellor hwearf
under neowelne næs ond ðær genyðerad wæs,
susle gesæled syððan æfre, (8.25?)
wyrmum bewunden, witum gebunden, (16.21?)
hearde gehæfted in helle bryne
æfter hinsiðe. Ne ðearf he hopian nó,
þystrum forðylmed, þæt he ðonan mote
of ðam wyrmsele, ac ðær wunian sceal
awa to aldre butan ende forð
in ðam heolstran hám, hyhtwynna leas. XI

Hæfde ða gefohten foremærne blæd
Iudith æt guðe, swa hyre god uðe,
swegles ealdor, þe hyre sigores onleah.
Þa seo snotere mægð snude gebrohte
þæs herewæðan heafod swa blodig (13.11)
on ðam fætelse þe hyre foregenga,
bláchleor ides, hyra begea nest,
ðeawum geðungen, þyder on lædde,
ond hit | ða swa heolfrig hyre on hond agea*f*, 205v
(hige)þoncolre, ham to berenne,
Iudith gingran sinre. Eodon ða gegnum þanonne (13.12)
þa idesa bá, ellenþriste,
oðþæt hie becomon, collenferhðe,
eadhreðige mægð, ut of ðam herige,

---

134 hie *Thorpe*] hie hie.

þæt hie sweotollice  geseon mihten
þære wlitegan byrig  weallas blican,
Bethuliam. Hie ða beahhrodene
feðelaste  forð onettan,
oð hie glædmode  gegán hæfdon
to ðam wealgate. Wiggend sæton,
weras wæccende  wearde heoldon
in ðam fæstenne,  swa ðam folce ǽr
geomormodum  Iudith bebéad,
searoðoncol mægð,  þa heo on sið gewat,
ides ellenróf. Wæs ða eft cumen
leof to leodum,  ond ða lungre het (13.13)
gleawhydig wíf  gumena sumne
of ðære ginnan byrig  hyre togeanes gán,
ond hi ofostlice  in forlæton
þurh ðæs wealles geat,  ond þæt word acwæð
to ðam sigefolce: "Ic eow secgan mæg
þoncwyrðe þing,  þæt ge ne þyrfen leng |
*mu*rnan on mode:  eow ys metod bliðe*e*, 206r
cyninga wuldor;  þæt gecyðed wearð
geond woruld wide,  þæt eow ys wuldorblæd
torhtlic toweard  ond tir gifeðe
þara læðða  þe ge lange drugon."
    Þa wurdon bliðe  burhsittende,
syððan hi gehyrdon  hu seo halige spræc (13.14)
ofer heanne weall. Here wæs on lustum;
wið þæs fæstengeates  folc onette, (13.15)
weras wif somod,  wornum ond heapum,
ðreatum ond ðrymmum  þrungon ond urnon
ongean ða þeodnes mægð  þusendmælum,
ealde ge geonge. Æghwylcum wearð

---

141 wealgate] *with* weal *added above the line with mark of insertion.*
142 heoldon] heordon *with* r *altered to* l.
144 Iudith *Ettmüller*] iudithe.
150 forlæton] forleton *with tagged* e *for* æ, *and the second* o *changed from* e.
165 þeodnes *Junius*] þeoðnes.

men on ðære medobyrig  mod areted,
syððan hie ongeaton  þæt wæs Iudith cumen
eft to eðle,  ond ða ofostlice
hie mid eaðmedum  in forleton.
Þa seo gleawe het,  golde gefrætewod,
hyre ðinenne  þancolmode
þæs herewæðan  heafod onwriðan  (13.19)
ond hyt to behðe  blodig ætywan
þam burhleodum,  hu hyre æt beaduwe gespeow.
Spræc ða seo æðele | (to e)*al*lu(m) þa(m) folce:  206v
"Her ge magon sweotol(e), (si)gerofe hæleð,
leoda ræswan,  on ðæs laðestan
hæðenes heaðorinces  heafod starian,
Holofernus  unlyfigendes,
þe us monna mæst  morðra gefremede,
sarra sorga,  ond þæt swyðor gyt
ycan wolde,  ac him ne uðe god
lengran lifes,  þæt he mid læððum us
eglan moste:  ic him ealdor oðþrong
þurh godes fultum.  Nu ic gumena gehwæne
þyssa burgleoda  biddan wylle,
randwiggendra  þæt ge recene eow
fysan to gefeohte,  syððan frymða god,  (14.2)
árfæst cyning,  eastan sende
leohtne leoman.  Berað linde forð,
bord for breostum  ond byrnhomas,
scire helmas  in sceaðena gemong,
fyllan folctogan  fagum sweordum,
fæge frumgaras.  Fynd syndon eowere
gedemed to deaðe  ond ge dóm agon,
tír æt tohtan,  swa eow getacnod hafað
mihtig dryhten  þurh mine | (h)and."  (13.18)  207r
Þa wearð snelra werod  snude g(e)gearewod,  (14.7)
cenra to campe.  Stopon cynerofe
secgas ond gesiðas,  bæron sigeþufas,

---

179 starian *Junius*] stariað.
195 frumgaras] *with the first* r *corrected from* u.
201 sigeþufas *Ettmüller*] þufas.

foron to gefeohte forð on gerihte,
hæleð under helmum, of ðære haligan byrig
on ðæt dægred sylf. Dynedan scildas,
hlude hlummon. Þæs se hlanca gefeah
wulf in walde, ond se wanna hrefn,
wælgifre fugel: wistan begen
þæt him ða þeodguman þohton tilian
fylle on fægum; ac him fleah on last
earn ætes georn, urigfeðera;
salowigpada sang hildeleoð,
hyrnednebba. Stopon heaðorincas,
beornas to beadowe, bordum beðeahte,
hwealfum lindum, þa ðe hwile ær
elðeodigra edwit þoledon,
hæðenra hosp. Him þæt hearde wearð
æt ðam æscplegan eallum forgolden
Assyrium, syððan Ebreas
under guðfanum gegan hæfdon
to ðam fyrdwicum. Hie ða fromlice
leton forð fleogan flana scuras, |
(hilde)*n*ædran of hornbogan, 207v
strælas st(edeh)earde. Styrmdon hlude
grame guðfrecan, garas sendon
in heardra gemang. Hæleð wæron yrre,
landbuende, laðum cynne,
stopon styrnmode, stercedferhðe;
wrehton unsofte ealdgeniðlan
medowerige. Mundum brugdon
scealcas of sceaðum scirmæled swyrd,
ecgum gecoste, slogon eornoste
Assiria oretmæcgas,
niðhycgende. Nanne ne sparedon
þæs herefolces, heanne ne ricne,
cwicera manna þe hie ofercuman mihton. XII
Swa ða magoþegnas on ða morgentíd
ehton elðeoda ealle þrage,

---

207 wistan *Cook*] westan.
234 ricne *Grein*] rice.

oðþæt ongeaton ða ðe grame wæron,
ðæs herefolces heafodweardas,
þæt him swyrdgeswing swiðlic eowdon
weras Ebrisce. Hie wordum þæt
þam yldestan ealdorþegnum
cyðan eodon, wrehton cumbolwigan
ond him forhtlice færspel bodedon,
medowerigum morgencollan,
atolne ecgplegan. Þa ic ædre gefrægn
slegefæge hæleð | slæpe tobredon 208r
ond wið þæs bealofullan b*ú*rgeteldes (14.8)
werigferhðe hwearfum þringan,
Ho(lo)fernus. Hogedon aninga
hyra hlaforde hilde bodian,
ærðonðe him se egesa onufan sæte,
mægen Ebrea. Mynton ealle (14.13)
þæt se beorna brego ond seo beorhte mægð
in ðam wlitegan træfe wæron ætsomne,
Iudith seo æðele ond se galmoda,
egesfull ond afor. Næs ðeah eorla nán
þe ðone wiggend aweccan dorste (14.10)
oððe gecunnian hu ðone cumbolwigan
wið ða halgan mægð hæfde geworden,
metodes meowlan. Mægen nealæhte,
folc Ebrea, fuhton þearle
heardum heoruwæpnum, hæfte guldon
hyra fyrngeflitu, fagum swyrdum,
ealde æfðoncan. Assyria wearð
on ðam dægweorce dom geswiðrod,
bælc forbiged. Beornas stodon
ymbe hyra þeodnes træf þearle gebylde,
sweorcendferhðe. Hi ða somod ealle (14.9)
ongunnon cohhetan, cirman hlude
ond gristbitian —gode orfeorme—
mid toðon, torn þoligende. Þa wæs hyra tires æt ende, |

---

249 werigferhðe *Grein*] weras ferhðe.
251 hilde *Leo*] hyldo.
266 dægweorce *Cook 1904*] dæge weorce.

*ea*des ond ellendæda. Hogedon þa eorlas awe*cc*(an) 208v
(hy)ra winedryhten: him wiht ne speow.
Þa wear(ð) sið ond late sum to ðam arod
þara beadorinca, þæt he in þæt búrgeteld (14.13)
niðheard neðde, swa hyne nyd fordráf.
Funde ða on bedde blacne lic(gan) (14.14)
his goldgifan gæstes gesne,
lifes belidenne. He þa lungre gefeoll
freorig to foldan, ongan his feax teran,
hreoh on mode, ond his hrægl somod,
ond þæt word acwæð to ðam wiggendum
þe ðær unrote ute wæron:
"Her ys geswutelod ure sylfra forwyrd,
toweard getacnod, þæt þære tide ys
mid niðum neah geðrungen, þe (we) sculon nu losian,
somod æt sæcce forweorðan. Her lið sweorde geheawen,
beheafdod healde*n*(d) ure." Hi ða hreowigmode (14.16–17)
wurpon hyra wæpen ofdune, gewitan him werigferhðe
on fleam sceacan. Him mon feaht on last, (15.1)
mægeneacen folc, oð se mæsta dæl (15.3)
þæs heriges læg hilde gesæged
on ðam sigewonge, sweordum geheawen,
wulfum to willan ond eac wælgifrum
fuglum to | frofre. Flugon ða ðe lyfd*o*(n) 209r
*l*aðra lindwig; him on laste for (15.4)
sweot Ebrea sigore geweorðod,
dom(e) gedyrsod. Him feng dryhten god
fægre on ful(t)u(m), frea ælmihtig.
Hi ða fromlice fagum swyrdum,
hæleð higerofe, herpað worhton
þurh laðra gemong, linde heowon,
scildburh scæro(n). Sceotend wæron

---

287 nu *Kluge*] *not in MS.*
292 mægeneacen] *with superscript* a *and mark of insertion.*
297 lindwig] lind *followed by more than one letter, the first of which is probably wynn. Malone (1961), 35, and in the facsimile, reads* wig.
298 sigore] *superscript with mark of insertion.*

guðe gegremede, guman Ebrisce,
þegnas on ða tíd þearle gelyste
gárgewinnes. Þær on greot gefeoll
se hyhsta dæl heafodgerimes
Assiria ealdorduguðe,
laðan cynnes. Lythwón becóm
cwicera to cyððe.
Cirdon cynerofe,
wiggend on wiðertrod, wælscel oninnan,
reocende hrǽw. Rúm wæs to nimanne (15.7)
londbuendum on ðam laðestan,
hyra ealdfeondum unlyfigendum
heolfrig hereréaf, hyrsta scyne,
bord ond bradswyrd, brune helmas,
dyre madmas. Hæfdon dómlice
on ðam folcstede fynd oferwunnen
eðelweardas, ealdhettende
swyrdum aswefede. Hie on swaðe reston,
þa ðe him to life laðost wæron |
(cwi)cera cynna. (Þ)a seo cneoris eall, 209v
mægða *mærost*, anes monðes fyrst, (15.13)
wlanc, wundenlocc, (w)ægon ond læddon
to ðære beorhtan byrig, Bethuliam,
helmas ond hupseax, hare byrnan,
guðsceorp gumena golde gefrætewod,
mare madma þonne mon ænig
asecgan mæge searoþoncelra.
Eal þæt ða ðeodguman þrymme geeodon,
cene under cumblum on compwige
þurh Iudithe gleawe lare,
mægð modigre. Hi to mede hyre (15.14)
of ðam siðfate sylfre brohton,
eorlas æscrofe, Holofernes (16.23)

---

319 fynd] *with* n *altered from* r.
322 wæron] *the only word of the last line of text (which is additional to the normal twenty).*
329 mare *Mossé*] mærra.
332 on *Rieger*] 7.

sweord ond swatigne helm, swylce eac side (b)yrnan
gerenode readum golde, ond eal þæt se rinca baldor
swiðmod sinces ahte oððe sundoryrfes, (15.14)
beaga ond beorhtra maðma, hi þæt þære beorhtan idese
ageafon gearoþoncolre.
Ealles ðæs Iudith sægde (16.1)
wuldor weroda dryhtne, þe hyre weorðmynde geaf,
mærðe on moldan rice, swylce eac mede on heofonum,
sigorlean | (in) sweg*l*es wuldre, þæs ðe heo ahte soðne geleafan
to ða(m) ælmihtigan. Huru æt þam ende ne tweode
þæs lea*n*(e)*s* *ð*(e heo) *l*(a)nge gyrnde. Þæs sy ðam leofan dryhtne
wu(ldor) to widan aldre, þe gesceop wind ond lyfte,
rodera*s* *ond* r(u)me grundas, swylce eac reðe streamas
ond *swe*(g)*l*(es) dreamas *þ*urh *his sylf*(es miltse).

344 sigorlean] *with six lines following in an early modern hand (imitating insular script) at the foot of the folio.*
347 gesceop *Junius*] gesceow.

# Commentary

**1b** *tweode*: Dobbie and Timmer, following Kaluza (1895), 384, close the line with this word. Earlier editors read *tweode gifena* as the last words of the first line. The general absence from *Jud* of light hypermetric a-verses suggests that *gifena* belongs to 2a, as does the parallel between the opening and closing hypermetric groups: *tweode* ends l.345. The earlier reading is not, however, impossible (see also notes to 2a and 90a). Attempts to supply the missing part of the line are speculative, beyond the probability that *tweode* was preceded by *ne* or some other negative form .

**2a** *gifena in ðys ginnan grunde*: triple alliteration is rare, but not unparallelled, elsewhere in hypermetric a-verses, cf. *Sea* 106a *Dol biþ se þe him his dryhten ne ondrædeþ*, and see Hieatt (1974), 238–9, who counts more than a dozen clear examples, mainly in poems that do not strictly conform to normal alliterative practices (e.g. *Max I*). See also pp.25–6.

**4** *hyldo*: either gen. sing. and dependent on *þearfe* (so Cook, Timmer), or acc. sing. and parallel to *mundbyrd* (see Bright (1889), 243f; Holthausen (1889), 448). As *þearf* takes a dependent gen. in l.92, and enjambement is pervasive in the poem, the former is perhaps likelier. *Hehstan* ... *hehstan*: alliteration on the same word occurs also in l.340, *beorhtra* ... *beorhtan*, but rarely elsewhere in O.E. poetry (see *Dan* 265, Farrell (1974), 62–3, and, above, p.88).

**5a** *waldend*: the poet makes unusually frequent use of verbal nouns of agency in *-end*. The simplex forms (ll.5, 45, 61, 69, 73, 81, 141, 258, 283, 289, 304, 312) are uninflected in the nom. and acc. pl. The cpd. forms (ll.11, 17, 19, 20, 27, 33, 42, 82, 96, 159, 188, 226, 233, 314, 320) take *-e* in these cases from the adjectival declension.

**5b–6b** *ðæs* ... *ðe*: 'on this account ... because'.

**7a** *ðam ælmihtigan*: the collocation of dem. and weak adj. (as noun) is common in the poem, particularly with reference to Holofernes. Unambiguous examples are (of God) *ælmihtig*, 7, 345; (of Judith) *æðele*, 176, *gleaw*, 171, *halig*, 160; (of Holofernes) *atol*, 75, *bealofull*, 100, *deofolcund*, 61, *galmod*, 256, *inwid*, 28, *lað*, 314, *modig*, 52, *rice*, 68, *stiðmod*, 25, *unlæd*, 102, *unsyfre*, 76. It is sometimes not clear whether the adjs. function as adj. or noun (ll.20, 44, 48, 57, 178, 205, 248, 256). See further C178b.

**7b–34a** The poet elaborates on the feast in 12.10 of the source, and presents a perversion of the heroic banquet as seen in *Beo*. Hume (1974), 73, remarks on the heavy stress on the drunkenness, and the absence of words for joy (*dream, wynn*) which normally characterise the feelings of the participants. Hill (1975), 16, concludes that the poet understood 'the Christian concept of perverted imitation [of good] as a manifestation of evil'. A similar scene is found in *Dan* 700f. In both of these, and elsewhere in the poetry (e.g. *Beo* 1008–1237, 2032–56), disaster follows swiftly after drinking in the mead-hall.

**7b** *Hōlofernus*: the first vowel is long, and so the name may fill a complete verse (see Campbell, §§548–58). Foreign proper names beginning with a vowel are often spelled with an inorganic <*h-*> by the scribes (e.g. *Habrahame* in *And*), but alliterate with vowels (so here and in ll.21, 46, 180, 336). In l.250 (as in 273) *hogedon* is unstressed, and *Holofernus* alliterates with *aninga*.

**9a** *girwan up swæsendo*: hypermetric a-verses with three main stresses usually display double alliteration. Pope (1966), 153–4, suggests reading *girwan up gyteswæsendo*, but *Jud* does not always conform to the strictest alliterative practices. *Girwan up* is usually translated as a phrasal verb, 'serve up', 'dress up', but it is unusual in O.E. for a particle to follow a non-finite part of the verb, and Denison (1985), 41–2, views this as 'the possible example of completive *up* in O.E. which is hardest to dismiss'. Prof. Stanley has suggested to me that *up swæsendo* may be a cpd., with *up* in the sense 'superior', 'royal'. *Up* usually means 'up', 'upper' or 'above' in cpds., but may have acquired metaphorical sense through association with the heavenly in cpds. such as *upcund*, *upeard*, *upheofon*, *uprodor*, *upweg*.

**12a** *ræswan*: either nom. pl., parallel to *hie* (10) and *rond-wiggende* (11) and sub. of *comon*, or dat. sing., and parallel to *þeodne*, with the sub. understood.

**12b** *þy feorðan dogor*: by contrast with some O.E. poetic narratives, *Jud* makes little use of parenthetic statements. The detail is taken over from the source (12.10), and, though the poet usually omits material irrelevant to the main events, he preserves some time markers, perhaps for reasons of narrative coherence (cf. 13.1 and ll.28 and 34, 14.2 and 189–90a, 14.7 and 204a, 15.13 and 324b). Chamberlain (1975), 146, speculates that this remark makes more sense if the audience had been told in the missing opening that Judith asked the elders to pray for five days to gain God's favour (8. 32).

**14a** *ælfscinu*: etymologically, 'elf-bright', 'beautiful as a nymph'. The Vulgate adds to the detailed description of Judith decking herself, the remark that, because of the virtue of her purpose, her beauty was miraculously increased (10. 4), and, consequently, everyone marvelled at her beauty (10. 7, 14, 18). Perhaps, then, the cpd. means 'wonderfully beautiful' (see Stuart (1972), 22, and cf. *sunsciene* (*Jul* 229), *wlitesciene* (*GenB* 527) and the epithet *mæg ælfscieno* for Sarah in *GenA* 1827, 2731 as descriptions of feminine beauty). *Ælf-* is a common O.E. name element, and, if meaningful in this context, it must have had complimentary sense. In other contexts (e.g. *ælfadl*, 'nightmare', *ælfsiden*, 'nightmare', *ælfðone*, 'nightshade'), it had a negative one. For discussion, see Jente (1921), 172–3 and Swanton (1988), 297.

**15a** *to ðam symle*: the phrase is quite common (e.g. *Beo* 489, 2104, *Dan* 700, *Dream* 141) but elsewhere lacks the dem.. There is a tendency for traditional phrasing to be filled out with dems. and possessives in late verse (see Scragg (1981), 29, and 53).

**16a** *wlance*: von Lindheim (1951), 34–8, suggests that *wlanc* here has the sense 'lusting'. Woolf (1975), 204 and n.22, argues for a pejorative meaning, especially in formulaic combination with *wingal*, but notes that this 'will depend upon the moral seriousness of the poem in which they occur'. *Wlanc* alliterates here with *win-* (cf. *Rid* 14. 17 *wlonce to wine*, *Sat* 93 *wloncra winsele*), but not with *wingal* (but note l.26 *medugal*). Early M.E. provides examples of pejorative *wlanc* (e.g. *The Owl and the*

*Nightingale* 489, and for discussion, see Stanley (1972), 145). If we accept a positive translation, then the description of the Assyrian officers' bearing or feelings is straightforward (perhaps, though, with some sense of how soon they are to be disabused of their false dignity); if a negative one is to be preferred, then this may be taken as moral comment from the narrator. Gordon translates 'exulting', Bradley 'insolent', Cook gives 'lordly, stately', and Timmer 'stately, proud'; von Rüden (1978), 137, suggests 'merry'. See also C26a.

**16b** *weagesiðas*: *wea*, 'misery', 'evil', suggests two senses for the cpd.: 'companions in misery', or 'companions in crime'. Both are applicable. On the spellings *wæg-, weg-*, and weakened apprehension of the etymological sense of the first element, or confusion with *weg*, 'way', see Scragg (1992), 472.

**17b–31** The poet here touches on the image of the cup of death, or *poculum mortis*, which is frequently to be found in medieval literature, and which appears to have both Christian and pre-Christian sources. That the adj. *deop*, 'deep', is associated with the cup of death may explain the description of the drinking goblets as *bollan steape*, 'deep cups' (see Russom (1988), 176–7: 'A drinking cup that was deep ... would produce that deep slumber to which death is so often compared'). Russom notes further that in O.E. poetry, as here, 'the advent of death is typically concealed from the doomed man' (177).

**19b** *Hie þæt fæge þegon*: this addition to the source (and the similar asides in 63–5, 272b, and 274b) strips the narrative of suspense but invests it with dramatic irony: our knowledge of the imminence of their doom makes their careless self-indulgence seem the height of folly. In the telling of a well known story there can be no uncertainty as to the outcome of the action and, in general, O.E. poets did not use suspense. For the suggestion that *fæge*, 'doomed', might imply condemnation of the Assyrians, see Gillam (1962), 175: 'it is almost always the bad who are *fæge*'.

**22** On the alliteration, see p.26, n.90.

**23–5** The poet does not, at this point, directly translate the Vulgate statement that Holofernes drank 'exceeding much wine, so much as he had never drunk in his life' (12.20) preferring dramatic representation to narratorial comment (but cf. 67b–9a). The general's excessive noise and laughter signals his imminent downfall. Tucker (1959), 222–6, compares the exultation of Grendel in *Beo* 730 'not knowing that one of the night's victims would be himself'. Robinson (1993a), 113, n.33, compares Byrhtnoth's laughter in *Mald* 147 with a scene of laughter before a murder in Layamon's *Brut*, and concludes that this may be 'a conventional dramatic signal that a mortal blow is imminent at the moment when the threatened person least expects it'. Magennis (1992), 198–200, gives examples of excessive laughter in a wide range of O.E. religious literature, and locates a possible source in Ecclesiasticus 21.23. Loud laughter is also associated with the vice of drunkenness in O.E. poetry: both are avoided by the seafarer (*Sea* 19–21), and in *JDay II* 262ff. laughter and drunkenness are amongst the joys of the world which lead to the damnation of the soul. On the parallel with Jordanes' account of the death of Attila the Hun, see C281b–2. On the unusual sequence of verbs in 23 and 25b, see Brodeur (1968), 107–8, who compares ll.162–4 and 270–1.

**24a** *þæt mihten*: either (a) *þæt* = conj. with subj. *mihten* in a clause of purpose ('He laughed ... in order that men could hear from far away how ... '), or (b) *þæt* = conj. with indic. *mihton* (with *-en* for *-on*) in a clause of result ('He laughed ... with the result that men could hear afar how ... ') or (c) *þæt* = dem. pron. as obj. of *mihton ... gehyran*, and a new sentence begins at l.24 ('Men could hear that from afar: how ... '). Holofernes intends to get drunk and seduce Judith; he surely does not care whether others can hear his carousing or not, so (a), a clause of purpose, is unlikely, but the fact that his noisiness results in a general disturbance is indicative of his excessive licentiousness, so both (b) and (c) are plausible. Confusion of verb inflexions in *-n* is sporadic in the text; cf. *-en* for *-on* in the result clause in ll.136–7.

**26a** *medugal*: the invitation in l.8 is to a wine party, but here Holofernes is 'drunk with mead', and, similarly, his men are *medowerig*, 229, 245, but also *winsæd*, 71. O.E. poets speak indiscriminately of different alcoholic drinks. Neither *beor* nor *ealo*, however, occurs in *Jud* (though DOE gives 'mead' as a sense of *beor*). Professor Swanton has suggested to me that the poet may have felt that ale and beer were insufficiently exotic drinks for an Assyrian general and his men.

**26a, 52b** *modig*: here in the pejorative sense 'proud, arrogant' (contrast 334). Ælfric also uses the word in this sense of Holofernes (Assmann (1889), 114, l.410). The picture of him as the perversion of the heroic leader encouraged such pejoration; cf. C16a, and the use of *swiðmod* (30, 339), and *þearlmod* (66, contrast 91). The phrase *modig 7 medugal* is unique, but it may have been formed by analogy with *wlanc 7 wingal*, and, like that formula, may have pejorative connotation.

**26b–7** *manode ... þæt hi gebærdon wel*: if *gebǣran* means 'to carry, or behave oneself properly', i.e. to pay attention to etiquette (cf. *Beo* 1012, *Finn* 38 *sel gebæran*), then Holofernes' exhortation is ironic in view of his designs on Judith and his general excess (see C7b–34a). The non-ironic translation 'cry out in joy, enjoy' is, however, also possible, and, if correct, then 27b could be a clause of result ('with the result that they enjoyed themselves greatly').

**28–34a** Bately (1984), 7–8, notes the influence of Biblical imagery in the presentation of the approach of night and concludes that the language is 'appropriate both to temporal, and to spiritual, and to eternal darkness, a fact which is brought home ... by the verbal and syntactical parallelisms of the three main clauses, with their verbs of related meaning, and the three subordinate clauses dependent on them, with the first and third both introduced by *oðþæt*, and the second amplifying the first'.

**28a** *se inwidda*: Timmer and Campbell (1938), 112, take the form as a weak adj. from *inwidd(e)* used nominally. It occurs only once elsewhere at *Brun* 46. See C7a.

**28b** *ofer ealne dæg*: the indefinite adj. of quantity *eal* frequently leads the noun, and is stressed and alliterates, in phrases of time. Cf. l.237b, and see C306a. The stressing of proclitic adjs. is dealt with by Slay (1952).

**29a** *dryhtguman sine*: originally *sin* functioned as the possessive 'his/her', and *his*, *hyre* as the genitives 'of him, of her' (cf. Latin *suus* and *ejus*). *Sin* progressively became confined to poetry, and *his*, *hyre* were used in both capacities. In *Jud* the possessive *sin* is always inflected in a post-nominal position requiring a stressed disyllable (29a, 99a, 132a), whilst possessive *his*, *hyre* are unstressed proclitics.

**31a** *oferdrencte his duguðe ealle*: either the verb is 3rd. sing. pret. indic., with *ealle* acc. sing. fem. agreeing with *duguðe*, or *oferdrencte* is a past participle modifying *ealle* (nom. pl. masc.), and *duguðe* is gen. sing. and dependent on *ealle*. In the first case, the subject, Holofernes, may be assumed, and the clause parenthetic, or *sinces brytta* in 30a may be the subject (so translate: '—he inebriated all the troop—'). In the second, the verse-phrase varies *hie* in 30b (so translate: 'until they, all the drunken troop, lay unconscious'). *Deaþ* and *drencan* are collocated elsewhere in the poetry (see for example *Ex* 34a *deaðe gedrenced*, *Whale* 30 *in deaðsele drence bifæsteð,* and cf. *Jud* 107 *druncen ... dead*; for discussion, see Doane (1978), 266).

**31b** *swylce*: where the conj. *swylce* means 'as if', the mood of the verb is normally subj. (see Mitchell, 2. §§3370–81); the form *wæron* is either a reverse spelling following centralisation of unstressed inflected vowels, or a very rare indic. in this type of clause.

**31b–2a** The first part of the simile is transparent: they are unconscious and so seem dead, which in a moral sense they are, and in a literal sense they are soon to be. The second is oxymoronic: they are flooded with wine (*oferdrencte*) as if drained of virtue (*agotene*); the moral sense reverses the literal. Foster (1892), 68, notes the rareness and simplicity of simile in O.E. poetic usage, with which this poem is 'in full accord', but the image here is more complex than he allows. Astell (1990), 123–4, sees in this the influence of 'Ambrose's notion that their drunken sleep ... symbolizes their spiritual destruction, [but] the poet makes the comparison explicit'. For further discussion, see Greenfield (1972), 96–100. The concatenation of these ideas (unconsciousness, death, drunkenness) is repeated in ll.106–7, in words which echo 30–1.

**32a** *agotene*: *ageotan* usually means 'to pour out, shed' (a liquid, frequently blood, e.g. *GenA* 984, *And* 141, 1449, *GuthA* 522). Here the sense is figurative, 'to drain (of good)', elsewhere illustrated by *Ex* 515 *ageat gylp wera*.

**33a** *fylgan*: Cook emends to *fyllan*, 'to fill up, replenish', but the verb *fylgan* may mean 'to attend to, serve', see BTS *fylgean*, II.1.d., '*to attend to* a person medically'.

**33b** *oðþæt* occurs at 30b, 33b, 134a, 238a. It is usually the conj. 'until'. For the possibility that it may be an adv. meaning 'at length' or 'and then', see Stanley (1974), 139–64, Mitchell (1978), 390–4, and Mitchell, 2. §2754. In 30b, 134a, 238a, there is no sense of a transition in the narrative, and the *oðþæt* clause completes the action of the main clause, so that the conj. is much the likelier; the clause that begins in 33b can, however, be construed as marking a shift in the narrative to a new theme ('At length, night closed in on the sons of men. Then ... '). The difficulty is made more acute by the uncertain meaning of *fylgan* in 33a.

**34b** *niða geblonden*: 'infected with evil', cf. *And* 675, *HomFr I* 16.

**36** *bedreste: gehlæste*: restoration of *a* in place of *æ*, with subsequent i-mutation to *æ*, gives *-ræste* (see Campbell § 193(c)); the line may originally have rhymed.

**36b, 37a** The Vulgate states (10.3) that Judith adorned herself with bracelets, earrings, rings and all her ornaments. For the possibility that these phrases in the poem, and similar ones at 138b, 171b, may have martial connotation, see Damico (1990), 183–4, and notes to 171b, and 327–9.

**39b** *bearhtme*: either 'in an instant' (< *bearhtm*, 'twinkling') and varying *hraðe* in 37, or, more probably, 'noisily' (< *bearhtm*, 'tumult').

**43b, 255a, 268a** *træf*: the meaning 'tent', rendering *tabernaculum* is confined to *Jud*. *And* 842 *tigelfagan trafu* seems to refer to tiled constructions in the pagan city of Mermedonia. Elsewhere *træf* occurs in three cpds.: *Beo* 175 *hærgtræf*, 'heathen temple', *And* 1691 *helltræf*, 'hellish building', *El* 926 *wearhtræf*, 'dwelling of the damned'. These may suggest that *træf* had, for the poet, an association with the heathen and hellish which *geteld* did not (see Huppé (1970), 163, and Berkhout and Doubleday (1973), 630–4; but note Lendinara (1993), 323, on *geteld* as a prose word). If so, its description as *wlitig* in 255a refers only to a surface or illusory beauty. See also C57a.

**45a** *inne*: though *inne* may be construed as an independent adv., 'inside', it is probably to be taken with the preceding *þær*, 'wherein' (see 50b *ðær inne*, 'therein'). Cf. *JDay II* 38 *Ne þær owiht inne ne belife*.

**47a** *fleohnet*: the word occurs elsewhere only twice in glosses of *canopeum* (cf. *fleogryfte*, *micgnet*). Holofernes' *canopeum* in the source is 'woven with purple and gold and emeralds and precious stones' and is a display of great wealth. This is abbreviated to *eallgylden ... fæger*, but the poet adds the seemingly original detail that it is a kind of 'two-way mirror': he can spy on his retainers whilst they cannot see him. Holofernes' distrust of his men may have been suggested to the poet by Hrabanus Maurus's interpretation of the canopy as *insidias ... dolosae cogitationis* ('the snares of deceitful thought'), but, equally, the use of the net in the psalms of the trickster tricked may be relevant. For further discussion, see pp.59–60, 78–9, and n.310, and Berkhout and Doubleday (1973). Huppé's notion, (1970), 163–4, that the canopy implies 'the mysterious presence of a god-like figure' seems far-fetched given that there is nothing mysterious about Holofernes in the mead-hall.

**47b** Sweet and Cook omit the ampersand as superfluous to the sense, but the emendation is unnecessary: 'There was a mosquito net, beautiful, all-golden and hung around the general's bed'; see DOE *and*, A.1.a.ii., 'joining syntactically disparate units, perhaps involving anacoluthon'.

**49a** *wlitan þurh*: adverbial use of *þurh* is rare; BT and Wullen (1911), 497, offer only this instance and *PPs* 77. 15 *He sæ toslat ... and hi foran þurh* in the poetry; there are no citations from the prose. With *wlitan þurh* cf. *þurhwlitan*, 'to see through' (see *ChristC* 1283, 1331), and with *faran þurh* cf. *þurhfaran*, 'to pass through'.

**51b** *ond on hyne nænig*: see DOE *and* B.3.a., '*ond* in *ond hyne nænig* comes close in sense to "but, yet" and perhaps even to "though"'. The context seems to be adversative: Holofernes could see through the net, and [yet] no-one could see him.

**54b** *on reste gebrohton*, 57a *gebroht on his burgetelde*, 125b–7a *gebrohte ... on ðam fætelse*: perfective *gebringan* (i.e. that form of *bringan* which expresses completed or finished action) is not, as Mod.E. *bring* is, a verb of motion, but one of rest, and so is followed by *on* + dat. (rather than acc.). *-getelde* and *fætelse* are unambigously dat.; the fem. *reste* is ambiguous in case but the syntax suggests the dat.. See Belden (1903), and Klaeber (1950), xciii.

**55** Ettmüller emends to *snelferhðe*, but there is no reason beyond the correcting of the alliteration to support the suggestion. Malone, 110, suggests that the scribe's original 'probably had *stunde* "at once" ... but the scribe wrote its synonym *snude* instead, influenced by the *sn* he was about to write in *snoteran*'. On the form *sterced-*, see p.20.

**56a** *hearran*: a rare poetic word, occurring outside *GenB* only in late poetry (*Mald* 204, *DEdw* 32), and possibly *Dan* 392 (or more probably *herran*, there, is a scribal error for *heran*, 'servants'). Green (1965), 417–21, regards it as a loan-word from O.S. into O.E. The spelling may suggest confusion or blending with *hēarra*, comp.of *hēah*, 'high', in the sense 'superior'. The alliterative collocation of *hæleþ: halig* (here and in 203) occurs quite often (*Ex* 388, 394, *And* 885, 996, 1054, 1607, *El* 1203, *ChristB* 461, 534). Frank (1972), 220–1, compares and contrasts the near homophonic attraction of *hæleþ:halig* and *mann*, 'man': *mān*, 'sin'.

**57a, 248b, 276b** *burgeteld*: the cpd. is confined to this poem. It may vary *træf*, but more probably *træf* denotes the entire tent (which the warriors stand around in 267–8), whilst this term refers to the bedroom—*cubiculum* in the source—which one of the Assyrians dares to enter in 275–7. Note *bur* as defined in BTS: '*A (private, inner) chamber* (as distinguished from the *heall*)'. That the words for Holofernes' dwelling are a unique cpd. and a simplex in an unparallelled sense (*træf*, 'tent') perhaps shows the poet straining his lexical resources to convey the full sense of the source. See also note to 43b, and Lendinara (1993), 321–2. On the construction in 57a, see C54b.

**58b** *ða beorhtan idese*: the same epithet occurs in 340b. Terms literally meaning 'bright' are quite often used of the heroine (14 *scinu*, 43 *torhtan*, 254 *beorhte*), but the epithets in which they appear have no exact parallel in the poetic corpus. DOE cites this usage in illustration of *beorht* sense E.4., 'resplendent, beautiful ... (of people)'; cf. *GenA* 1728 *wlitebeorht ides* of the beautiful Sarah. But Judith's chasteness and moral purity, rather than simply her physical beauty, may be more relevant; see DOE sense D.5., 'effulgent, radiant, glorious (of the righteous)'. *Torht* is similarly ambiguous. Hieatt (1980), 254, notes that this language 'probably associates her with the light emanating from God [in ll.189–91]'. The matter is complicated in ll.58 and 254 by the fact that the narrator is at those points recording the thoughts of Holofernes and the Assyrians respectively; if the adj. is felt to be in the voice of the narrator, the moral sense is probable, if it is in the reported thought, then the physical sense is certain, for the Vulgate tells us repeatedly that Holofernes and the Assyrians admire Judith's beauty.

**59b** *wuldres dema*: either 'the judge of glory', i.e. the one who portions out the glory of heavenly reward, or 'the ruler of glory' (cf. *And* 661 *sigedema* for *dema* in this sense, and see Brooks (1961), 84). Epithets for God which comprise *wuldres* with a noun meaning 'ruler' or 'prince' (e.g. *wuldres ealdor*, *wuldres cyning*, *wuldres wealdend*) are common in the poetry, but this epithet is unique, as is *se hehsta dema* (4a, 94b). Most of the poet's epithets for God may be found elsewhere in the corpus; that these two cannot, may suggest that the poet was keen to develop the theme of the power of God's judgement—an evident theme of the source. Poetic epithets with *dema* and *demend* are listed in Marquardt (1938), 282–3.

**60b** *he him þæs ðinges gestyrde*: BTS *gestiran*, II.l.d., gives examples of this construction with dat. of pers. and gen. of action.

**61a** *dryhten dugeða waldend*: two formulaic epithets, *dugeða dryhten* (cf. *And* 698, *El* 81, *ChristB* 782, *Phoen* 494) and *dugeða waldend* (cf. *And* 248), overlap in *apo koinou* construction. Although there are no examples in the corpus of the first phrase in the order *dryhten dugeða*, *ChristA* 428, *Sat* 580 *dryhten weoroda, And* 621 *dryhten gumena*, *Beo* 2402, 2901 *dryhten Geata* suggest that the word order in formulas with *dryhten* and a noun in the gen. plural was reversible. The usual punctuation, with a comma after *dryhten*, disrupts this structure. On formulaic embedding in hypermetric verse, see Nicholson (1963).

**61b** *gewat*, **290** *gewitan*: this verb is commonly followed by an inf. of motion (*neosan*, *sceacan*), often with a pleonastic pron. (*him*, 290). Cf. the construction in ll.11–12. *Se deofulcunda*: on Holofernes' devilishness, see pp.76–9.

**62** The line is incomplete, but there is no lacuna in the sense. Cook and Sweet, following Koeppel (1893), supply *gangan* after *galferhð*, making a complete normal line which interrupts the hypermetric cluster (cf. 96a which is normal, but in a hypermetric group). Schmitz (1910), 40, takes *galferhð gumena ðreate* as a complete hypermetric a-verse in a line which lacks a b-verse. Such gaps occur sporadically in the poetry, but only very rarely in hypermetric verse (according to Bliss, 162–8, only elsewhere at *Res* 1). They may result from scribal error, or a looser style. Bliss (1971) notes their frequency in *Max I*, compares the systematic use of short lines in O.N. *ljóðaháttr* and concludes that short lines 'may have been intended as such by the poet' (at 449). Moffat (1992), 819–21, however, shows that scribal interference seems to be responsible for a number of examples in poems for which we have two versions. Loss here is more probable than not, but more than one reconstruction is possible.

**63–5** See C19b.

**65b** *swylcne he ær æfter worhte*: *wyrcan æfter* = 'to strive after, work for'; *swylcne* stands in apposition to *ende*. Hence: 'such [i.e. his end] he had worked for'.

**66a** *þearlmod ðeoden gumena*: the epithet that is used here of Holofernes is used by Judith in l.91 seemingly incongruously of God. Cf. the heroine's ironic use of 'my lord' in the Vulgate (e.g. 12.12–13, where Vagao refers to Holofernes as 'my lord', and Judith replies to him using the same phrase, apparently of the same person, but covertly of God); see also pp.77–8.

**66b** *on ðysse worulde*: the dem. is stressed and alliterates although it is not displaced from its normal syntactic position. Fakundiny (1970), 138–9, and Leslie (1966), 79–80, list other examples of alliterating *þes* in formulas of place with *woruld*. The stress here draws attention to the contrast between this world and the next.

**67b–9a** Grein and Sweet take the second *swa* in 68b to mean 'as if'. But as Mitchell, 2. §2870, points out, 'there was clearly no pretence about it'. Other examples of *swa* ... *swa* meaning 'so ... that' are cited by Mitchell, 2, §§2869–70.

**68b–9a** *he nyste ræda nanne on gewitlocan*: '(so drunk that) he forgot all his designs'.

**71b** *wærlogan*: etymologically 'faith-falsifier'. Malone (1946), 150, remarks that 'Holofernes plays two parts: that of *leodhata* "tyrant" (in his relationship to his subjects) and that of *wærloga* "traitor, rebel" (in his relationship to his Lord)'. If so, this is another example of oxymoron in the poem (cf. 31–2 *oferdrencte/ agotene*, 268–9 *gebylde/ sweorcendferhðe*). BT, however, offers the sense 'a faithless, perfidious person', which is literally applicable to Holofernes because of his explicit intention to abuse the covenant between host and guest and symbolically appropriate for a devilish figure. Satan is called *wærloga* in *And* 613, 1297, *Jul* 455, *Whale* 37. The semantic development of the word is discussed by Roberts (1979), 298. See C61b.

**74a** *þēowen*: the metre establishes the diphthong as long; see Campbell, §593 (2), f. 2, 'the short diphthong is metrically well established in *þeowe* (Gen. 2747, &c.), but *þeowen* may have *ēo* from *þēow* (Jud. 74)', and Fulk (1992), 146–52. *Þrymful*: BT offers the sense 'mighty', and so Hamer's translation, but Judith is only inspired with *ellen*, 'courage', 'strength', by an act of divine grace following her prayer (94b–5a), so the sense 'glorious' or 'illustrious' is to be preferred.

**75a** *þone atolan*: the adj. is frequently used substantively of the devil in *Sat* (ll.382, 411, 485, 680, 716, 725); see C61b.

**76b** *unsyfra*: the prefix alliterates in preference to the adv. *ær* (which is in the initial dip). The poem conforms to the practice of *Beo* in the treatment of *un-*: when stressed it alliterates (see Kendall (1982), 52).

**77b, 103b** *wundenlocc*: this rare detail of physical description of Judith may derive from the mention in the Vulgate (10.3) of her braided or plaited locks. Elsewhere the cpd. occurs only once, in *Rid* 25 of the *ceorl*'s daughter who is *wif wundenlocc*. The Hebrews, however, are also described as *wundenlocc* in l.325, and so perhaps it means 'curly-haired' and does not refer to 10.3. See C325a.

**79a** *scurum heardne*: 'hard (or 'hardened'?) in the storm of battle' cf. *Beo* 1033, *And* 1133 *scurheard*, *Hildebrandslied* 64 *scarpen scurim*. Garmonsway (1980), 85, takes *Beo* 1033, *scurheard*, 'as an allusion to the quenching of blades to harden them, since it follows a reference to files, which obviously alludes to the processes of smithying'. Wrenn (1988), 265, suggests that the first element of *regnheard*, *Beo* 326, 'supernaturally hard' became confused with *regn*, 'rain', and so 'the nearly synonymous *scur* could be substituted as alliteration demanded' (Hamer, 140). Though these ideas are attractive, the image of battle as storm is a figurative commonplace in O.E. verse and elsewhere. See *Jud* 221b *flana scuras*, 223b, *styrmdon*; *Beo* 3116 *isernscur*, 3117 *stræla storm*.

**80b–98a** Judith draws the sword in ll.77b–80a, but 20 lines elapse before she seizes Holofernes and strikes. Delaying the narrative climax heightens the dramatic tension, but as the gap is filled with Judith's prayer and the statement that God answered it the postponement of the beheading may show that the real interest lay in the theme of the efficacy of rightful prayer. Judith makes two speeches in Holofernes' bedchamber in the source, the second of which, delivered between drawing the sword and cutting his neck, is brief: 13.9: Strengthen me, O Lord God, at this hour. On Judith's prayer, see Hill (1981) and Bzdyl (1982).

**81a** *be naman nemnan*: perhaps echoing OT paronomasia; see Frank (1972), 222. In 'naming his name', she appears to invoke the three persons of the Trinity: *frymða god*, God the Father, *bearn alwaldan*, God the Son, and *frofre gæst*, God the Holy Ghost. See pp.74–5.

**86a** Frank (1992), 100, notes that seven out of eight instances of *þryness*, 'Trinity', in the verse alliterate and are in collocation with *þrymm*, 'majesty' (*El* 177, *GuthA* 646, *ChristB* 599, *Jul* 726, *And* 1685, *KtHy* 40). As she points out, O.E. writers tend 'to pick out happy verbal coincidences, whose very naturalness in the language suggests doctrinal inevitability' (106, n.17). See also Keiser (1919), 63–5.

**87–9** McPherson (1980), 115–16, notes the use of *homoioteleuton*, the use of identical word-endings, in *geomor*, *ealdor*, *sigor* (and there is also much other repetition of *-or-* in ll.87–93).

**90a** Bliss scans as a1e (2A1a) with the verb in the dip. Elsewhere in the corpus this type rather frequently opens with a finite verb carrying ornamental alliteration (e.g. *Dream* 64a, 75a, *Phoen* 630a, *Dan* 59a). But here a non-alliterating inf., which—as a clause non-initial stressed element—should alliterate and be stressed, opens the verse. If the verb is unstressed, this is one of only three light hypermetric a-verses in the poem, and the only light hypermetric a-verse opening with an unstressed stressed element in the corpus of hypermetric verse scanned by Bliss, 162–8. If it is treated as a normal verse with an extended initial dip, it would be the only such verse in the corpus with an unstressed and prefixed inf. in the initial dip (see Stanley (1975), 324–5). Vetter (1872), 40, and Schmitz (1910), 42, reverse *mote* and *geheawan*, an ingenious suggestion which corrects the alliteration, but there are a few other departures from strict alliterative conventions in the poem. Pope (1966), 129, n.15, unconvincingly suggests *gemearcian* for *geheawan*. *Morðres bryttan*: in stark opposition to 93a *tires brytta* and applied to a devil in *And* 1170 (note also the epithets *hearmes brytta* and *synna bryttan* for the devil in *Seasons* 166 and *El* 957, and see Marquardt (1938), 298).

**91a** *þearlmod þeoden gumena*: see C66a.

**93a** *torhtmod tires*: *torht* and *tir* are often found in alliterative collocation in O.E. poetry (so also 157).

**93b** *me is þus torne on mode*: with *torn* used adverbially. The phrasing is possibly a variation of a more familiar idiom: see BT *weorc*, VII, *wesan weorce (on mode)*, with dat. of the noun and dat. of the pers., 'to be painful to a person (at heart)', e.g. *Beo* 1418. See C94a and C97b.

**94a** *hate on hreðre minum*: *hate* is probably an adv. and the phrase parallels and varies 93b *torne on mode*; the syntax is echoed again in 97b *rume on mode*.

**94b–7a** The comments on the power of rightful prayer are an addition to the source, and a Christian commonplace; see for example Boethius, *De Consolatione Philosophiae* V, pr. 6: 'Nor vainly are our hopes placed in God, nor our prayers, which when they are right cannot be ineffectual'.

**95a** *mid elne onbryrde*: heroic courage, more normally a male virtue in such literature, is granted to Judith by divine intervention. On the heroising of Judith here, see pp.67–70.

**96a** *herbuendra*: a normal verse in a hypermetric cluster. Timmer states that 96b is not hypermetric (assuming syncopation of *seceð*?), but Bliss, 163, scans it a1e (2A1a). The change of metre—whether it involves the a-verse or the whole line—does not justify Timmer's speculation that 'Line 96 (and perhaps 95b) may well be an addition by a scribe'. Normal verse occasionally interrupts hypermetric clusters elsewhere (cf. *Max I* 60–1 and see Bliss, 162–8).

**97a** *mid ræde*: probably the noun *ræd* in the sense 'wisdom' (the phrase having semi-adverbial function and meaning 'advisedly', 'properly'), but see also Grein who construes it as the adj. *ræde*, 'prompt', 'ready', in agreement with *geleafan* and parallel to *rihte*.

**97b** *rume on mode*: Kaske (1982), 23–4, notes similar uses of *rum* in contexts involving wisdom (*ræd*) in *GenB* 519, *Beo* 278, *El* 1240 and sees a possible echo of Ps. 118.32 ('I have run the way of your commandments, since you widened my heart'). The parallel phrasing of 93b, 94a, and 97b brings out the theme of the power of divine grace: the answering of her prayer produces an elation as great as was her previous distress.

**98a** *haligre*: dat. sing. fem. 'for the holy (woman)'. Hamer mis-translates 'in the Holy One'.

**98b** *þone hæðenan mannan*, 110a *þone hæðenan hund*, 179a *hæðenes heaðorinces*: most of the epithets for Holofernes occur elsewhere in the poetic corpus, often with heroic flavour or positive connotation (e.g. *folces ræswa*, *eorla dryhten*, *goldwine gumena*, *wigena baldor*), but these pejorative phrases with *hæþen* are specific to the poem. The poet's stress on the heathenism of Holofernes displays his particular re-interpretation of the story: the conflict between Hebrew and Assyrian is one between Judaeo-Christian and pagan.

**99b** *wið hyre weard*: 'towards her'; for the construction *wiþ* + gen. + *weard* see BT *wiþ*, ix.1.(a); cf. *to* + dat. + *weard*.

**100a** *bysmerlice*: the usual sense is 'shamefully', but the shame is Holofernes', not Judith's, so 'ignominiously' is to be preferred. As man and warrior, he is shamed by his powerlessness when a woman attacks him. The disgrace of a man's death at the hands of a woman is noted in Judges 9.52–4, but it is not surprising that an O.E. poet should view the event in this light.

**102–3** *eaðost ... wel*: 'so she could best manage him properly'.

**103b–111a** The Vulgate states more concisely: *Et percussit bis in cervicem eius* (13.10: 'And she struck twice upon his head'). The narrative climax is drawn out by repetition (*Sloh ða ... þæt; Sloh ða ... þæt*) and variation (*wundenlocc/ ides ellenrof; þone feondsceaðan/ þone hæðenan hund*). By slowing down the pace of the action, the narrator appears to relish the violence of the double act, but see also C80b–98a.

**110a** *þone hæðenan hund*: the earliest example of this meiosis which occurs later quite frequently (see MED *hound*, 2b.(b)). The pejorative use of *hound* for pagans or lapsed Christians derives from the Bible (see 1 Samuel 17.43, 2 Kings 8.13, 2 Peter 2.22). See C98b.

**110b–11a** In the Vulgate, Judith rolls away Holofernes headless body (*et evolvit corpus eius truncum*); here, with a slight change which may derive from an OL reading, his head rolls to the floor as a consequence of the heroine's second blow. That the head of this bestial (note *hund,* 110a) and gluttonous figure should gravitate to the earth may show that the poet symbolically linked the two: cf. *Cura Pastoralis*, Sweet (1871), 154, 18–20: 'the beasts, because of the greediness of their desires, always look at the ground'.

**111a** *forð on ða flore*: see Sievers-Cook, §274, n.1: '**flōr** has ... acc. sing. always **flōr**'; but Campbell, §614, notes that no fem. *u-stem* nouns are 'free from the influence of the *ō*-stems', and the acc. sing. *flore* shows this influence. Venezky-Healey list seven unambiguous instances of fem. acc. sing. *flor* (four in the phrase *on þa flor*, all four in prose), and five such instances of *flore* (four in the phrase *on þa flore*, two in poetry). The change from *gefeoll ... on þa flor* in the O.E. prose Boethius to the complete a-verse *feol on þa flore* in the verse (see Sedgefield (1899), 8, ll.3–4, and 153, l.81) suggests that the assimilation to the *ō*-stem was useful to the poets.

**111b** *leap*: elsewhere only in Ælfric's *De Falsis Deis* translating *corpora*, which Pope (1967–8), 702, glosses 'dead body, corpse'. The sense may be a metaphorical extension of the better attested meaning '(wicker) basket (for chaff, fish, eels)'. Metaphors of the body as a vessel or container are frequent in O.E. verse (see cpds. in *-fæt, -cofa*). When Holofernes' spirit passes elsewhere (*gæst ellor hwearf*), his *leap* is left behind, *gesne* ('void, empty').

**112b–21** The grim fate reserved for Holofernes' soul is an addition to the source, which makes no comment on the matter at this point. The depiction of Hell as a place beneath a cliff (113a *under neowelne næs*) filled with serpents (115a *wyrmum*, 119a *wyrmsele*) is found elsewhere in O.E. poetry (e.g. *Sat* 89–105, 132–6) and prose (esp. Blickling Homily 17, Morris (1874–80), 209–11). The motif of the cliff perhaps derives from the

Apocalypse of Peter (see James (1953), 510), and is common (see Wright (1993), 130).

**112b** *gæst ellor hwearf*: the periphrasis for death is a formula, cf. *Beo* 55b *fæder ellor hwearf*. There is no mystery in *Jud* as to the place indicated by *ellor*.

**113** The rhyme *næs:wæs* necessitates stress on *wæs* which is a departure from the poet's normal practice with this form.

**116b** *in helle bryne*: though Cook, Sweet and Timmer take *helle bryne* as a cpd., Terasawa (1994), 47, 74–5, shows that there are metrical criteria for interpreting the sequence as a gen. phrase: cpds. in which the first element comprises a long, or a closed, stressed stem syllable, together with an unstressed syllable (so-called '*hilde*-type' cpds.) may not contain a second element that is resolvable. Hutcheson (1995), 50, n.49, on the other hand, suggests emending to *hellbryne*.

**116–17** The continued alliteration was probably induced by the association of *hell* and *hinnsiþ* (see *GenB* 718, 721, *Sat* 454, *Whale* 68 and the alliteration of *hinfarð* and *hellea* in O.S. *Heliand* 1038).

**120** Campbell (1971), 163–4, suggests that the eternal nature of the damnation—emphatically conveyed here by the adverbial tautology—was prompted by the commentary of Hrabanus Maurus (see *PL* 109, col.572, *ad perditionem perpetuam*), for it is not from the source; but this fate is apt for a devilish figure and need not have had a specific source.

**121a** *in ðam heolstran ham*: *heolstor* as adj. is rare; in verse, there is only *El* 763 *heolstor hofu* (see Gradon (1958), 55). It occurs in glosses, though *heolstrig* is commoner. Napier (1900), 177, gloss 93, *de latebrosis*: *of heolestrum* suggests the senses 'hidden, secret', as well as 'dark'. Holofernes' new 'dark home' constrasts with the *ham* of Judith (131b), Bethulia, whose walls shine invitingly. See also C137b. Note that, though *ham* is strong masc. dat. sing., the endingless locative is 'frequent with the words *dæg*, *hām*, *morgen*' (Campbell, §572).

**123a** *æt guðe,* **175b** *æt beadowe*: the narrator twice refers to the beheading as a 'battle', but Holofernes is in no condition to put up a fight. The poet may be thinking of the wider spiritual meaning of the event: the defeat of evil by good. These, and other terms for war, weapons and armour, are sometimes used in O.E.

poetry with spiritual connotation: see for example *Jul* 382–401 (*beado* 385, *guþ* 393, 397), and for discussion Hermann (1976), 1–9.

**125b** *gebrohte*: for the construction, see C54b and Klaeber (1929), 230.

**127b–9b** *þe ... on*: translate 'in which'. *Foregenga*: the sense 'attendant' occurs only here. The usual meaning is 'a predecessor', but note the gloss *for. gencga: antecessor*, 'one who goes before' (Goossens (1974), 193, no. 689, with missing letter) and cf. Gothic *faura-gaggja*, 'a steward'. See also C132a.

**128b** *hyra begea nest*: 'both their food'; *hyra* must be a proclitic possessive adj. (rather than a sentence particle, as in 'the food of both of them') in order to avoid a violation of Kuhn's first law. See also C130b.

**130a, 316a** *heolfrig*: the adj. is found only in *Jud* and was probably formed from the poetic noun *heolfor*, by analogy with *blod/blodig* (130a *swa heolfrig* varies 126b *swa blodig*).

**130b** *hyre on hond*: Cook gives *hyre* as dat. sing., so giving a breach of Kuhn's first law. If *hyre* is gen. sing., it can function as a proclitic possessive adj. without violating this law.

**132a** *gingran sinre*: though the comp. fem. is used substantively elsewhere, the sense 'handmaid' (translating *ancillae* 13. 11) is not elsewhere attested, but cf. *gingre* 'deputy', in the O.E. Bede (Miller (1890–8), 340), and *geongra*, *gingra*, masc., 'attendant, servant'. The phrase *gingran sine*, 'his followers', occurs twice in *And* (ll.427, 847), so the wording here may show the poet feminising a traditional formula. See C127b and pp.68–70.

**136b** *mihten*: see C24a.

**137b** *weallas blican*: given that it is night (see 13.1, 'and when it was grown late', 13.16, 'and lighting up lights'), it is not clear how the walls can shine, but the motif is probably not to be considered too literally and may be anagogic. The same formula is used in *MSol* 236a of Jerusalem, and the shining walls of the New Jerusalem are often mentioned in descriptions of paradise (see for example Patch (1950), 112–13, 118–19). The contrast between the *ham* of Holofernes (121) and that of Judith (131) may be considered an analogue of the opposition between heaven and hell. The parallel with the shining cliffs of *Beo* 222 *brimclifu* *blican* is inexact: there it is plainly day-time. Cf. also l.326a *to ðære beorhtan byrig*.

**138a, 326b** *Bēthūliam*: the name occupies a whole verse and to scan and alliterate normally requires an initial, stressed long syllable; cf. C7b. But see Bright (1899), 348–51, for criticism of the view that the accommodation of the Latin accentuation to O.E. metre required lengthening of the initial vowel.

**139a** *feðelaste*: Cook glosses acc. pl., but as Timmer and Dobbie argue, the form is more probably dat. sing., 'with pace', 'at speed'.

**144b** *Iudith*: the MS form *Iudithe* is kept by Timmer, but the uninflected form is required for the subject. His suggestion that the spelling is evidence of the weakening of unstressed syllables is implausible. The loss of such syllables would have to be very advanced for a scribe to feel that final *-e* had no phonetic significance and could be placed in positions where it was historically impossible. Dobbie may be right to suggest that the error stemmed from confusion with the preceding dat., despite the difference of gender.

**149b**: *hyre togeanes gán*: apparently with double alliteration in the b-verse on palatal and velar; see pp.25–6, 42, and cf. *Mald* 32b *mid gafole forgyldon*, 192b *guþe ne gymdon*. It is otherwise extremely rare, but note *Ex* 38b *frumbearna fela*.

**150** *forlæton*: inf., with *-on* for *-an* (see pp.14–15).

**158a** *þara læðða*: the gen. is difficult and the verse is short, though not impossibly so, being the only example in *Jud* of a1b. Early commentators assumed textual loss, but Imelmann (1908), 7, explains it as a gen. of cause, 'for the afflictions'; Mitchell, 1. §1293, compares Ælfric's *Catholic Homilies* i. 36. 3 *to edleane his geswinces* and ii. 590. 15 *wite þæs weorces*. It is, however, the only example in *Jud* of a light verse of type a which is not clause-initial (for this rule in *Beo*, see Kendall (1991), 34–6, and Stanley (1992)), and so may be corrupt.

**161b–6a** On the style, see Stanley (1994), 152–3 and also Brodeur (1968), 107–8.

**161b** *on lustum*: the idiom is usually in the singular (*And* 1023, 1140, 1573, *El* 138, *Whale* 26). In the plural, it occurs only here and in *GenB* 473. Timmer, 10–11, and l.161n., sees the correspondence as evidence of the poet's familiarity with *GenB*, but in both the poets use the plural as a rhetorical device, a type of enallage, to convey the immensity of the joy. *GenB*, 467–76, describes the pleasures that follow from eating the fruit of the tree of life. Here, the Bethulian army is 'in ecstasies' at the return of the heroine against all odds.

**162** The opening dip violates Kuhn's second law. There are a few somewhat similar exceptions in *Beo*, listed by Kendall (1991), 76–7, section (e). His explanation of these (that the dem. might function occasionally as a sentence particle) is not relevant here: *ðæs* does not refer back to the preceding clause. Perhaps an ampersand has dropped out from the beginning of the line, but see also 341b, and Momma (1997), 72–5, for a survey of failure to observe this law in the corpus.

**165a** *þeo[d]nes*, MS *þeoðnes*: Timmer's theory of the confusion of *d* and *ð* in O.E. orthography is 'not borne out by the scribe's practice' (Malone, 111). Dittographic error is likelier, as Malone suggests (cf. *Beo* 1362b MS. *stanðeð*).

**167a** *medobyrig*: the application of this term to Bethulia demonstrates to Magennis (1983), 337, that 'drinking can still function as symbolic of good communal life, the seat of which in *Jud* is Bethulia', but at other points mead is linked to the vice of the Assyrians (26 *medugal*, 229, 245 *medowerig* and 31–2). By metonymy, *medo* in combination with a word for place stands for 'mead-hall' (cf. *Beo* 924 *medostig*, 'path to the mead-hall', 1643 *meodowong*, 'plain near the mead-hall'), so that *medoburg* means 'city with a mead-hall'. The metonymic transfer may have caused the disassociation of the word and the drink in this type of cpd..

**167b** *areted*: the unsyncopated, tri-syllabic form is required by the metre. Cf. ll.87a, 116a, 155b.

**170a** *hie*: either acc. sing. fem. referring to Judith, with the sub. *hie*, 'they', understood from 168a, or *hie* is the sub., and the obj., Judith, is understood from 168b.

**171b** *golde gefrætewod*: the phrase may refer to the jewellery listed in 10.3 of the source, but the same phrasing is used of war-gear in 328b. Perhaps the poet thought of Judith's jewellery as her armour. See also C36b and C327–9.

**174–9** For the taking and displaying of the head of a defeated enemy, cf. 1 Maccabees 7.47, and *Beo* 1647–50; see Bremmer

(1996), 124–6, for other examples both biblical and A-S. The poet omits the hanging of the head from the city walls (14.1, 7).

**177a** *Her ge magon ...* : an exception to the usual verb-sub. word-order after *her* in the verse: see Stanley (1994), 88–9.

**178b** *laðestan*: here and elsewhere (e.g. 44, 48, 57 etc.), the function of the adj. is ambiguous; read either 'Of the most odious, heathen warrior', or, with the adj. used absolutely (i.e. in a nominal sense), 'of the most odious one, of the heathen warrior'. Given the strong and frequent use of enjambement in the poem, and the fact that the adjs. here are proximate (*laðestan* line final, *hæðenes* next line, initial), the first reading is more natural; where other linguistic material separates adj. and noun (as in 44–6 *se rica ... Holofernus*), the latter interpretation is likelier.

**181–2a** *þe us monna mæst morðra gefremede, sarra sorga:* Timmer translates 'most of the murders of men', with *monna* dependent on *morðra* and the phrase *monna mæst morðra* functioning as the obj. of *gefremede*. Better sense is produced by taking *mæst morðra* as the obj.; so translate 'who, of [all] men, perpetrated the greatest of crimes, of grievous woes, against us'. For similar syntax and phrasing, see *Beo* 2645a–6a *he manna mæst mærða gefremede, dæda dollicra,* and *Dream* 79–80a *þæt ic bealuwara weorc gebiden hæbbe, sarra sorga.* It is possible, however, that the construction is *apo koinou*: 'who, most (*mæst*) of [all] men, perpetrated the greatest (*mæst*) of crimes ... '.

**186b–8a** Either *burgleoda* and *randwiggendra* vary *gumena* and depend on *gehwæne* ('each of the men, of these citizens ... of the soldiers'), or both *burgleoda* and *randwiggendra* depend on *gumena* (so Hamer: 'to every man among the citizens and warriors'), or *burgleoda* depends on *gumena* and *randwiggendra* on *gehwæne* (so Bradley: 'each man among these citizens, each shield-wielding soldier').

**189a** *fysan*: pres. subj. 2nd. pers. pl., with *-an* for *-en*. (see pp.14–15).

**189b** The clause introduced by *syððan* may be subordinate either to the clause in 188b–91a (' ... that you prepare yourselves for battle after God sends the dawn', so Timmer, and Hamer's translation), or to the clause that begins in 191b ('after God sends the dawn, carry your shields forward', so Sweet, Dobbie, and Hamer's text), or it may be *apo koinou* and taken with the preceding and following clauses (on this, see Mitchell, 2. §§3796–99). Bately (1985), 421–2 points out that in prose 'the subordinate clause introduced by *siþþan* frequently opens a sentence', whilst in verse 'the normal position ... is after the main clause'; most of the seven exceptions that she isolates in verse can, as here, readily be repunctuated.

**190b** *sende*: pres. subj., translating the future perfect *exierit* (14.2), in a clause of time: 'after God shall have sent forth (the sun)'.

**192b** *byrnhomas*: *hapax legomenon*, but cf. *WaldA* 17 *byrnhomon* (acc. sing. of weak *byrnhoma*?).

**194–5** The continued alliteration and assonance of *fagum*: *fæge* suggests word-play.

**194a** MS *fyllan*: Sweet, Timmer, following Ettmüller, emend to *fyllað*, with the verb parallel to *berað*, 191. *Fyllan* could be pres. subj. lst. pers. pl., 'let us cut down ... ', with *-an* for *-en* (cf. *fysan*, 189a), but Judith does not, in the rest of the speech, involve herself in the imminent action. The form is, more likely, an uninflected inf. indicating purpose after a verb of motion: 'carry shields forwards ... in order to cut down' (see Mitchell, 2. §§2940–51, and Callaway (1913), 136).

**196** *Deaþ* and *dom* form a common alliterative collocation in O.E. poetry: see Kock (1917), 175–8, and Quirk (1963), 156–7. The Christian poet dealing with the theme of battle naturally associated death, glory and judgement. The shift from the verb *gedemed* to the etymologically related noun *dom* is an instance of *polyptoton* (play on words from the same root, but with different forms), a frequent trope in O.E. prose and verse.

**198b** *þurh mine hand*: the possessive leads the noun in alliteration in this phrase. See Fakundiny (1970), 136–7 and 262: 'This pattern has the effect of particularizing the noun and is thus clearly rhetorical' (at 136); cf. *Ex* 262b, *ChristC* 1379b, *Jul* 493b, *Beo* 558b. But possessives are infrequent with parts of the body in O.E., and so in this context may be stressed like lexical adjs. (note exceptions such as *GenA* 1809, *PPs* 73.3.4, 87.5.4). *Ex* 262 is lexically identical to *Jud* 198: both Moses and Judith make clear to their followers that divine power operates through their hands (an emphasis which derives from the source).

**200b** *stopon* (followed by cpd.): note the repetition in 212b and 227a; on the incremental pattern in O.E. poetic narrative, see Bartlett (1935), 49–61, and cf. *Beo* 702b–21a.

**201b** [*sige*]*þufas*: the b-verse lacks an alliterating word. Ettmüller, followed by most eds., adds *sige-* by analogy with *sigebeacen*, *sigebeam*. Because the cpd. is *hapax legomenon*, the emendation is uncertain. There are no surviving cpds. with *þuf.*

**205** The alliteration on the cluster *hl-* may have onomatopoeic effect (as at l.23, but see also pp.27–8 and 45–6), echoing the noise of the preparations for battle. Only six lines in the corpus contain *hl-* alliteration carried across three alliterative positions: *Az* 85, *Phoen* 25, *Rim* 28, *Rid* 33.3, *Jud* 23, 205. *Hlude*, 'loudly' occurs in three of these. *Rim* 28 rhymes *hlynede:dynede* as in *Jud* 23. *Rid* 33.3 and *Jud* 23 deal with the theme of laughter, *Rim* 28 with the noise of harp and song, *Jud* 205 with the tumult of battle. These similarities suggest the effect is traditional.

**205b–12a, 296–7a** As is usual in O.E. poetic battle narrative, the wolf, raven and eagle—the beasts of battle—alerted by the noisy preparations for war (204b–5a), appear in anticipation of carrion; see Fry (1972), and Griffith (1993). The diction and the motifs here are conventional, the only unique feature being the description of the wolf as *hlanca*, 'lean' (but the implication that the beast is ravenous is appropriate, and the idea is also associated here with the birds, cf. 207a, 295b *wælgifre*/*-um*, 210a *ætes georn*). The reappearance of the beasts later, in the midst of the battle, is unusual but not unparallelled, cf. *El* 27–30, 52–3, 111–14. On the unusual syntax, see pp.37–41.

**206–7** The collocation *wulf: wæl* (see 295 and *Ex* 164, *El* 28, 112, *Beo* 3027, *Mald* 96) perhaps motivated the continued alliteration. See C116–17.

**209b–12a** Sweet and Dobbie punctuate with commas at the end of 210 and 211, and so Hamer translates: 'Behind them flew the eagle keen for carnage, dewy-winged with feathers dark, the horny-beaked one sang a song of battle', with *salowigpada* and *hyrnednebba* describing the eagle. Timmer has a semi-colon after 211a so that *salowigpada* agrees with *earn*, but *hyrnednebba* may refer to the eagle or the raven. However, in *Fort* 37 and *Brun* 61, *salowigpad* refers explicitly to the raven, and this bird is *saluwigfeðera* in *GenA* 1448 and *sealobrun* in *Finn 35*. The words *salo* and *salowig* are nowhere used of the eagle. *Hyrnednebba* in its single other occurrence in *Brun* 62 describes the raven. The punctuation here, with a semi-colon at the end of 210 follows Cook (1904): 209b–10 concern the eagle, 211–12a refer back to the raven of 206–7. Accordingly, *fleah* in 209b does not confer 'stress and alliteration on the coordinate verb *sang* in 211b' (Orton (1985), 153–4).

**209b** The eagle follows behind the wolf and raven, which may suggest that *ac* has continuative rather than adversative function, cf. *Beo* 804, 1448, 1576, and, possibly, *GenB* 847. Cook gives '*and(?)*' in his glossary; Timmer, 'and' (and so Gordon). Glogauer (1922), 21–2, allows the continuative as his fourth function of *ac*, but Mitchell, 1.§1769, is doubtful of its existence, and Schücking (1904), §50, does not allow it. Perhaps translate 'but then'.

**210b, 211a** *urigfeðera*, *salowigpada*: these forms in *-ig* occur only in cpds. (cf. *Phoen* 153 *haswigfeðra*).

**211b** *sang hildeleoð*: on the abnormality, see pp.31 and 37–41.

**219a** *guðfanum*: the cpd. is unusual in register—its first element is poetic, but the cpd. is virtually confined to the prose. This is its only use in O.E. poetry.

**220a** *fyrdwicum*: O.E. *wic*, like Latin *castrum*, is used in the plural with the singular sense 'camp', (e.g. *castra* 13.12). Note also *roderum* in l.5 and *heofonum* in l.343 with singular sense, and the general use in ecclesiastical Latin of the plural *caeli*, 'heaven'.

**222a** *hildenædran*: in their power to give deadly wounds, and, in some respects, in shape, arrows are like snakes. The cpd. occurs also in *El* 119, 141; cf. *Mald* 47, 146 *ætterne/ættryne ord*, 'poisoned point': the metaphor is traditional. For further parallels and discussion, see Cook (1900), 148–50, and Meissner (1921), 145–6, 153–4.

**222b** *hornbogan*: either a bow 'curved like a horn', or 'tipped with horn' (see OED, *horn* 17b, 'each tip or end of a bow' and 28, 'made of horn, as *horn bow*').

**223a** *stedehearde*: a unique word. Jiriczek (1929) implausibly suggests that the first element is loaned from O.N. *steði*, 'anvil', but this should normally give O.E. **steþe*. As most O.E. cpds.

which are *hapax legomena* are comprised of common elements, it is likelier that A-S readers would connect the first element with the common word *stede*, either in the root sense, 'position', giving the sense 'hard in position', 'firmly fixed', or in the extended sense 'firm' (cf. *stedefæst*, 'firmly fixed'), giving a tautologous cpd., with the first element in an intensifying function, and the meaning 'very hard' (cf. *Mald* 156 *forheard* [*gar*], 'the very hard [spear]').

**227** The adjs. in this line belong to the clause containing the verb *stopon*; if the second began the following clause, the verb *wrehton* would acquire positional stress, and should have to alliterate. Punctuation is accordingly required at the end of l.227 to indicate the clause boundary.

**228b** *ealdgeniðlan*: the cpd. is used in *And* of the devil (1341) and the heathen Mermedonians (1048). Cpds. with similar sense and devilish associations occur: see C315a, C320b, and pp.76–7.

**229a, 245a** *medowerige*: the cpd. occurs only in *Jud* (cf. *symbelwerig*), and was suggested by the statement in the Vulgate that 'they were all overcharged with wine' (13.2). On the implications of syllabic *-ig-* for the poem's date, see p.46.

**230b** *scirmæled*: *hapax legomenon*, 'brightly adorned', cf. *GenA* 1992 *hringmæled*, 'ring-adorned', *Ex* 125, *GuthB* 1288, *scirwerod*, 'enveloped in brightness'.

**233a** *niðhycgende*: if *nið* has pejorative sense, the cpd. means 'evil-schemers', and varies the direct obj. *oretmæcgas*, but, if it has the neutral sense 'battle', the cpd. means 'those thinking about battle', and in the nom. pl. it functions either as the sub. of *slogon* in l.231, or of *sparedon* in 233. In *ChristC* 1107, this cpd. is used of those who crucify Christ and so is pejorative. Gordon and Hamer take it as referring to the Assyrians, and translate 'contrivers of evil', and 'the cruel-hearted ones' respectively; Bradley construes it as an adj. describing the Hebrews ('retainers ... set about the Assyrian warriors ... intending to spite them'). On the meanings of *nið*, see Corso (1980).

**234b** MS *heanne ne rice*: Timmer emends to the pl. *heane ne rice*, but the usual emendation to the sing. *heanne ne ricne* is to be preferred given the sing. antecedent *nanne* (233).

**237b** See C28b.

**239b** *heafodweardas*: meaning either 'chief guards' (so BT, Cook and Timmer), or 'those who perform *heafod-weard*, guarding the (lord's) head' (see BTS), perhaps rendering *exploratores*, 'watchmen', 14.3. If the latter sense is relevant, there may be irony: the guards have failed to protect Holofernes' head. If it is a pun, cf. Judith's word-play on *caput* as 'head' and 'chief' in 13.27.

**243b** *cumbolwigan*: 'standard warrior'; as the term is used both of Holofernes (259) and his men (243), it should be regarded as a periphrasis for 'warrior', rather than having its literal sense. The word occurs only in *Jud*.

**245b** *morgencollan*: it is morning in the Vulgate when the Assyrians approach Holofernes' tent (14.8), but the poet here also touches upon an O.E. poetic convention: morning, especially early morning, as a time of distress, cf. *Beo* 2894 *morgenlong*, 3022 *morgenceald*, *Res* 96 *morgenseoc*, and see Stanley (1955), 434–5. The second element, *-colla*, is unattested elsewhere. Pogatscher (1908), 258, connects it with *cwelan*, 'to die', *cwalu*, 'torment, slaughter', and **cyllan*, 'to kill'. 'Morning-slaughter' fits the context well.

**246b** *ædre*: advs. of time modifying the obj. of *gefrignan* or its dependent inf. phrase are placed before *gefrignan*; cf. *Beo* 2752.

**249a** MS *weras ferhðe* is meaningless: Körner and Cook add *werig-*, and so Timmer. Grein reads *werigferhðe*, with *weras* erroneously for *werig-*, and this is perhaps the simplest explanation. The cpd. occurs at 290b in a hypermetric verse of the form a1d (2A1a). Identical scansion of the cpd. in *weras werigferhðe* would produce an unusual D type.

**249b** *hwearfum*: the alliteration *w: hw* is irregular, but not unparallelled. Cf. *GuthA* 263 *hwearfum wræcmæcgas, woð up astag*. Both occurrences of the noun *hwearf*, 'crowd', in the poetry alliterate on *w-* perhaps suggesting a change from *hw-*\\ > *w-*\\, or a by-form *wearf* (cf. Layamon's *Brut*, 1036 *warf*, 8727 *wærf*, and see OED *wharf*). But note Roberts (1979), 138, for the possibility that *hwearfum* in *GuthA* 263 is in the dip. See also pp.27–8, 45–6, and for further examples Blake (1961), 165–6.

**250b** The verb is in the dip, and the line has vocalic alliteration.

**251b** MS *hyldo*: *hyldo*, 'loyalty', is meaningful here ('to declare their loyalty to their lord', cf. *PPs* 94.1.3 *urum hælende hyldo gebeodan*), but it is unclear why the Assyrians should choose this moment to do so. The source has 'to arouse their leader for the battle' (14.3), and hence the emendation to *hild*, 'battle'. Either the scribe understood *hyldo* for *hilde* (see Sisam (1953), 43. n.l, 'there are such errors due to the religious preoccupations of the copyists', n.b. *hyldo* in the common sense 'grace'; and cf. *And* 393, 1508, 1585 where *heofon*, 'heaven', has been substituted for *geofon*, 'ocean'), or *hyldo* may be a late spelling of *hilde* with <*y*> for <*i*>, and <o> for <e> by centralisation (so Malone (1930), 116).

**257a** *afor*: used in the *Leechdoms* to mean 'rough'; here, and in its only other poetic occurrence, *GuthA* 519, in the (metaphorical?) sense 'fierce, ferocious', but only here does it denote a quality of character.

**260b** *hæfde geworden*: see BTS *geweorþan*, V.l.a. (a), for the impersonal construction with acc. of pers., and action not stated; cf. Ælfric's 'Preface to Genesis', *he deð swa swa hine sylfne gewyrð* (Crawford (1969), 80, l.108ff.). BT translate 'how pleased the warrior had been with the maid'; Dobbie offers 'How the warrior had decided [to act] toward the holy maid'. The sense of *geweorþan* is perhaps better preserved if 259b–60 are rendered 'how it had turned out for the warrior with the holy woman'. Timmer cites the impersonal construction in *GenB* 387 to show the influence of that poem on *Jud*, but the syntax is frequent in O.E.; see Doane (1991), 273, and for discussion of impersonal *geweorþan* Klaeber (1919), and (1926), 365.

**263b** *hæfte*: Grein emends to *hæste* 'violently', and so Cook, Sweet, Timmer, and BTS. Dobbie, following Kern (1877), 210ff, assumes an otherwise unattested *hæft* (cf. O.N. *heipt*, 'battle'). Cassidy-Ringler and BT argue for use of *hæft*, 'hilt', for 'sword' (by synecdoche), as frequently happens with *ord*, 'point', and *ecg*, 'edge', in the poetry. Timmer regards it as improbable that singular *hæfte* should vary plural *fagum swyrdum*, but cf. *Mald* 124a *mid orde*, 126a *mid wæpnum*. *Hæft*, 'hilt', occurs elsewhere in verse only in the cpd. *hæftmece*, *Beo* 1457a, where the reference to the hilt appears to be redundant (Hrunting, like all swords, having a hilt). O.E. *hilt*, 'hilt', is not used to mean 'sword'.

**265a** *ealde æfðoncan*: scan as 1D1 with elision of *-e* before the stressed vowel, and cf. the same formula in *Jul* 485, with omission of *-e* in the manuscript. Cf. C271b.

**265b** *Assyria wearð*: elsewhere, in 218a, 232a, 309a, the proper name occupies an entire verse in lines of vocalic alliteration, and must, accordingly, have four syllables with the first receiving the most stress, and *-ia* disyllabic. This being so, the scansion of 265b produces a sub-type of E unknown in *Beo*: / \ x x | /. By contraction, or slurring, *-ia* might be treated as monosyllabic, giving type 3E2; or, if *wearð* is treated as part of the dip of the next a-verse (giving d2c in 266a), 265b would scan as 1*D*1.

**268b** *gebylde*: Jost (1954), 217, following Cosijn (1894), 444, emends to *geblyde*, postulating an adj. **geblyged*, 'terrified' (cf. *GuthB* 941 *ungeblyged*, 'undismayed'). Grein (1912), 80, assumes a verb *gebyldan* = *contristare*, *anxiare*. Timmer and Cook offer 'excite' as a sense of *(ge-)byldan*, 'to make bold'. The normal sense 'emboldened' may, however, be correct, if ironic: in 257–61, the Assyrians are too afraid to wake Holofernes; in 269–72, they pluck up sufficient courage to make noise and gnash their teeth in a vain attempt to arouse him; in 275–7, driven by need, one of their number becomes so brave that he enters the general's tent. The elements of *sweorcendferhð* are transparent in meaning (*sweorcend*, 'darkening', *ferhþ*, 'spirit, mind'), but the cpd. is *hapax legomenon* and does not directly translate the Vulgate, so its exact sense is uncertain. 'Downcast' can hardly be right if the Assyrians are 'emboldened', but if they are 'sombre', or 'gloomy', the juxtaposition of *þearle gebylde* and *sweorcendferhðe* is not contradictory. The discovery of the body leads to a change of mood from gloom to despair, where, in the source, they are confident before this event (see 14.12).

**270a** *cohhetan*: *hapax legomenon*, glossed by Sweet as 'make a noise, cough', and translated by Grein as 'lärmen' ('to make a row'). Timmer notes 'the meaning is really "to cough"', but the source has *perstrepentes* (14.9), 'making a great noise', and *cirman*, which apparently varies *cohhettan*, means 'make a noise', 'shout'. The verb 'cough' is not recorded in English, according to

MED, before the fourteenth century, and the O.E. verb with this sense is *hwostan*. Perhaps the sense of **cohhian* is to be related to that of cognate forms like M.H.G. *kuchen*, 'to blow', *kichen*, 'to breathe heavily', Ger. *keuchen*, 'to gasp'. According to Marckwardt (1942), 279, the suffix in *cohhettan* represents an 'unsustained durative', indicating repeated or continous action where the repetition is not regular, and the verb means 'raise a tumult'. But the semantic shift from this to 'cough' is quite considerable, so perhaps it means 'clear the throat noisily and frequently', 'hawk and hem repeatedly': if so, the poet here lends the scene a touch of dramatic, even comic, realism.

**271–2a** The punctuation follows Jost (1954), 218, who notes that *gristbitian (mid) toþum* is a formulaic phrase, and translates: 'They began to shout aloud and gnash—deprived of all virtue—their teeth, suffering grief'.

**271b** *gode orfeorme*: the phrase occurs in *And* 406, 1617, and *Vain* 49. The source demonstrates in *And* 406 that *god* means 'good' (see Brooks (1961), 76), whilst the variation *wuldor-cyninge* in *Vain* 50a suggests that 'God' is the correct reading in 49b. The context here supports either reading and, as Cassidy-Ringler suggest, a play on words may be intended: that those who are alienated from God should gnash their teeth and suffer grief would seem entirely appropriate to a Christian (cf. Matt 13.41–2); and the Assyrians have already been described in 32a as 'deprived of virtue'. The scansion is unproblematic, with resolution if the first stress is short; and elision if it is long (but see Fulk (1992), 142, n.5). Word-play on 'God' and 'good' is common in Ælfric (see Pope (1967–8), 132–3, and n.2) and occasional in O.E. poetry (e.g. *Max I* 120).

**272b** *Þa wæs hyra tires æt ende*: an impersonal construction which does not require a sub., cf. *Beo* 223–4, *ChristC* 1028–9, *JDay I* 2, and see DOE *BĒON*, B 16, for analogous constructions.

**273b–4a** The enjambement of alliteration led early editors, including Cook, to place *aweccan* at the head of 274a. As 273a is hypermetric and 274b normal in metre, 273b and 274a are likely to have been expanded and normal respectively. Placing the verb at the end of 273b achieves this pattern.

**274b** The dramatic irony of the attempt to waken Holofernes is sharpened by the poet's use of understatement: they did not succeed at all. The phrasing of 273b–4 is somewhat similar to that of Ælfric at the same point in his version of the story: '*ac hi woldon elles mid gehlyde hine awreccan. Ða þa him þæs ne speow þurh heora hludan spræce* ... ' (see Assmann (1889), 113). Cook, lxvi, lists certain verbal correspondences between Ælfric's homily and the poem and notes with some scepticism that these 'might suggest that he was acquainted with the latter', but Ælfric does not use any of the distinctive poetic words or formulas of the poem, and his translation method is quite different, following the source much more closely than the poet does. The slight verbal resemblances between the two are those that we might expect to find in two translations of the same text by speakers of the same language.

**275ff** The bold Assyrian who ventures into Holofernes' tent is not named in the poem, but in the source he is Holofernes' personal servant, the eunuch Vagao (14.13–14). The poet consistently removes references to figures other than the central pair, and where a secondary figure is mentioned, as here, he remains anonymous and is referred to by prons. only (275 *sum*, 276 *he* etc., and see Foster (1892), 75).

**275b** *sum to ðam arod*: the metre is irregular. If *arod* is stressed, the verse must be scanned as 1E1 (with *to ðam* proclitic on *arod*), a type which does not occur in regular verse; if the dem. is stressed, the verse is 1A2a, an a-verse type (cf. C306a). In partitive gen. construction the indefinite pron. *sum* generally follows the gen. (e.g. *Mald* 164b *lidmanna sum*, *Beo* 1240b *beorscealca sum*) and is stressed; it may be stressed and alliterate when it precedes and is separated from its dependent gen. noun, as here (*beadorinca*, 276a), but such verses are very rare in O.E. verse (see Slay (1952), 6–10, and Rissanen (1986), 203, but cf. ll.233–4 *nanne ... þæs herefolces*). *Arod*, 'ready', is found elsewhere only in prose. The coincidence of metrical abnormality, unusual syntax and prosaic vocabulary may be significant: the DOE entry for *arod* records two prose instances of the phrase *arod to* in both of which the prep. follows the adj., and so the accommodation of a prose idiom to the requirements of the metre may be the root of the irregularity. Translate: 'Finally, one of the warriors steeled himself to that [*lit.* became ready to such an extent ... ] and ventured into the inner chamber'.

**278b** *blacne*: 'pale, of the pallor of death, or fear of death', cf. *Ex* 204 *wigblac*, *Beo* 2488 *[heoro]blac*, *Sawles Warde his leor deaðlich ant blac* (Bennett, Smithers, Davis (1974), 249, ll.65–6), and see MED, *blok* (1).

**279b** See n.93.

**280a** The formula occurs in *El* 877, *GuthB* 1338 with the noun in the dat., rather than the gen.. Dobbie notes occasional use of the gen. case after other verbs of separation prefixed with *be-*.

**280b–1a** *He þa ... gefeoll freorig to foldan*: the alliterative enjambement results from the expansion of the a-verse formula *feallan (þa) to foldan* to include the word *freorig*, 'shivering', 'cold (from shock, fear)'. The breaking of the cliché underpins the striking realism of the detail, which is an addition to the source. The motif occurs (at a different point, and of a different figure) in the Vulgate: Achior, upon seeing the head of Holofernes, 'fell upon his face upon the earth, and his soul swooned away' (13.29).

**281b–2** His rending of his garments is a detail from the Vulgate (14.14), but the additional melodramatic gesture, his tearing out of his hair, is not. Cf. 1 Esdras 8.71: 'And as soon as I had heard these things, I rent my clothes, and my holy garment, and plucked the hair from off my head and beard, and sat me down sad and full of heaviness', and also the grief of the Huns at the death of Attila in Jordanes' *Getica*: 'Then, as in the custom of that race, they plucked out the hair of their heads' (see Mierow (1915), 123). The bold Assyrian's display is not, however, an expression of grief for his lord, but one motivated by the realisation of the imminence of his own demise, as his subsequent speech makes clear. On the resemblances between the account of Attila's death and that of Holofernes, see Klaeber (1913), 260–1, and (1927), 257–8. If, as Klaeber argues in the latter, Jordanes was influenced by the biblical Judith, these resemblances do not show the influence of Jordanes on the O.E. poem. The correspondence of the motif of the tearing out of hair, in both, but not in the Vulgate, may derive from the OL phrase *et luctu* (see Lewis and Short *luctus* II A 'The external signs of sorrow in one's dress and gestures').

**282a** On the alliteration, see pp.29–30 and n.111.

**285–6** Two constructions appear to overlap: 'Here our own destruction is made manifest, shown to be imminent' and 'Here [it] is shown that the time is near ... '

**287–8** Grein and Cook arrange and emend these lines as follows:

'[nu] mid niðum neah geðrungen,
þe we [life] sculon losian somod,
æt sæcce forweorðan'.

Their editions accordingly contain 350 lines of text rather than 349. The metre of this arrangement is not entirely satisfactory: 288b seems short, and 289a, if normal, has anacrusis but only single alliteration, and, if hypermetric, is an otherwise unattested a1a(1A*1a). Kluge's arrangement is to be preferred: with the addition of *nu* to provide alliteration in 287, two metrically acceptable expanded lines result. Klaeber (1913), 258, supplies *nyde*, 'by necessity' instead of *nu*, drawing attention to uses of *nyde* with *sculan*. Cf. also *GuthB* 934 *þurh nydgedal neah geþrungen*. However, advs. of time often occur with *losian*, and *her*, *nu* and *sculan* are frequently collocated (e.g *GenB* 799–820). Foster (1892), 47, objects that *nu* should not alliterate; examples are rare in strict verse (*GuthA* 49, *Beo* 1174) but are commoner in looser metre (*PPs* 78.4.3, 79.6.2, 149.1.2, *Met* 8.7, 10.53, 21.5).

**290–1** *gewitan him ... sceacan:* cf. C61b. and see *GenA* 858, *Brun* 53, *Beo* 26, 234 for examples of *gewitan* with 'ethic' use of *him*.

**291–2** Jost (1954), 218, rightly notes the awkwardness of the transition from the indefinite pron. *mon*, 'one', to a noun with collective sense, *folc*, 'people' and suggests emending the MS reading *hī mon* (=*him mon*) to *him on*, so translating, 'the mighty army fought behind them ... '. The emendation is attractive, but here as elsewhere (see 47b, 127b–9, 271–2a) the slightly strained syntax may be the poet's own.

**297a** *lindwig*, MS *lindw..* (?): Grein and Cook emend *laðra lindwiggendra* (giving an isolated hypermetric verse); Dobbie suggests *lindwerod*, and compares with *El* 142a *laðra lindwered,* but it is doubtful whether there was space in the MS for five letters after *lind* (Junius reads *lind ;*). Malone tentatively reads *lindwig*, with *wig* meaning either 'army', with concrete sense (so Malone, and cf. *Dan* 5 where *wig* is varied by *wigena mænieo,* 'a host of warriors'), or 'prowess', in an abstract one. If so, *lindwig* is either acc. and the obj. of *flugon* (from transitive *fleon*, 'to flee'), or nom., varying *ða ðe lyfdon*, and the sub. of *flugon* (from intransitive *fleogan,* 'to flee'). So translate either 'The survivors fled the shield-army [or 'the shield-prowess'] of their foes', or 'The survivors, the shield-army of foes, fled'.

**299b–300a** *feng ... on fultum*, 'gave (them) help', 'came to (their) aid', cf. *Summons* 9 *fo on fultum*, and see BTS *fon*, III.1.c.(a).

**304a** *scildburh*: in a fashion typical of O.E. poetry, a foreign army fights in a recognisable A-S or Germanic manner. Cf. *El* 652, where Helena speaks of a shield-wall at the siege of Troy.

**306a** *þegnas on ða tid*: probably 1A*2a with stress and alliteration on the dem., and secondary stress on the noun. Cf. *Beo* 197, 790, 806 *on þæm dæge*, 736 *ofer þa niht*, *JDay II* 177 *Hwæt miht þu on þa tid þearfe gewepan?*, and the stress pattern in modern English phrases such as 'in those days', 'at that time'. For discussion, see Hutcheson (1995), 159, n.13. Possibly, however, the etymologically correct absence of inflection in the acc. sing. of the fem. *i*-stem noun *tid* is an example of scribal hypercorrection of *tide*, and the verse should be scanned as 1A*1b (though this metrical-grammatical type usually shows double alliteration), with acc. *-e* by analogy with the fem. *ō*-stems (see Campbell §604).

**310a** *laðan cynnes*: almost always in *Jud*, the weak adj., when in collocation with a noun, is preceded by a dem.. 310a and probably 347a (see C347a) are the only exceptions. For the use of the weak adj. after a gen., see Mitchell, 1. §113. The lack of weak adjs. not preceded by dems. may be an indicator of lateness of date, but dems. may have been inserted by scribes accustomed to late prose usage.

**311–12** Probably referring to the Hebrews who are called *cynerofe* in l.200; if so *wiðertrod* means 'retirement'. However in *GenA* 2084 *wiðertrod* refers to the retreat of a defeated foe. If *cynerofe* can be translated 'very famous' (BT offers 'royally famous'), these lines may refer to the retreat of the Assyrians.

**312b** *wælscel*: Dobbie connects the second element of this *hapax legomenon* with O.I. *skellr*, 'smiting', and the Corpus and Harley gloss *concisium:scelle* (Lindsay (1921), 47, C777;

Oliphant (1966), 107, C1908), with the whole meaning 'carnage'; but DML, following Lindsay, take *concisium* as a spelling of *conchylium*, 'shell-fish or shell'. Huppé (1970), 184, offers the meaning 'slaughter-shells', i.e. 'corpses', but *scell*, 'shell', is fem. not neut. and the context demands a pl. form, which would accordingly be inflected. Possibly *scel* is related to *scolu*, 'band, troop', and the cpd. means 'heaps of slain' (so Hamer). Alternatively, it may be a noun related to the verb *scellan*, 'to sound', hence 'slaughter noise'; if so, the cpd. varies *reocende hræw*, but different senses are appealed to. *Oninnan*: the adverbial suffix *-an* indicates 'place from which' (Campbell, §677); in collocation with *on*, *innan* is here used as a prep. governing the acc., expressing the idea of movement from within, 'from amidst'.

**315a** *ealdfeondum*: the Assyrians are the ancient enemies of the Hebrews; the same term is used of the Babylonians in *Dan* 57, 453 and, elsewhere, in the singular, of Satan or, in the plural, of his minions (*ChristB* 567, *GuthA* 141, 203, 218, 365, 390, 475, *Phoen* 401, 449). See also C228b and C320b. Ælfric in his homily on Judith interprets the main event of the story as an allegory of the Church's defeat of 'the old enemy', Satan (*þæt is Cristes cyrce ... þe mid cenum geleafan þam ealdum deofle of forcearf þæt heafod* Assmann (1889), 115, ll.413–16).

**317a** *bradswyrd*: Dobbie is probably correct to argue that this word, here and in the same formula in *Mald* 15, is a cpd., given the later form *broadsword* and the fact that the second foot of type 1A2 regularly contains a cpd.; but cf. *Beo* 2509a, 2638a and *Mald* 237.

**320b** *ealdhettende*: 'the old enemy' (see C228b, C315a). Cf. *Beo* 1776 *ealdgewinna* (of Grendel), *Pan* 34 *fyrngeflita* (of the enemy of the panther, who symbolises God), *And* 1346 *fyrnsceaþa* (of a devil), *Ex* 50 *ealdwerige* (of the Egyptians).

**324b** *anes monðes fyrst*: translating *per dies autem triginta* (15. 13: 'for thirty days'). The lack of alliteration and stress on *an* possibly indicates a weakening from the full numerical sense (contrast ll.64, 95). See further Foster (1892), 18, but note also Mitchell, 1. §§220–35, esp. 232–5, and Fulk (1992), 248.

**325a** *wundenlocc*: the cpd. is used in ll.77 and 103 of Judith. Rieger suggests that its use here is an error resulting from scribal confusion of *mægþ*, 'woman', and *mǣgþ*, 'tribe, race', but there is nothing to substantiate this speculation.

**327–9, 337–40** In his enumeration of the spoils, the poet borrows the rhetoric but changes most of the substance of the Vulgate. In particular, the cattle, beasts and household stuff (15.8, 14) are replaced by armour and weapons, and the giving of these to Judith both heroises and masculinises her. For the giving of a defeated leader's war-gear to his killer, cf. *Beo* 2616–18.

**329a** *mærra madma*: the gen. appears to lack a governing noun. Rieger suggests supplying *worn* or *fela* after *madma*, but the rare, heavier types of D, 1D*4–6 are otherwise absent from the poem. Timmer supplies *ma* at the opening of the b-verse, placing the alliterating *mon* in the dip. Sweet places *ma* at the end of the a-verse, but triple alliteration results. Cassidy-Ringler retain the MS form and explain the gen. phrase either as the descriptive complement of *guðsceorp* or *golde* (with somewhat strained sense), or as a partitive complement of *eal* in 331a, (with severe syntactic disjunction). Mossé emends to *mare madma*, but also suggests *mærran madmas*. Both make good sense. The first is the solution adopted here. Note, however, that partitive genitives occur rarely in the verse with no governing word expressed (e.g. *Beo* 1366–7, *El* 324–5, *And* 303, and see Mitchell, 2. §1302).

**330a** On the postponed position of the metrically monosyllabic auxiliary *mæge*, see n.157.

**338a** *readum golde*: the meaning of this formulaic phrase (cf. *GenA* 2406, *Dan* 59, *Rid* 48.6) has been much discussed. Barley (1974), 18–19, argues that the semantic boundaries of O.E. *read* and Mod.E. *red* are not coterminous, *yellow* covering O.E. *geolo* and part of the area of *read*. *Readum golde* is, accordingly, in his view 'yellow gold' (note that *fealo*, 'yellow'(?), is also used of the colour of gold, e.g. *Mald* 166 *fealohilte*). But see also MED *gold*, 1(c) *red* ~, 'gold with a small alloy of copper to enhance its color'.

**338b–9b** The word-order is disjunctive, the verb *ahte* interrupting the coordinate genitives *sinces oððe sundoryrfes* which depend on *eal* (so translate, maintaining the disjunction: 'and all that the lord of warriors, the arrogant one, of treasure owned or personal wealth'). Similar disjunctions with the verb interrupting the syntax occur elsewhere in the poem (e.g. ll.166–7, 195–6).

**341b** The verse breaks Kuhn's Law of Clause Openings: on the poet's inconsistent treatment of *eal*, see n.110.

**341–2** *sægde wuldor ... dryhtne*: Timmer states that this expression does not occur elsewhere, but note *El* 1116–17 *sægdon wuldor gode*.

**344–9** Timmer, apparently misinterpreting Sisam (1953), 65, n.2, states that the last six lines in the MS have been copied from the Junius transcript, but Malone, 113, dates the early modern hand to c.1600, predating the transcript. That the copier imitates Insular script and therefore sometimes uses that form of Insular *s* with the long descender below the line (e.g. *þæs*, twice, l.346) confirms that these lines were originally written by Scribe B, for this *s* is entirely absent from the work of Scribe A.

**345a** Sweet, Cook, Timmer add *a*, 'ever', at the beginning of the verse 'in conformity with l.7a' (Timmer), but the echo between the beginning and end of the surviving text is not exact enough to justify emendation on that basis. The verse may be scanned as hypermetric without the addition (as a1b (1D1) rather than 1A1b (1D1)) and makes sense as it stands.

**346–9** Campbell (1988) 6–7, 28–9, observes that a homiletic prayer of thanksgiving is a prevalent terminal motif of O.E. poems, and compares the ends of *And*, *Phoen* and *Sea*, but remarks on the unique interpretation of the convention in *Jud*. See also pp.75–6, and n.259.

**347a** *to widan aldre*: *widan* may have *-an* for dat. sing. neut. strong *-um*, but the phrase occurs quite often with *-an* (*GenA* 1015, *And* 938, 1721, *ChristC* 1514, *GuthA* 636), whilst *to widum aldre* is unattested. The form is therefore probably weak, showing earlier syntax preserved in a poetic formula. On the occurrence of weak adjs. without dems. in the poetry, and the implications for dating, see Amos (1980), 110–24.

**349a** Pope (1966), 100, suggests adding *sæs* at the beginning of the verse in order to make a regular three-stress hypermetric a-verse, but it may be scanned as hypermetric with the anacrusis rather than the number of stresses indicating the verse type, (a1a (2A1a)). *OrW* ends with a similar expanded line, a1a (2A1a), a1e (2A1a).

# Bibliography

Volumes of the Patrologia Latina, and Monumenta Germaniae Historica are excluded. For brief references to dictionaries, see List of Abbreviations.

## 1. Transcript and Facsimiles

mid-17th cent. F. Junius, 'Fragmentum historiæ Judith, etc.', now Bodleian Library, MS Junius 105. [Junius]

1963 K. Malone, *The Nowell Codex (British Museum Cotton Vitellius A. xv, Second ms)*, EEMF 12 (Copenhagen). [Malone]

1991 F.C. Robinson and E.G. Stanley, *Old English Verse Texts from Many Sources: a Comprehensive Collection*, EEMF 23 (Copenhagen). [Robinson and Stanley]

## 2. Editions

1698 E. Thwaites, *Heptateuchus, Liber Job, et Evangelium Nicodemi; Anglo-Saxonice. Historiæ Judith Fragmentum; Dano-Saxonice* (Oxford), part II, 21–6.

1834 B. Thorpe, *Analecta Anglo-Saxonica: A Selection in Prose and Verse from Anglo-Saxon Authors of Various Ages; with a Glossary* (London). [Thorpe]

1838 H. Leo, *Altsächsische und Angelsächsische Sprachproben* (Halle). [Leo]

1849 L.F. Klipstein, *Analecta Anglo-Saxonica*, vol.2 (New York). {ll.15–349}

1850 L. Ettmüller, *Engla and Seaxna Scopas and Boceras* (Quedlinburg and Leipzig).

1857 C.W.M. Grein, *Bibliothek der Angelsächsischen Poesie* (Göttingen), 2nd edn., R.P. Wülker, II, 1894 (Leipzig). [Grein]

1858 L.G. Nilsson, *Judith, Fragment af ett fornengelskt Qväde* (Copenhagen).

1861 M. Rieger, *Alt- und angelsächsisches Lesebuch* (Giessen). [Rieger]

1880 K. Körner, *Einleitung in das Studium des Angelsächsischen*, Part II (Heilbronn). [Körner]

1888 A.S. Cook, *Judith, an Old English Epic Fragment* (Boston), 2nd edn., 1889. [Cook]

1888 F. Kluge, *Angelsächsisches Lesebuch* (Halle). [Kluge]

1893 G.E. MacLean, *An Old and Middle English Reader* (New York). {ll.122–235}

1904 A.S. Cook, *Judith, an Old English Epic Fragment* (Boston and London). [Cook 1904]

1915 J. Zupitza and J. Schipper, *Alt- und mittelenglisches Übungsbuch*, 12th edn., A. Eichler (Vienna and Leipzig). {ll.122–235}

1919 A.J. Wyatt, *An Anglo-Saxon Reader Edited with Notes and Glossary* (Cambridge). {ll.15–121, 246b–291a}

1921 A.S. Cook, *A First Book in Old English*, 3rd edn. (London). {ll.159–235, 291b–341a}

1945 F. Mossé, *Manuel de l'anglais du Moyen Âge des origines au XIVe siècle*, I, *Vieil-anglais* (Paris). {ll.159–235, 291b–349} [Mossé]

1952 B.J. Timmer, *Judith* (London), rev. edn., 1978 (Exeter). [Timmer]

1953 E.V.K. Dobbie, *Beowulf and Judith*, The Anglo-Saxon Poetic Records IV (New York). [Dobbie]

1955 F.P. Magoun, *The Poems of British Museum ms Cotton Vitellius A.XV: Beowulf (fol. 132a–201b) and Judith (fol. 202b–209b)* (Cambridge, Mass.).

1967 H. Sweet, *Sweet's Anglo-Saxon Reader in Prose and Verse*, 15th edn., D. Whitelock (Oxford). [Sweet]

1971 F.G. Cassidy and R.N. Ringler, *Bright's Old English Grammar and Reader*, 3rd edn. (New York). [Cassidy-Ringler]

## 3. Translations

1857 C.W.M. Grein, *Dichtungen der Angelsachsen* (Göttingen), 119–28. [Grein]

1926 R.K. Gordon, *Anglo-Saxon Poetry* (London), 352–8. [Gordon]

1970 R. Hamer, *A Choice of Anglo-Saxon Verse* (London), 135–57. [Hamer]

1982 S.A.J. Bradley, *Anglo-Saxon Poetry: An Anthology of Old English Poems in Prose Translation with Introduction and Headnotes* (London), 495–504. [Bradley]

## 4. General works and other editions

Bliss, A., *The Metre of 'Beowulf'*, 2nd edn. (Oxford, 1967). [Bliss]

Campbell, A., *Old English Grammar* (Oxford, 1959). [Campbell]

Cameron, A., *et al.*, *Old English Word Studies: A Preliminary Author and Word Index*, Toronto Old English Series 8 (Toronto, 1983). [Cameron]

Greenfield, S.B. and F.C. Robinson, *A Bibliography of Publications on Old English Literature to the End of 1972* (Toronto, 1980). [Greenfield and Robinson]

Hickes, G., *Linguarum veterum Septentrionalium Thesaurus Grammatico-criticus et Archaeologicus*, 2 vols (Oxford, 1703–5). [Hickes]

Hogg, R.M., *A Grammar of Old English* (Oxford, 1992). [Hogg]

Holthausen, F., *Altenglisches Etymologisches Wörterbuch* (Heidelberg, 1934). [Holthausen]

Ker, N.R., *Catalogue of Manuscripts containing Anglo-Saxon* (Oxford, 1957). [Ker]

Madan, F. and H.H.E. Craster, *A Summary Catalogue of Western Manuscripts in the Bodleian Library at Oxford* (Oxford, 1937). [Madan]

Mitchell, B., *Old English Syntax*, 2 vols (Oxford, 1985). [Mitchell]

Searle, W.G., *Onomasticon Anglo-Saxonicum: A List of Anglo-Saxon Proper Names from the Time of Beda to that of King John* (Cambridge, 1897). [Searle]

Sievers, E., *An Old English Grammar*, ed. and trans. A.S. Cook (Boston, 1903). [Sievers-Cook]

Venezky R.L. and A. di Paolo Healey, *A Microfiche Concordance to Old English* (Delaware, 1980). [Venezky-Healey]

Wanley, H., *Antiquæ Septentrionalis Liber Alter* (Oxford, 1705). [Wanley]

## 5. STUDIES and other works and editions cited (works of relevance to the literary interpretation of the poem are preceded by the symbol *)

Adams, E.N., *Old English Scholarship in England from 1566–1800*, Yale Studies in English 55 (New Haven, 1917).

Amos, A.C., *Linguistic Means of Determining the Dates of Old English Literary Texts*, Medieval Academy Books 90 (Cambridge, Mass., 1980).

Assmann, B., ed., *Angelsächsische Homilien und Heiligenleben* (Kassel, 1889).

*Astell, A.W., 'Holofernes's head: *tacen* and teaching in the Old English *Judith*', *ASE* 18 (1989), 117–33.

Auerbach, E., *Literary Language and Its Public in Late Latin Antiquity and in the Middle Ages*, trans. R. Mannheim (London, 1965).

Barley, N.F., 'Old English colour classification: where do matters stand?', *ASE* 3 (1974), 15–28.

Bartlett, A.C., *The Larger Rhetorical Patterns in Anglo-Saxon Poetry*, Columbia University Studies in English and Comparative Literature 122 (New York, 1935).

Bately, J., 'Time and the passing of time in *The Wanderer* and related Old English texts', *E&S* 37 (1984), 1–15.

——, 'Linguistic evidence as a guide to the authorship of Old English verse: a re-appraisal, with special reference to *Beowulf*', in *Learning and Literature in Anglo-Saxon England: Studies Presented to Peter Clemoes on the Occasion of his Sixty-Fifth Birthday*, ed. M. Lapidge and H. Gneuss (Cambridge, 1985), 409–31.

——, ed., *The Anglo-Saxon Chronicle: A Collaborative Edition, Volume 3, MS A* (Cambridge, 1986).

Belanoff, P.A., 'The fall (?) of the Old English female poetic image', *PMLA* 104 (1989), 822–31.

*——, 'Judith: sacred and secular heroine', in *Heroic Poetry in the Anglo-Saxon Period: Studies in Honor of Jess B. Bessinger*, Studies in Medieval Culture 32, ed. H. Damico and J. Leyerle (Kalamazoo, 1993), 247–64.

Belden, H.M., 'Perfective *ge-* in Old English *bringan* and *gebringan*', *EStn* 32 (1903), 366–70.

Belsheim, J., ed., *Libros Tobiæ, Judit, Ester ante Hieronymum latine translatos, ex codice olim Freisingensi nunc Monacensi* (Throndhjem, 1893).

Bennett, J.A.W., 'The history of Old English and Old Norse studies in England from the time of Francis Junius till the end of the eighteenth century', unpublished D.Phil. thesis (Oxford University, 1938).

——, G.V. Smithers and N. Davis, eds., *Early Middle English Verse and Prose*, 2nd edn. (Oxford, 1974).

*Berkhout, C.T., and J.F. Doubleday, 'The net in *Judith* 46b–54a', *NM* 74 (1973), 630–4.

Biggs, F.M., *et al.*, *Sources of Anglo-Saxon Literary Culture: A Trial Version* (Binghamton, 1990).

Binz, G., review of Cook (1904), in *EStn* 36 (1906), 130.

Blake, N.F., 'A note on "HW" in Old English', *N&Q* 206 (1961), 165–6.

Bliss, A., 'The OE long diphthongs *ĒO* and *ĒA*', *EGS* 3 (1949–50), 82–7.

——, 'Single half-lines in Old English poetry', *N&Q* 216 (1971), 442–9.

——, 'Auxiliary and verbal in *Beowulf*', *ASE* 9 (1981), 157–82.

Bodden, M.C., 'The preservation and transmission of Greek in early England', in *Sources of Anglo-Saxon Culture*, ed. P.E. Szarmach and V.D. Oggins, Studies in Medieval Culture 20 (Kalamazoo, 1986), 53–63.

Bogaert, M., 'La vieille version latine de Judith dans la Bible d'Oxford Bodléienne, Auct. E. infra 1–2', *Studia Patristica* 10 (1970), 208–14.

Boyle, L.E., 'The Nowell Codex and the poem of *Beowulf*', in *The Dating of Beowulf*, ed. C. Chase, Toronto Old English Series 6 (Toronto, 1981), 23–32.

Bremmer Jr, R.H., 'Grendel's arm and the law', in *Studies in English Language and Literature: 'Doubt Wisely', Papers in Honour of E.G. Stanley*, ed. M.J. Toswell and E.M. Tyler (London, 1996), 121–32.

Bright, J.W., review of Cook (1888), in *MLN* 4 (1889), 240–4.

——, 'Proper names in Old English verse', *PMLA* 14 (1899), 347–68.

Brink, B.A.K. ten, *'Beowulf': Untersuchungen*, Quellen und Forschungen 62 (Strassburg, 1888).

*Brodeur, A.G., 'A study of diction and style in three Anglo-Saxon narrative poems', in *Nordica et Anglica: Studies in Honour of Stefán Einarsson*, ed. A.H. Orrick (The Hague, 1968), 98–114.

Brooks, K.R., ed., *Andreas and the Fates of the Apostles* (Oxford, 1961).

Brown, M.P., 'A new fragment of a ninth-century English bible', *ASE* 18 (1989), 33–43.

Burnam, J.M., ed., *Commentaire anonyme sur Prudence d'après le manuscrit 413 de Valenciennes* (Paris, 1910).

Bzdyl, D.G., 'Prayer in Old English narratives', *MÆ* 51 (1982), 135–51.

Cable, T., 'Metrical style as evidence for the date of *Beowulf*', in *The Dating of Beowulf*, ed. C. Chase, Toronto Old English Series 6 (Toronto, 1981), 77–82.

Calder, D., *Cynewulf*, Twayne's English Authors Series 327 (Boston, 1981).

Callaway, M., Jr, *The Infinitive in Anglo-Saxon* (Washington, 1913).

Cameron, A., *et al.*, 'A reconsideration of the language of *Beowulf*', in *The Dating of Beowulf*, ed. C. Chase, Toronto Old English Series 6 (Toronto, 1981), 33–75.

Campbell, A., ed., *The Battle of Brunanburh* (London, 1938).

——, 'The Old English epic style', in *English and Medieval Studies Presented to J.R.R. Tolkien on the Occasion of his Seventieth Birthday*, ed. N. Davis and C.L. Wrenn (London, 1962), 13–26.

*Campbell, J.J., 'Schematic technique in *Judith*', *ELH* 38 (1971), 155–72.

*——, 'Ends and meanings: modes of closure in Old English poetry', *Medievalia et Humanistica* ns 16 (1988), 1–49.

Carnicelli, T.A., ed., *King Alfred's Version of St. Augustine's 'Soliloquies'* (Cambridge, Mass., 1969).

Carr, C.T., *Nominal Compounds in Germanic*, St Andrews University Publications 41 (London, 1939).

Catholic Truth Society, trans., *The Holy Bible: Douay Version translated from the Latin Vulgate (Douay, A.D. 1609: Rheims, A.D. 1582)* (London, 1956).

Cavill, P., 'Sectional divisions in Old English poetic manuscripts', *Neophil* 69 (1985), 156–9.

*Chamberlain, D., '*Judith*: a fragmentary and political poem', in *Anglo-Saxon Poetry: Essays in Appreciation for John C. McGalliard*, ed. L.E. Nicholson and D.W. Frese (Notre Dame, 1975), 135–59.

Charles, R.H., ed. and trans., *The Apocrypha and Pseudepigrapha of the Old Testament in English* (Oxford, 1913).

Clayton, M., 'Ælfric's *Judith*: manipulative or manipulated?', *ASE* 23 (1994), 215–27.

Clubb, M.D., review of Malone (1963), in *PQ* 43 (1964), 558–67.

Cook, A.S., ed., *The Christ of Cynewulf: A Poem in Three Parts, The Advent, The Ascension, and The Last Judgment*, 2nd edn. (Boston, 1909).

Corso, L., 'Some considerations of the concept "Nið" in *Beowulf*', *Neophil* 64 (1980), 121–6.

Cosijn, P.J., 'Anglosaxonica', *BGdSL* 19 (1894), 441–61.

Crawford, S.J., ed., *The Old English Version of the Heptateuch, Ælfric's Treatise on the Old and New Testament and his Preface to Genesis*, EETS os 160, rev. edn. (London, 1969).

Cross, F.L. and E.A. Livingstone, *The Oxford Dictionary of the Christian Church*, 2nd edn. (Oxford, 1974).

Curtius, E.R., *European Literature and the Latin Middle Ages*, trans. W.R. Trask (London, 1953).

Damico, H., 'The Valkyrie reflex in Old English literature', in *New Readings on Women in Old English Literature*, ed. H. Damico and A. Hennessey Olsen (Bloomington, 1990), 176–90.

Dancy, J.C., comm. and trans., *The Shorter Books of the Apocrypha: Tobit, Judith, Rest of Esther, Baruch, Letter of*

*Jeremiah, Addition to Daniel, and Prayer to Manasseh*, The Cambridge Bible Commentary (Cambridge, 1972).

Davidson, C., 'Differences between the scribes of *Beowulf*', *MLN* 5 (1890), 43–5.

Denison, D., 'The origins of completive *up* in English', *NM* 86 (1985), 37–61.

Dietrich, F., '*Hycgan* und *hopian*', *ZfdA* 9 (1853), 214–22.

Doane, A.N., ed., *'Genesis A': A New Edition* (Madison, 1978).

——, ed., *The Saxon Genesis: An Edition of the West Saxon 'Genesis B' and the Old Saxon Vatican 'Genesis'* (Madison, 1991).

Donoghue, D., *Style in Old English Poetry: The Test of the Auxiliary* (New Haven, 1987).

*Doubleday, J.F., 'The principle of contrast in *Judith*', *NM* 72 (1971), 436–41.

Dunning, T.P., and A.J. Bliss, eds., *The Wanderer* (London, 1969).

Fakundiny, L., 'The art of Old English verse composition', *RES* 21 (1970), 129–42, 257–66.

Farrell, R.T., ed., *'Daniel' and 'Azarias'* (London, 1974).

Förster, M., 'Die Beowulf-Handschrift', *Berichte über die Verhandlungen der Sächsischen Akademie der Wissenschaften* 71, number 4 (Leipzig, 1919).

*Foster, T.G., *'Judith': Studies in Metre, Language and Style, with a View to Determining the Date of the Old English Fragment and the Home of its Author*, Quellen und Forschungen 71 (Strassburg, 1892).

Fraipont, J., ed., *Sancti Fulgentii Episcopi Ruspensis Opera*, Corpus Christianorum, series Latina, 91 and 91A (Turnholt, 1968).

Frank, R., 'Some uses of paronomasia in Old English scriptural verse', *Speculum* 47 (1972), 207–26.

——, 'Late Old English *þrymnys* "Trinity": scribal nod or word waiting to be born?', in *Old English and New: Studies in Language and Linguistics in Honor of Frederic G. Cassidy*, ed. J.H. Hall, N. Doane and D. Ringler (New York and London, 1992), 97–110.

*Fry, D.K., 'Imagery and point of view in *Judith* 200b–231', *ELN* 5 (1967–8), 157–9.

*——, 'Type-scene composition in *Judith*', *An Med* 12 (1972), 100–19.

Fulk, R.D., *A History of Old English Meter* (Philadelphia, 1992).

Garmonsway, G.N., *et al.*, trans., *'Beowulf' and its Analogues* (London, 1980).

Gatch, M. McC., *Preaching and Theology in Anglo-Saxon England: Ælfric and Wulfstan* (Toronto, 1977).

Gerritsen, J., 'British Library ms Cotton Vitellius A. xv–a supplementary description', *ES* 69 (1988), 293–302.

Gillam, D.M.E., 'The connotations of O.E. *fæge*: with a note on Beowulf and Byrhtnoð', *SGG* 4 (1962), 165–201.

Glogauer, E., *Die Bedeutungsübergänge der Konjunktionen in der angelsächsischen Dichtersprache* (Leipzig, 1922).

Glunz, H.H., *History of the Vulgate in England from Alcuin to Roger Bacon* (Cambridge, 1933).

Gneuss, H., 'A preliminary list of manuscripts written or owned in England up to 1100', *ASE* 9 (1981), 1–60.

Godden, M., ed., *Ælfric's Catholic Homilies: The Second Series: Text*, EETS ss 5 (London, 1979).

——, 'Biblical literature: the Old Testament', in *The Cambridge Companion to Old English Literature*, ed. M. Godden and M. Lapidge (Cambridge, 1991), 206–26.

Gollancz, I., *The Cædmon Manuscript of Anglo-Saxon Biblical Poetry: Junius XI: in the Bodleian Library* (Oxford, 1927).

Goossens, L., 'A chronology for the falling together of lOE *hr* and *r*', *ES* 50 (1969), 74–9.

——, ed., *The Old English Glosses of MS. Brussels, Royal Library, 1650 (Aldhelm's 'De Laudibus Virginitatis')* (Brussels, 1974).

Gradon, P.O.E., ed., *Cynewulf's Elene* (London, 1958).

——, 'Studies in late West-Saxon labialization and delabialization', in *English and Medieval Studies Presented to J.R.R. Tolkien on the Occasion of his Seventieth Birthday*, ed. N. Davis and C.L. Wrenn (London, 1962), 63–76.

Green, D.H., *The Carolingian Lord: Semantic Studies on Four Old High German Words: balder, frô, truhtin, hêrro* (Cambridge, 1965).

Greenfield, S.B., *The Interpretation of Old English Poems* (London, 1972).

Gretsch, M., 'The language of the "Fonthill Letter"', *ASE* 23 (1994), 57–102.

Griffith, M.S., 'The method of composition of Old English verse translation with particular reference to "The Metres of Boethius", "The Paris Psalter" and "Judgment Day II"', unpublished D.Phil. thesis (Oxford University, 1985).

——, 'Poetic language and the formula in Old English poetry', in *Sentences: Essays Presented to Alan Ward on the Occasion of his Retirement from Wadham College, Oxford*, ed. D.M. Reeks (Southampton, 1988), 155–66.

—— 'Convention and originality in the Old English "beasts of battle" typescene', *ASE* 22 (1993), 179–99.

Grimm, J and W., ed., *Das Lied von Hildebrand und Hadubrand* (Cassel, 1812).

Grinda, K.R., 'Pigeonholing Old English poetry', *Anglia* 102 (1984), 305–22.

Hamer, R., *Old English Sound Changes for Beginners* (Oxford, 1967).

Hastings, J., *A Dictionary of the Bible, Dealing with its Language, Literature, and Contents, Including the Biblical Theology*, 5 vols (Edinburgh, 1900).

*Heinemann, F.J., '*Judith* 236–291a: a mock heroic approach-to-battle type scene', *NM* 71 (1970), 83–96.

Herbison, I., 'The idea of the "Christian epic": towards a history of an Old English poetic genre', in *Studies in English Language and Literature: 'Doubt Wisely', Papers in Honour of E.G. Stanley*, ed. M.J. Toswell and E.M. Tyler (London, 1996), 342–61.

*Hermann, J.P., 'The theme of spiritual warfare in the Old English *Judith*', *PQ* 55 (1976), 1–9.

Hessels, J.H., *A Late Eighth-Century Latin-Anglo-Saxon Glossary preserved in the Library of the Leiden University (MS. Voss. Qo Lat. No. 69)* (Cambridge, 1906).

Hetherington, M.S., *The Beginnings of Old English Lexicography* (Spicewood, 1980).

Heusler, A, *Deutsche Versgeschichte, mit Einschluss des altenglischen und altnordischen Stabreimverses*, 2nd edn. (Berlin, 1956).

Heyworth, P.L., ed., *Letters of Humfrey Wanley: Palaeographer, Anglo-Saxonist, Librarian, 1672–1726* (Oxford, 1989).

Hieatt, C.B., 'Alliterative patterns in the hypermetric lines of Old English verse', *MP* 71 (1974), 237–42.

*——, '*Judith* and the literary function of Old English hypermetric lines, *SN* 52 (1980), 251–7.

Hill, J.M., 'Figures of evil in Old English poetry', *Leeds Studies* 8 (1975), 5–19.

Hill, T.D., 'Sapiential structure and figural narrative in the Old English *Elene*', *Traditio* 27 (1971), 159–77.

*——, 'Invocation of the Trinity and the tradition of the *Lorica* in Old English poetry', *Speculum* 56 (1981), 259–67.

Hofer, O, 'Über die Entstehung des angelsächsischen Gedichtes *Daniel*', *Anglia* 12 (1889), 158–204.

Holthausen, F., review of Kluge (1888), in *LGRPh* 10 (1889), 445–9.

Hoover, D.L., *A New Theory of Old English Meter*, American University Studies, Series 4, 14 (New York, 1985).

Hughes, K., 'Some aspects of Irish influence on early English private prayer', *Studia Celtica* 5 (1970), 48–61.

Hulbert, J.R., 'The accuracy of the B-scribe of *Beowulf*', *PMLA* 43 (1928), 1196–9.

Hume, K., 'The concept of the hall in Old English poetry', *ASE* 3 (1974), 63–74.

*Huppé, B.F., *The Web of Words: Structural Analyses of the Old English Poems 'Vainglory', 'The Wonder of Creation', 'The Dream of the Rood', and 'Judith', with Texts and Translations* (Albany, 1970).

Hutcheson, B.R., *Old English Poetic Metre* (Cambridge, 1995).

Imelmann, R., review of Cook (1904), in *Beibl* 19 (1908), 1–8.

James, M.R., trans., *The Apocryphal New Testament* (Oxford, 1953).

Jente, R., *Die mythologischen Ausdrücke im altenglischen Wortschatz*, Anglistische Forschungen 56 (Heidelberg, 1921).

Jiriczek, O.L., 'Die Bedeutung von ae. *stede-heard* (*Judith* 223)', *EStn* 64 (1929), 212–18.

Jost, K., review of Timmer (1952), in *ES* 35 (1954), 214–18.

Kaluza, M., 'Die Schwellverse in der altenglischen Dichtung', *EStn* 21 (1895), 337–84.

*Kaske, R.E., '*Sapientia et fortitudo* as the controlling theme of *Beowulf*', in *An Anthology of 'Beowulf' Criticism*, ed. L.E. Nicholson (Notre Dame, 1963), 269–310.

——, '*Sapientia et fortitudo* in the Old English *Judith*', in *The Wisdom of Poetry: Essays in Early English Literature in Honor of Morton W. Bloomfield*, ed. L.D. Benson and S. Wenzel (Kalamazoo, 1982), 13–29, 264–8.

Kastovsky, D., 'Semantics and vocabulary', in *The Beginnings to 1066*, ed. R.M. Hogg, Cambridge History of the English Language 1 (Cambridge, 1992), 290–408.

Kedar, B., 'The Latin translations', in *Mikra: Text, Translation, Reading and Interpretation of the Hebrew Bible in Ancient Judaism and Early Christianity*, ed. M.J. Mulder, Compendia Rerum Iudaicarum ad Novum Testamentum, section 2, I, 299–338.

Keiser, A., *The Influence of Christianity on the Vocabulary of Old English Poetry*, Illinois Studies in Language and Literature 5 (Urbana, 1919).

Kendall, C.B., 'The prefix *un-* and the metrical grammar of *Beowulf*', *ASE* 10 (1982), 39–52.

——, *The Metrical Grammar of 'Beowulf'*, Cambridge Studies in Anglo-Saxon England 5 (Cambridge, 1991).

Kern, H., 'Een Paar bedorven Plaatsen', *Taalkundige Bijdragen* I (1877), 210–14.

Kiernan, K.S., *Beowulf and the Beowulf Manuscript* (New Brunswick, 1981).

Klaeber, F., 'Notes on Old English poems', *JEGP* 12 (1913), 252–61.

——, 'Concerning the functions of Old English *geweorðan* and the origin of German *gewähren lassen*', *JEGP* 18 (1919), 250–71.

——, 'Zur jüngeren *Genesis*', *Anglia* 49 (1926), 361–75.

——, 'Attila's and Beowulf's funeral', *PMLA* 42 (1927), 255–67.

——, 'Jottings on Old English poems', *Anglia* 53 (1929), 225–34.

——, ed., *'Beowulf' and 'The Fight at Finnsburg'*, 3rd edn. with first and second supplements (Boston, 1950).

Kock, E.A., 'Domen över död man', *Arkiv för Nordisk Filologi* 33 (1917), 175–8.

Koeppel, E., 'Zu *Judith* V. 62', *Archiv* 90 (1893), 140–1.

Krapp, G.P., and E.V.K. Dobbie, eds., *The Exeter Book*, The Anglo-Saxon Poetic Records III (New York, 1936).

Kuhn, H., 'Zur Wortstellung und -betonung im Altgermanischen', *BGdSL* 57 (1933), 1–109.

Kuhn, S.M., ed., *The Vespasian Psalter* (Ann Arbor, Mich., 1965).

Laistner, M.L.W., 'The Latin versions of Acts known to the Venerable Bede', *Harvard Theological Review* 30 (1937), 37–50.

Lapidge, M, 'Aldhelm's Latin poetry and Old English verse', *CL* 31 (1979), 209–31.

Lass, R., and J.M. Anderson, *Old English Phonology*, Cambridge Studies in Linguistics 14 (Cambridge, 1975).

Lawrence, J., *Chapters on Alliterative Verse* (London, 1893).

Lehmann, W.P., *The Development of Germanic Verse Form* (Austin, Tex., 1956).

Lendinara, P., 'The Old English renderings of Latin *tabernaculum* and *tentorium*', in *Anglo-Saxonica: Festschrift für Hans Schabram zum 65. Geburtstag*, ed. K.R. Grinda and C-D. Wetzel (Munich, 1993), 289–325.

Leslie, R.F., ed., *The Wanderer* (Manchester, 1966).

——, 'Analysis of stylistic devices and effects in Anglo-Saxon literature', in *Old English Literature: Twenty-two Analytical Essays*, ed. M. Stevens and J. Mandel (Lincoln, Nebr., 1968), 73–81.

Levison, W., 'Sigolena', *Neues Archiv der Gesellschaft für ältere deutsche Geschichtskunde* 35 (1910), 219–31.

Lindheim, B. von, 'Traces of colloquial speech in Old English', *Anglia* 70 (1951), 22–42.

Lindsay, W.M., ed., *The Corpus, Épinal, Erfurt and Leiden Glossaries*, Publications of the Philological Society 8 (London, 1921).

*Locherbie-Cameron, M., 'Wisdom as a key to heroism in *Judith*', *Poetica* 27 (1988), 70–5.

Lucas, P.J., 'Some aspects of *Genesis B* as Old English verse', *Proceedings of the Royal Irish Academy*, Section C, 88 (1988), 143–78.

——, 'The place of *Judith* in the *Beowulf*-manuscript', *RES* 41 (1990), 463–78.

*——, '*Judith* and the woman hero', *YES* 22 (1992), 17–27.

——, ed., *Exodus*, rev. edn. (Exeter, 1994).

Luick, K., *Historische Grammatik der Englischen Sprache*, 2 vols (Oxford, 1964).

Lutz, A., 'Spellings of the *waldend* group–again', *ASE* 13 (1984), 51–64.

*Magennis, H., 'Adaptation of biblical detail in the Old English *Judith*: the feast scene', *NM* 84 (1983), 331–7.

——, 'Images of laughter in Old English poetry with particular reference to the *hleahtor wera* of *The Seafarer*', *ES* 73 (1992), 193–204.

*——, 'Contrasting narrative emphases in the Old English poem *Judith* and Ælfric's paraphrase of the book of Judith', *NM* 96 (1995a), 61–6.

——, 'Attitudes to sexuality in Old English prose and poetry', *Leeds Studies* 26 (1995b), 1–27.

Malone, K., 'When did Middle English begin?', *LM* 7 (1930), 110–17.

——, 'Plurilinear units in Old English poetry', *RES* 19 (1943), 201–4.

——, 'Variation in *Widsith*', *JEGP* 45 (1946), 147–52.

——, 'Some *Judith* readings', in *Festschrift zum 75. Geburtstag von Theodor Spira*, ed. H. Viebrock and W. Erzgräber (Heidelberg, 1961), 32–7.

Marckwardt, A.H., 'The verbal suffix *-ettan* in Old English', *Language* 18 (1942), 275–81.

Marquardt, H., *Die altenglischen Kenningar: ein Beitrag zur Stilkunde altgermanischer Dichtung*, Schriften der Königsberger Gelehrten Gesellschaft, 14. Jahr, Heft 3 (Halle, 1938).

Marsden, R., 'Old Latin intervention in the Old English *Heptateuch*', *ASE* 23 (1994), 229–64.

——, *The Text of the Old Testament in Anglo-Saxon England*, Cambridge Studies in Anglo-Saxon England 15 (Cambridge, 1995).

McPherson, C.W., 'The influence of Latin rhetoric on Old English poetry', unpublished D.Phil. thesis (University of Washington, 1980).

Meissner, R., *Die Kenningar der Skalden: Ein Beitrag zur skaldischen Poetik* (Bonn and Leipzig, 1921).

Meroney, H., 'The early history of *down* as an adverb', *JEGP* 44 (1945), 378–86.

Mierow, C.C., trans., *The Gothic History of Jordanes* (Cambridge, 1915).

Miller, T., ed., *The Old English Version of Bede's 'Ecclesiastical History of the English People'*, EETS os 95, 96, 110, 111 (London, 1890–8).

Mitchell, B., 'Old English "OÐÞÆT" adverb?', *N&Q* 223 (1978), 390–4.

——, *et al.*, 'Short titles of Old English texts, *ASE* 4 (1975), 207–21.

——, *et al.*, 'Short titles of Old English texts: addenda and corrigenda', *ASE* 8 (1979), 331–3.

Moffat, D., 'Anglo-Saxon scribes and Old English verse', *Speculum* 67 (1992), 805–27.

Momma, H, *The Composition of Old English Poetry*, Cambridge Studies in Anglo-Saxon England 20 (Cambridge, 1997).

Morris, R., ed., *The Blickling Homilies of the Tenth Century*, EETS os 58, 63 73 (London, 1874–80).

Murphy, M., 'Edward Thwaites, pioneer teacher of Old English', *DUJ* 73, ns 42 (1980–1), 153–9.

*Mushabac, J., '*Judith* and the theme of *Sapientia et fortitudo*', *Massachusetts Studies in English* 4 (1973), 3–12.

Napier, A.S., ed., *Old English Glosses Chiefly Unpublished* (Oxford, 1900).

*Nelson, M., '*Judith*: a story of a secular saint', *Germanic Notes* 21 (1990), 12–13.

Nichols, A.E., 'AWENDAN: a note on Ælfric's vocabulary', *JEGP* 63 (1964), 7–13.

*Nicholson, L.E., 'Oral techniques in the composition of expanded Anglo-Saxon verses', *PMLA* 78 (1963), 287–92.

Oakeshott, W., *The Two Winchester Bibles* (Oxford, 1981).

Ogilvy, J.D.A., *Books Known to the English, 597–1066* (Cambridge, Mass., 1967).

Oliphant, R.T., ed., *The Harley Latin-Old English Glossary Edited from British Museum MS Harley 3376* (The Hague, 1966).

*Olsen, A.H., 'Inversion and political purpose in the Old English *Judith*', *ES* 63 (1982), 289–93.

Orchard, A., 'Artful alliteration in Anglo-Saxon song and story', *Anglia* 113 (1995), 429–63.

Orton, P.R., 'Verbal apposition, coordination and metrical stress in Old English', *NM* 86 (1985), 145–58.

Parkes, M.B., *Pause and Effect: An Introduction to the History of Punctuation in the West* (Aldershot, 1992).

Patch, H.R., *The Other World According to Descriptions in Medieval Literature* (Cambridge, Mass., 1950).

Phillpotts, B.S., '*The Battle of Maldon*: some Danish affinities', *MLR*, 24 (1929), 172–90.

Plummer, C., ed., *Baedae Historia Ecclesiastica gentis Anglorum: Venerabilis Baedae opera historica*, 2 vols (Oxford, 1896).

Pogatscher, A., 'Etymologisches und Grammatisches', *Anglia* 31 (1908), 257–75.

Pope, J.C., *The Rhythm of 'Beowulf': An Interpretation of the Normal and Hypermetric Verse-Forms in Old English Poetry*, rev. edn. (New Haven, 1966).

——, ed., *Homilies of Ælfric: A Supplementary Collection*, EETS os 259, 260 (London, 1967–8).

*Pringle, I., '*Judith*: the homily and the poem', *Traditio* 31 (1975), 83–97.

Quirk, R., 'Poetic language and metre', in *Early English and Norse Studies: Presented to Hugh Smith in Honour of his Sixtieth Birthday*, ed. A. Brown and P. Foote (London, 1963), 150–71.

Remley, P.G., 'The Latin textual basis of *Genesis A*', *ASE* 17 (Cambridge, 1988), 163–89.

——, *Old English Biblical Verse: Studies in 'Genesis', 'Exodus' and 'Daniel'*, Cambridge Studies in Anglo-Saxon England 16 (Cambridge, 1996).

Rissanen, M., '*Sum* in Old English poetry', in *Modes of Interpretation in Old English Literature: Essays in Honour of Stanley B. Greenfield*, ed. P.R. Brown, *et al.* (Toronto, 1986), 197–225.

Roberts, J., 'A metrical examination of the poems *Guthlac A* and *Guthlac B*', *Proceedings of the Royal Irish Academy*, Section C, 71 (1971), 91–137.

——, ed., *The Guthlac Poems of the Exeter Book* (Oxford, 1979).

Robinson, F.C., 'God, death, and loyalty in *The Battle of Maldon*', in his *The Tomb of Beowulf and Other Essays on Old English* (Oxford, 1993a), 105–21.

——, 'The prescient woman in Old English literature', in his *The Tomb of Beowulf and Other Essays on Old English* (Oxford, 1993b), 155–63.

Robinson, P.R., 'Self-contained units in composite manuscripts of the Anglo-Saxon period', *ASE* 7 (1978), 231–8.

Rollinson, P.B., 'The influence of Christian doctrine and exegesis on Old English poetry: an estimate of the current state of scholarship', *ASE* 2 (1973), 271–84.

Rüden, M. von, *'Wlanc' und Derivate im Alt- und Mittelenglischen* (Frankfurt, 1978).

Russom, G., 'The drink of death in Old English and Germanic literature', in *Germania: Comparative Studies in the Old Germanic Languages and Literatures*, ed. D.G. Calder and T.C. Christy (Wolfeboro, 1988), 175–89.

Rypins, S., ed., *Three Old English Prose Texts in MS. Cotton Vitellius A xv*, EETS os 161 (London, 1924).

Sabatier, P., ed., *Bibliorum Sacrorum Latinae Versiones Antiquae* (Paris, 1751).

Schlemilch, W., *Beiträge zur Sprache und Orthographie spätaltenglischen Sprachdenkmäler der Übergangszeit 1000–1150*, SEP 34 (Halle, 1914).

Schmitz, T., 'Die Sechstakter in der altenglischen Dichtung', *Anglia* 33 (1910), 1–76, 172–218.

Schücking, L., *Die Grundzüge der Satzverknüpfung im 'Beowulf'*, SEP 15 (Halle, 1904).

Scragg, D.G., 'Accent marks in the Old English Vercelli Book', *NM* 72 (1971), 699–710.

——, ed., *The Battle of Maldon* (Manchester, 1981).

——, ed., *The Vercelli Homilies and Related Texts*, EETS os 300 (Oxford, 1992).

Sedgefield, W.J., ed., *King Alfred's Old English Version of Boethius' 'De Consolatione Philosophiae'* (Oxford, 1899).

*Shepherd, G., 'Scriptural poetry', in *Continuations and Beginnings*, ed. E.G. Stanley (London,1966), 1–36.

——, 'English versions of the Scriptures before Wyclif', in *The Cambridge History of the Bible*, II *The West from the Fathers to the Reformation*, ed. G.W.H. Lampe (Cambridge, 1969), 362–87.

Shippey, T.A., *Old English Verse* (London, 1972).

——, ed. and trans., *Poems of Wisdom and Learning in Old English* (Cambridge, 1976).

Sievers, E., 'Zur Rhythmik des germanischen Alliterationsverses', *BGdSL* 10 (1885), 209–314, 451–545; and 12 (1887), 454–82.

Sisam, K., *Studies in the History of Old English Literature* (Oxford, 1953).

Skeat, W.W., ed., *Ælfric's Lives of the Saints, being a Set of Sermons on Saints' Days Formerly Observed by the English Church*, EETS os 94, 114 (London, 1890 and 1900).

Sklar, E.S., '*The Battle of Maldon* and the popular tradition: some rhymed formulas', *PQ* 54 (1975), 409–18.

Slay, D., 'Some aspects of the technique of composition of Old English verse', *TPS* (1952), 1–14.

Squires, A., ed., *The Old English Physiologus*, Durham Medieval Texts 5 (Durham, 1988).

Stanley, E.G., 'Old English poetic diction and the interpretation of *The Wanderer*, *The Seafarer* and *The Penitent's Prayer*', *Anglia* 73 (1955), 413–66.

——, 'Spellings of the *Waldend* group', in *Studies in Language, Literature, and Culture of the Middle Ages and Later*, ed. E. Bagby Atwood and A.A. Hill (Austin, Texas, 1969), 38–69.

——, 'Studies in the prosaic vocabulary of Old English verse', *NM* 72 (1971), 385–418.

——, ed., *The Owl and the Nightingale* (Manchester, 1972).

——, 'Some observations on the A3 lines in *Beowulf*', in *Old English Studies in Honour of John C. Pope*, ed. R.B. Burlin and E.B. Irving Jr. (Toronto and Buffalo, 1974), 139–64.

——, 'Verbal stress in Old English verse', *Anglia* 93 (1975), 307–34.

——, 'The date of *Beowulf*: some doubts and no conclusions', in *The Dating of 'Beowulf'*, ed. C. Chase, Toronto Old English Series 6 (Toronto, 1981), 197–211.

——, 'Alliterative ornament and alliterative rhythmical discourse in Old High German and Old Frisian compared with similar manifestations in Old English', *BGdSL* 106 (1984), 184–217.

——, 'Ælfric on the canonicity of the book of Judith: *hit stent on leden þus on ðære bibliothecan*', *N&Q* 230 (1985), 439.

——, 'Parody in Early English literature', *Poetica* 27 (1988), 1–69.

——, 'Notes on Old English poetry', *Leeds Studies* 20 (1989), 319–44.

——, 'Initial clusters of unstressed syllables in half-lines of *Beowulf*', in *Words, Texts and Manuscripts: Studies in Anglo-Saxon Culture Presented to Helmut Gneuss on The Occasion of his Sixty-Fifth Birthday*, ed. M. Korhammer, K. Reichl and H. Sauer (Cambridge, 1992), 263–84.

——, *In the Foreground: 'Beowulf'* (Cambridge, 1994).

——, 'The dialect origins of late Old English verse', *Poetica* 42 (1995, for 1994), 1–21.

——, 'Old English poetry: "out of the people's warm mouth', *N&Q* 242 (1997), 6–21.

Stuart, H., 'The meaning of O.E. **ælfsciene*', *Parergon* 2 (1972), 22–6.

Suzuki, S., 'On the combination of type A verses into lines in *Beowulf*: a further consideration', *N&Q* 239 (1994), 437–9.

——, *The Metrical Organization of 'Beowulf': Prototype and Isomorphism*, Trends in Linguistics, Studies and Monographs 95 (Berlin, 1996).

*Swanton, M., 'Die altenglische Judith: Weiblicher Held oder frauliche Heldin', in *Heldensage und Heldendichtung im Germanischen*, ed. H. Beck (Berlin, 1988), 289–304.

Sweet, H., ed., *King Alfred's West-Saxon Version of Gregory's Pastoral Care*, EETS os 45, 50 (London, 1871).

Tatlock, J.S.P., 'Layamon's poetic style and its relations', in *The Manly Anniversary Studies in Language and Literature* (Chicago, 1923), 3–11.

Taylor, P.B., and P.H. Salus, 'The compilation of Cotton Vitellius A. XV', *NM* 69 (1968), 199–204.

Terasawa, J., *Nominal Compounds in Old English: A Metrical Approach*, Anglistica 27 (Copenhagen, 1994).

Thomson, H.J., ed., *Prudentius*, 2 vols (Cambridge, Mass., 1969).

Thwaites, E, unpublished letter to G. Hickes, undated (Oxford, 1697?) , Bod. Lib. MS Eng. hist. c.6, f.118.

Timmer, B., 'Sectional divisions of poems in Old English manuscripts', *MLR* 47 (1952), 319–22.

Tolkien, J.R.R., ed., *The Old English 'Exodus': Text, Translation, and Commentary*, ed. J. Turville-Petre (Oxford, 1981).

Tucker, S.I., 'Laughter in Old English literature', *Neophil* 43 (1959), 222–6.

Tupper, F., 'Notes on Old English poems', *JEGP* 11 (1912), 82–103.

Twysden, R., ed., *Historiæ Anglicanæ Scriptores Antiqui* (London, 1652).

*Tyler, E.M., 'Style and meaning in *Judith*', *N&Q* 237 (1992), 16–19.

——, 'How deliberate is deliberate verbal repetition', in *Studies in English Language and Literature: 'Doubt Wisely', Papers in Honour of E.G. Stanley*, ed. M.J. Toswell and E.M. Tyler (London, 1996), 508–30.

Vetter, F., *Zum Muspilli und zur germanischen Alliterationspoesie: Metrisches, Kritisches, Dogmatisches* (Vienna, 1872).

Weber, R., *Biblia Sacra iuxta Vulgatam Versionem* (Stuttgart, 1975).

Wells, D.M., 'The sections in Old English poetry', *YES* 6 (1976), 1–4.

Wenisch, F., *Spezifisch anglisches Wortgut in den nordhumbrischen Interlinearglossierungen des Lukasevangeliums*, Anglistische Forschungen 132 (Heidelberg, 1979).

——, '*Judith*—eine westsächsische Dichtung?', *Anglia* 100 (1982), 273–300.

Woolf, R., 'The devil in Old English poetry', *RES* 4 (1953), 1–12.

*——, 'Saints' lives', in *Continuations and Beginnings*, ed. E.G. Stanley (London, 1966), 37–66.

——, '*The Wanderer*, *The Seafarer*, and the genre of *Planctus*', in *Anglo-Saxon Poetry: Essays in Appreciation For John C. McGalliard*, ed. L.E. Nicholson and D.W. Frese (Notre Dame and London, 1975), 192–207.

*——, 'The lost opening to the *Judith*', in *Art and Doctrine: Essays on Medieval Literature*, ed. H. O'Donoghue (London, 1986), 119–24.

Wrenn, C.L., and W.F. Bolton, eds., *Beowulf with the Finnesburg Fragment*, 3rd edn., rev. (Exeter, 1988).

Wright, C.D., *The Irish Tradition in Old English Literature*, Cambridge Studies in Anglo-Saxon England 6 (Cambridge, 1993).

Wright, J., and E.M. Wright, *Old English Grammar*, 2nd edn. (London, 1914).

——, *An Elementary Middle English Grammar*, 2nd edn. (London, 1928).

Wullen, F., 'Die syntaktische Gebrauch der Präpositionen *fram*, *under*, *ofer*, *þurh* in der angelsächsischen Poesie', *Anglia* 34 (1911), 423–97.

Yerkes, D., ed., *The Old English Life of Machutus*, Toronto Old English Series 9 (Toronto, 1984).

# Appendix I

## Alliteration and Rhyme

### Alliteration

**A** The alliteration of velar and palatal *g-*:
(1) Lines alliterating only on the velar: 22 (*gold-:gumena:gyte-*), 32 (*agotene:goda:gumena*), 112 (*gesne:gæst*), 140 (*glæd-:gegan*), 148 (*gleaw-:gumena*), 171 (*gleawe:golde*), 186 (*godes:gumena*), 219 (*guð-:gegan*), 224 (*grame:guð-:garas*), 271 (*gristbitian: gode*), 279 (*gold-:gæstes*, but see also section (6)), 305 (*guðe: gegremede:guman*), 307 (*gar-:greot*), 328 (*guð-:gumena:golde*). Note also 62a (*gal-:gumena*) where the line is incomplete, and 83 which has ornamental velar alliteration.
(2) Lines alliterating only on the palatal: 2 (*gifena:ginnan: gearwe*), 149 (*ginnan:togeanes*).
(3) Lines in which the name *Iudith* alliterates:
(a) with the velar: 13 (*gleaw*), 123 (*guðe:god*), 256 (*gal-*), 333 (*gleaw*).
(b) with the palatal: 40 (*gyst-*), 132 (*gingran:gegnum*), 144 (*geomor-*), 168 (*ongeaton*), 341 (*ageafon:gearo-*).
(4) Lines which lack alliteration if the velar and palatal are not held to alliterate together: 9 (*girwan:gumena*), 238 (*ongeaton: grame*).
(5) Lines or verses with alliterative abnormality if velar and palatal are held to alliterate: 2a (*gifena:ginnan:grunde*, with triple alliteration), 149b (*togeanes:gan*, with double alliteration).
(6) Other abnormalities involving *g-* alliteration: 279 (*gold-: gæstes:gesne*, with double alliteration on velars in the b-verse).

**B**: Minor Alliterative Patterns (assuming the normal alliterative rules; with line or verse references):
(1) Consonant cluster alliteration:

(i) Throughout the line: 23 (*hl-*), 29 (*dr-*), 37 (*hr-*), 80 (*sw-*), 83 (*fr-*), 106 (*sw-*), 125 (*sn-*), 164 (*ðr-*), 199 (*sn-*), 205 (*hl-*), 214 (*hw-*), 240 (*sw-*), 247 (*sl-*), 282 (*hr-*), 321 (*sw-*).
(ii) In the a-verse: 5 (*fr-*), 55 (*sn-*), 86 (*ðr-*), 337a (*sw-*).
(iii) In one of two alliterating positions in the a-verse and in the b-verse: 30 (*sw-*), 57 (*br-*), 88 (*sw-*), 221 (*fl-*), 317 (*br-*).
(2) Crossed alliteration (including alliteration on syllables bearing secondary stress; with ab/ab pattern unless otherwise specified): 3 (aab/ab), 20 (aab/ab), 58 (aab/ab), 78, 83, 84 (abc/ac, if the second element of *alwalda* carried stress), 85, 112 (ab/abc), 135 (abc/ab), 137, 155, 165, 173, 215, 223 (aab/ab), 235, 237 (aab/ab), 253, 310, 325 (aab/ab), 339 (aab/ab). Note also l.150 with tertiary stress.
(3) Transverse alliteration: 331 (ab/ba); in addition, the alliteration on the finite verbs in the initial dip of 61 and 98 was possibly perceptible.
(4) Continued alliteration: 17–18, 57–8, 64–5, 75–6, 78–9, 88–9, 108–9, 116–17, 124–5, 130–1, 141–2, 148–9, 160–1, 164–5, 169–70, 174–5, 194–5, 206–7, 217–18, 220–1, 231–2, 300–1.
(5) Alliterative enjambement: 14–15, 28–9, 36–7, 38–9, 66–7, 85–6, 89–90, 95–6, 137–8, 155–6, 184–5, 211–12, 214–15, 235–6, 247–8, 272–3, 273–4, 280–1, 288–9, 290–1, 296–7, 310–11. With tertiary stress, note ll.41–2.

Rhyme:

The rhymes in sections 1a, 2a, and 3a should be regarded as truly rhyming; those in the other sections occasionally involve ornament (especially in combination with other devices), but some are no doubt either accidental or the product of the poet's grammar and appositive style.
(1) At the end of two stressed words within one verse:
(a) Of stem syllables (feminine rhyme): 23b.
(b) Of their unstressed inflected syllables, either in agreement, or in correlative or dependent relation (in many instances such masculine rhymes are grammatically inevitable): 3b, 4a, 4b, 10b, 17a, 20a, 25b, 51a, 66b, 70b, 97a, 98b, 163b, 164a, 164b, 166a, 179a, 182a, 194b, 201a, 214a, 234b (with emendation), 235a, 237b, 263a, 264b, 301b, 323a, 325b, 333b, 340a, 348a.

(2) At the end of two verses forming one alliterative line:
(a) Of stressed stem syllables (feminine rhymes, except 113): 2, 29, 60 (with lengthening before *-rd*, see Campbell, §283), 63, 113, 115, 123, 304. Line 202 has rhyme if the poet's form of *gerihte* lacked palatal umlaut (see Campbell, §§304–5). Note also the imperfect masculine rhymes, or strong assonance, in ll.110 (*hund/wand*) and 153 (*þing/leng*).
(b) Of syllables bearing different quantities of stress (feminine rhymes, except 299): 36 (see Campbell §193c, 194), 231, 272, 299. To these may be added the imperfect rhyme in l.20.
(c) Of unstressed inflected syllables (masculine rhymes), excluding *-e* and forms which became identical through levelling:
(i) On the same, or closely related, inflections (with case, number, gender, etc., given): 4 (*wk. noun, gsm.: -an*), 23 (*wk. verb, pret. 3 sg.: -de*), 33 (*dpm./dpn.: -um)*, 85 (*gsf./dsf.: -re*), 178 (*wk. noun, npm./superl. adj.,wk. gsm.: -an*), 201 (*mnp./map.: -as*), 222 (*wk. noun, apf./wk. noun, dpm.: -an*), 238 (*pret. 3 pl.: -on*), 315 (*noun, dpm./adj. dpm.: -um*), 334 (*adj., gsf.: -re/3 pers. pron., dsf.: hyre*), 348 (*apm.: -as*).
(ii) On different inflections: 173 (*wk. noun, gsm./verb, inf.: -an*), 208 (*wk. noun, npm.: -an/wk. verb, inf.: -ian*), 259 (*wk. verb, inf.: -ian/wk. noun, asm.: -an*), 281 (*wk. noun, dsf./verb, inf.: -an*).
(3) At the end of consecutive verses not forming an alliterative line:
(a) Of stem syllables (feminine rhyme): 348b–9a.
(b) Of the unstressed inflected syllables of stressed words (usually with apposition): 71b–2a, 81b–2a, 163b–4a (of both stressed words in each verse), 192b–3a, 245b–6a, 298b–9a (of both stressed words in each verse), 303b–4a, 317b –18a, 345b–6a.
(4) There are no examples of stressed syllables rhyming at the end of consecutive a-verses or consecutive b-verses, and the occasional rhyme of inflected syllables in these contexts is accidental.

# Appendix II

## Index to the scansion of *Judith*

| | | |
|---|---|---|
| 1 | | *def.* |
| 2 | 1A*1b(2A1a) | a1c(2A1a) |
| 3 | 1A*3b(2A1a) | a1d(2A1a) |
| 4 | 1A*1a(2A1a) | a1e(2A1a) |
| 5 | 2A1(2A1a) | a1c(1A1a) |
| 6 | 2A3(1A*1a) | 1d(1A*1a) |
| 7 | 1A1b(1D1) | a1e(2A1a) |
| 8 | 3A3(2A1a) | a1c(2A1a) |
| 9 | 2A1(1D1) | a1d(2A1a) |
| 10 | 1A*1a(3A1) | a1b(2A1a) |
| 11 | 2A1(1D1) | a1d(2A1a) |
| 12 | 2A1(2A1a) | a1c(2A1a) |
| 13 | 3B1b | 1A1b |
| 14 | 1D2 | 1A*1a |
| 15 | a1d | 2A1a |
| 16 | 1A*1a(1A1a) | a1c(1A1a) |
| 17 | 2A1(1D1) | a1c(2A1a) |
| 18 | 1A1b(1A*1a) | a1c(1A*1a) |
| 19 | 2A1(1D1) | a1b(2A1a) |
| 20 | 2A1(1D1) | a1c(1A*1a) |
| 21 | 2A1(2A1a) | a1b(2A1a) |
| 22 | 2A3a(ii) | d2a |
| 23 | 1A1a | 1A*1a |
| 24 | 3B1c(i) | 1A*1a |
| 25 | d2b | 1A*1a |
| 26 | 1A*2a(i) | 1A*1a |
| 27 | 1*D*1 | 3B1c(i) |
| 28 | d1b | 3B1b |
| 29 | 2A3a(ii) | 1A*1a |
| 30 | 2A3(2A1a) | a1d(2A1a) |
| 31 | 1A*1a(2A1a) | a1e(1A*1a) |
| 32 | 2A1(1A*1a) | a1c(2A1a) |
| 33 | 2A1(1D1) | a1b(2A1a) |
| 34 | 3A1(1A1a) | a1b(1A*1a) |
| 35 | 3B2a | 2A1a |
| 36 | d2b | 1A*1a |
| 37 | 1A*1a | 2C1a |
| 38 | 2*A*1 | 3B*1d |
| 39 | 3E2 | 2A1a |
| 40 | d1b | d1b |
| 41 | 1D*2 | d1b |
| 42 | 1*D*1 | 1A*1a |
| 43 | 3B1a | 2B1a |
| 44 | 3B1b | 1A*1a |
| 45 | 2A1a | 3E1 |
| 46 | 2*A*1 | d2b |
| 47 | 2A3b | d3c |
| 48 | 1A1a | d1b |
| 49 | 3B1b | 2A1a |
| 50 | d1a | 3B1b |
| 51 | 2A1a | 2C1b |
| 52 | 2A1a | 3B1c |
| 53 | 2A1a | 2C1b |
| 54 | 1A*1a(1A*1a) | a1c(1A*1a) |
| 55 | 1A*1a(2A1a) | a1c(2A1a) |
| 56 | 1A1b(2A1a) | a1c(2A1a) |
| 57 | 1A1b(1A1a) | a1c(1A*1a) |
| 58 | 2A1(2A1a) | a1c(2A1a) |
| 59 | 1A*1b(1A*1a) | a1d(2A1a) |
| 60 | 2A1(2A1a) | a1d(1A*1a) |
| 61 | 2A1(2A1a) | a1d(2A1a) |
| 62 | 2A3(2A1a) | --- |
| 63 | 1A*1a(2A1a) | a1e(1A1a) |
| 64 | 1A*1b(2A1a) | a1d(1A*1a) |
| 65 | 2A1(1D1) | a1d(2A1a) |
| 66 | 2A3(2A1a) | a1d(2A1a) |
| 67 | 1A*1b(2A1a) | a1c(1A*1a) |
| 68 | 1A*1b(2A1a) | a1d(2A1a) |
| 69 | d3b | 2A1a |
| 70 | 1A1b | 2A1a |
| 71 | 1D3 | d3c |
| 72 | 1D*3 | 1A*1a |

| | | |
|---|---|---|
| 73 | 2A1a | d1b |
| 74 | 2A1a | 1A*1a |
| 75 | a1d | 2A1a |
| 76 | 1A*1a | d1b |
| 77 | 1A*1a | d5c |
| 78 | 3E1 | 2A1a |
| 79 | 2A1a | 3B*1b |
| 80 | 2A1a | 3B1c |
| 81 | 2C1a | 2A1a |
| 82 | 1*D*1 | 2B1b |
| 83 | 3B1b | 3B1a |
| 84 | 1D1 | 2A1a |
| 85 | 2A1a | 1D1 |
| 86 | 3E1 | 1A*1b |
| 87 | 1A*1a | 2C1a |
| 88 | 1A*1a(1A*1a) | a1c(2A1a) |
| 89 | 1A1a(1A*1a) | a1d(2A1a) |
| 90 | a1e(2A1a) | a1d(1A*1a) |
| 91 | 2A3(2A1a) | a1c(2A1a) |
| 92 | 1A*1a(2A1a) | a1c(2A1a) |
| 93 | 2A3(2A1a) | a1d(1A*1a) |
| 94 | 1A*1a(2A1a) | a1c(2A1a) |
| 95 | 1A*1a(1A*1a) | a1c(1A*1a) |
| 96 | 1*D*1 | a1e(2A1a) |
| 97 | 1A*1b(1A*1a) | a1d(1A*1a) |
| 98 | 3A1(1A1a) | a1e(2A1a) |
| 99 | 1A*1a(2A1a) | a1c(1A*1a) |
| 100 | 2*A*1 | d1c |
| 101 | 1A*1a | 2A1a |
| 102 | d1c | 2A1a |
| 103 | 1A1 | d5b |
| 104 | d3b | 2A1a |
| 105 | 1*D*1 | 3B*1b |
| 106 | 3B1b | 3B1c(i) |
| 107 | 1A*2a(i) | 2B1b |
| 108 | 1D*1 | d1b |
| 109 | 1D5 | 2A1a |
| 110 | 3B1b | 3B1c(i) |
| 111 | 1A1b | 3B1b |
| 112 | 1A*1a | 3E2 |
| 113 | 3B1b | 3B1c(i) |
| 114 | 1A*1a | 2A1a |
| 115 | 1A*1a | 1A*1a |
| 116 | 1A*1a | 3B1a |
| 117 | d2b | 3B1c(i) |
| 118 | 1A*1a | 2C1b |
| 119 | d3b | 3B1b |
| 120 | 1A*1a | 3B1b |
| 121 | 3B1b | 3E2 |
| 122 | a1d | 3E2 |
| 123 | 1A*1a | 2C1c |
| 124 | 2A1a | 3B*1c |
| 125 | 3B1b | 1A*1a |
| 126 | d2a | 1A*1a |
| 127 | d1b | d2c |
| 128 | 2A3b | 3B1b |
| 129 | 1A*1a | 2A3a |
| 130 | a1d | 2B1c |
| 131 | 1*D*1 | 1A1a |
| 132 | 2A1(2A1a) | a1c(2A1a) |
| 133 | 3B1a | 2*A*1 |
| 134 | a1d | 2*A*1 |
| 135 | 3E2 | 1A1b |
| 136 | d1b | 2C1a |
| 137 | 3B1b | 2A1a |
| 138 | 1*D*1 | d2b |
| 139 | 2*A*1 | 1D1 |
| 140 | d2b | 2C1a |
| 141 | d3b | 2A1a |
| 142 | 1D1 | 2A1a |
| 143 | d1b | 3B1b |
| 144 | 2*A*1 | 2E1 |
| 145 | 3E2 | 2B1c |
| 146 | 1D5 | 2C2b |
| 147 | 1A1a | 3B1b |
| 148 | 3E2 | 2A1a |
| 149 | 3B1c(i) | 3B1c(i) |
| 150 | d1b | 1A1a |
| 151 | 3B1b | 2B1b |
| 152 | d2b | 3B1b |
| 153 | 3E2 | 3B1c(i) |
| 154 | 1A*1a | 2C1b |
| 155 | 2A1a | 3B1b |
| 156 | 2C1a | d5c |
| 157 | 2A1a | 2C1a |
| 158 | a1b | 3B1b |

| | | |
|---|---|---|
| 159 | a1c | 1*D*1 |
| 160 | a1d | 3B1b |
| 161 | 3B1b | 1A1b |
| 162 | d3b | 1D1 |
| 163 | 1D3 | 1A*1a |
| 164 | 1A*1a | 1A*1a |
| 165 | 3B1c(i) | 2*A*1 |
| 166 | 1A*1a | 3E1 |
| 167 | 1A2c(ii) | 1A1a |
| 168 | a1d | 3B1b |
| 169 | 1A1a | d1b |
| 170 | d2b | 1A1a |
| 171 | 3B1b | 1A*1a |
| 172 | d1b | 2*A*1 |
| 173 | d2a | 1A*1a |
| 174 | a1c | 1A*1a |
| 175 | d2a | 3B*1d |
| 176 | a1c | 1A*1a |
| 177 | a1d | 3E2 |
| 178 | 2A1a | d1b |
| 179 | 1D*2 | 2A1a |
| 180 | 2*A*1 | 1*D*1 |
| 181 | 3B1b | 1A*1a |
| 182 | 2A1a | 3B1b |
| 183 | 2A1a | 3B1c(i) |
| 184 | 2A1a | 3B1c(i) |
| 185 | 2A1a | 3B*1b |
| 186 | 2C1a | 3B*1b |
| 187 | d2b | 2A1a |
| 188 | 1*D*1 | 3B1b |
| 189 | 1A*1b | 3B1b |
| 190 | 2A1b | 2A1a |
| 191 | 2A1a | 3B1b |
| 192 | 1A1a | d3a |
| 193 | 2A1a | 3B*1a |
| 194 | 1D*3 | 2A1a |
| 195 | 1D*2 | 1A1b |
| 196 | 1A*1a | 2C1b |
| 197 | 1A1a | 3B1c(i) |
| 198 | 2A1a | 3B1a |
| 199 | 3B1b | 1A*1a |
| 200 | 1A*1a | d2b |
| 201 | 1A*1b | d2b |
| 202 | 1A*1b | 1A1b |
| 203 | 1A1b | 3B1c(i) |
| 204 | 3B1b | 2A1a |
| 205 | 2A1a | 3B*1b |
| 206 | 1A1a | 3B1b |
| 207 | 3E2 | 2A1a |
| 208 | d3c | 2A1a |
| 209 | 1A*1a | 2B1b |
| 210 | 1D5 | 2*A*1 |
| 211 | 2*A*1 | 1D5 |
| 212 | 2*A*1 | d2b |
| 213 | 1A*1a | 1A*1a |
| 214 | 2A1a | 3B1b |
| 215 | 1*D*1 | 2A1 |
| 216 | 3E1 | 3B1b |
| 217 | d3b | 1A*1a |
| 218 | 1*D*1 | d1b |
| 219 | d3b | 2C1a |
| 220 | d2b | d1b |
| 221 | 2C1b | 2A1a |
| 222 | 2*A*1 | d3a |
| 223 | 1D*2 | 2A1a |
| 224 | 1D3 | 2A1a |
| 225 | 3B*1a | 1A1b |
| 226 | 1*D*1 | 2A1a |
| 227 | 1D*2 | 2*A*1 |
| 228 | d1b | 1*A*1 |
| 229 | 1*D*1 | 2A1a |
| 230 | 1A*1a | 3E2 |
| 231 | 1A*1a | d1b |
| 232 | 1*D*1 | 2*A*1 |
| 233 | 1*D*1 | 1A*1a |
| 234 | d2a | 1A*1a |
| 235 | 2A1a | 2C1d |
| 236 | d2b | d5b |
| 237 | 1D*2 | 2A1a |
| 238 | a1c | 2C1b |
| 239 | d2a | 2*A*1 |
| 240 | d4b | 2A1a |
| 241 | 1D1 | 3B1a |
| 242 | d1a | 2*A*1 |
| 243 | 2A1a | d3b |
| 244 | d1b | 2A3a(i) |

| Line | | |
|---|---|---|
| 245 | 1*D*1 | 2*A*1 |
| 246 | 1D*3(i) | 3B*1b |
| 247 | 3E2 | 1A*1a |
| 248 | d1c | 1*A*1 |
| 249 | 2*A*1 | 2A1a |
| 250 | 2*A*1 | d1c |
| 251 | d1b | 2A1a |
| 252 | a1e | 2C1a |
| 253 | 1D1 | 2A1a |
| 254 | 3B1b | 3B1b |
| 255 | 3B1b | 1A*1a |
| 256 | 1A*1a | d2b |
| 257 | 1A*1a | 3B1b |
| 258 | a1c | 2A1a |
| 259 | d1c | d3c |
| 260 | 3B1b | 1A*1a |
| 261 | 2A1a | 1D1 |
| 262 | 1D1 | 2A1a |
| 263 | 1D*2 | 2A1a |
| 264 | d4b | 2A1a |
| 265 | 1D1 | *rem.* |
| 266 | d2b | 1A1a |
| 267 | 1A1a | 2A1a |
| 268 | 3B1d | 1A*1a |
| 269 | 2*A*1 | 2C1b |
| 270 | d1c | 2A1a |
| 271 | d2a | 1D1 |
| 272 | 2A1(1D1) | a1d(1A*1a) |
| 273 | 1A*1a(2A1a) | a1d(1A*1a) |
| 274 | d2b | 2B1a |
| 275 | 2B1b | *rem.* |
| 276 | d2b | d4d |
| 277 | 2A3a(i) | 2B1c |
| 278 | a1d | 2A1a |
| 279 | d3a | 2A1a |
| 280 | 1A*1a | 3B*1b |
| 281 | 1A*1a | 2C2c |
| 282 | 1A1a | 2C2b |
| 283 | 2B1b | d1b |
| 284 | d1b | 2A1a |
| 285 | a1c | 3B*1b |
| 286 | 1A*1a | 3B1c(i) |
| 287 | 2A1(1A1a) | a1d(1D1) |
| 288 | 1A1a(1A*1a) | a1b(1A*1a) |
| 289 | 2A1(2A1a) | a1b(2A1a) |
| 290 | 1A*1b(1A*1a) | a1d(2A1a) |
| 291 | 2C1a | 2B1b |
| 292 | 3E2 | 3B1b |
| 293 | 3B1a | 1A*1a |
| 294 | d2b | 1A*1a |
| 295 | 1A*1a | d2b |
| 296 | 1A*1a | 1A1b |
| 297 | 2A2(i) | 3B1b |
| 298 | 1D1 | 1A*1a |
| 299 | 1A*1a | 3B1b |
| 300 | 1A*1a | 1D1 |
| 301 | d1b | 2A1a |
| 302 | 1D2 | 2A3a(i) |
| 303 | 3B*1a | 2A1a |
| 304 | 2A3a(i) | 2A1a |
| 305 | 1A*1a | 1D1 |
| 306 | 1A*2a | 1A*1a |
| 307 | 1*A*1 | 2B1b |
| 308 | 3B1a | *rem.* |
| 309 | 1*D*1 | 2*A*1 |
| 310 | 2A1a | 2E1a |
| 311 | 1A*1a | d2b |
| 312 | 1A*2a(i) | 1A*3 |
| 313 | 3E1 | 1A1b |
| 314 | 1*D*1 | d1b |
| 315 | d2b | 1*D*1 |
| 316 | 2A2(i) | 2A1a |
| 317 | 1A2a(i) | 2A1a |
| 318 | 2A1a | d1b |
| 319 | d3b | 1A1b |
| 320 | 2*A*1 | 1*D*1 |
| 321 | 1A*1a | 2C1b |
| 322 | a1d | 2A1a |
| 323 | 2A1a | 3B1b |
| 324 | 2A1a | 3B1b |
| 325 | 1D5 | 1A*1a |
| 326 | 3B1c(i) | 1*D*1 |
| 327 | 1A*2a(i) | 2A1a |
| 328 | 2A3a(i) | 1A*1a |
| 329 | 2A1a | 2C1b |
| 330 | 3B1a | 1*D*1 |

| | | |
|---|---|---|
| 331 | 1A2b(ii) | 1A*1a |
| 332 | 1A*1b | d2a |
| 333 | d1a | 2A1a |
| 334 | 1D1 | 3B1b |
| 335 | d3b | 2A1a |
| 336 | 1D*2 | 2A1 |
| 337 | 1A1a(3E1) | a1c(2A1a) |
| 338 | 2A1(2A1a) | a1d(2A1a) |
| 339 | 2A3(2A1a) | a1b(2A1a) |
| 340 | 1A*1a(2A1a) | a1d(2A1a) |
| 341 | 2A1(1D1) | a1c(2A1a) |
| 342 | 2A1(2A1a) | a1c(3E2) |
| 343 | 1A*1a(2A1a) | a1c(1A*1a) |
| 344 | 1A*3a(2A1a) | a1e(1A*1a) |
| 345 | a1b(1D1) | a1d(1A*1a) |
| 346 | 1A*1b(2A1a) | a1c(2A1a) |
| 347 | 1A*1a(2A1a) | a1c(1A1a) |
| 348 | 1A*1a(2A1a) | a1c(2A1a) |
| 349 | a1a(2A1a) | a1b(2A1a) |

JUDITH

## Table I

The main metrical types are listed in the same way as Table I, Appendix C, in Bliss, 122–3. Three columns give the number of a-verses with double alliteration (1), the number of a-verses with single alliteration (2), and the number of b-verses (3).

| | (1) | (2) | (3) |
|---|---|---|---|
| 1. Type a1 | 0 | 18 | 0 |
| 2. Type a2 | 0 | 0 | 0 |
| 3. Type d1 | 0 | 19 | 16 |
| 4. Type d2 | 0 | 20 | 11 |
| 5. Type d3 | 1 | 10 | 6 |
| 6. Type d4 | 2 | 0 | 1 |
| 7. Type d5 | 0 | 0 | 4 |
| 8. Type e1 | 0 | 0 | 0 |
| 9. Type 1*A*1 | 0 | 1 | 2 |
| 10. Type 1*D*1 | 0 | 17 | 6 |
| 11. Type 2*A*1 | 0 | 13 | 12 |
| 12. Type 3*E*1 | 0 | 0 | 0 |
| 13. Type 1A1 | 12 | 1 | 14 |
| 14. Type 1A2 | 2 | 1 | 0 |
| 15. Type 1A*1 | 33 | 5 | 39 |
| 16. Type 1A*2 | 5 | 0 | 0 |
| 17. Type 1A*3 | 0 | 0 | 1 |
| 18. Type 1A*4 | 0 | 0 | 0 |
| 19. Type 1D1 | 3 | 5 | 7 |
| 20. Type 1D2 | 2 | 0 | 0 |
| 21. Type 1D3 | 3 | 0 | 0 |
| 22. Type 1D4 | 0 | 0 | 0 |
| 23. Type 1D5 | 4 | 0 | 1 |
| 24. Type 1D6 | 0 | 0 | 0 |
| 25. Type 1D*1 | 1 | 0 | 0 |
| 26. Type 1D*2 | 8 | 0 | 0 |
| 27. Type 1D*3 | 3 | 0 | 0 |
| 28. Type 1D*4 | 0 | 0 | 0 |
| 29. Type 1D*5 | 0 | 0 | 0 |
| 30. Type 1D*6 | 0 | 0 | 0 |
| 31. Type 2A1 | 10 | 21 | 54 |
| 32. Type 2A2 | 2 | 0 | 0 |
| 33. Type 2A3 | 5 | 2 | 3 |
| 34. Type 2A4 | 0 | 0 | 0 |
| 35. Type 2B1 | 0 | 2 | 11 |
| 36. Type 2B2 | 0 | 0 | 0 |
| 37. Type 2C1 | 3 | 2 | 18 |
| 38. Type 2C2 | 0 | 0 | 3 |
| 39. Type 2E1 | 0 | 0 | 2 |
| 40. Type 2E2 | 0 | 0 | 0 |
| 41. Type 3B1 | 7 | 22 | 47 |
| 42. Type 3B2 | 0 | 1 | 0 |
| 43. Type 3B*1 | 0 | 2 | 11 |
| 44. Type 3E1 | 2 | 2 | 2 |
| 45. Type 3E2 | 5 | 3 | 5 |
| 46. Type 3E3 | 0 | 0 | 0 |
| 47. Type 3E*1 | 0 | 0 | 0 |
| 48. Type 3E*2 | 0 | 0 | 0 |
| 49. Type 3E*3 | 0 | 0 | 0 |
| 50. Remainders | 0 | 0 | 3 |
| Defective | 0 | 1 | 2 |
| Hypermetric | 65 | 3 | 68 |
| Total | 175 | 174 | 349 |

## Table II

This Table is the same as Table IV, Appendix C, in Bliss, 128, and converts the data of Table I into percentages. The first column following each type gives the percentage of a-verses with double alliteration to the total of a-verses of each type; the second gives the proportion of a-verses to the total number of verses of each type. Figures are in italics where the number of examples is too small to be reliable.

| | (1) | (2) |
|---|---|---|
| Type a1 | 0 | 100 |
| Type d1 | 0 | 54 |
| Type d2 | 0 | 65 |
| Type d3 | 9 | 65 |
| Type d4 | *100* | *67* |
| Type d5 | *0* | *0* |
| Type 1*A*1 | *0* | *33* |
| Type 1*D*1 | 0 | 74 |
| Type 2*A*1 | 0 | 52 |
| Type 1A1 | 92 | 48 |
| Type 1A2 | *67* | *100* |
| Type 1A*1 | 87 | 49 |
| Type 1A*2 | *100* | *100* |
| Type 1A*3 | *0* | *0* |
| Type 1D1 | 38 | 53 |
| Type 1D2 | *100* | *100* |
| Type 1D3 | *100* | *100* |
| Type 1D5 | *100* | *80* |
| Type 1D*1 | *100* | *100* |
| Type 1D*2 | 100 | 100 |
| Type 1D*3 | *100* | *100* |
| Type 2A1 | 32 | 36 |
| Type 2A2 | *100* | *100* |
| Type 2A3 | 71 | 70 |
| Type 2B1 | 0 | 15 |
| Type 2C1 | 60 | 22 |
| Type 2C2 | *0* | *0* |
| Type 2E1 | *0* | *0* |
| Type 3B1 | 24 | 38 |
| Type 3B2 | *0* | *100* |
| Type 3B*1 | 0 | 15 |
| Type 3E1 | *50* | *67* |
| Type 3E2 | 63 | 62 |

## Table III

This Table is based on Table I, Appendix D, in Bliss, 129–30, and gives the distribution of the main types of hypermetric verse. Types that do not occur in *Judith* have been omitted, but Bliss's numbering has been retained. Types are listed at the left-hand side, and the three columns to their right give the same information as those in Table I, above.

| | (1) | (2) | (3) |
|---|---|---|---|
| 1. a(1A) | 0 | 0 | 4 |
| 2. a(1A*) | 0 | 0 | 21 |
| 3. a(1D) | 0 | 1 | 1 |
| 4. a(2A) | 0 | 2 | 41 |
| 7. a(3E) | 0 | 0 | 1 |
| 9. 1A(1A) | 1 | 0 | 0 |
| 10. 1A(1A*) | 3 | 0 | 0 |
| 11. 1A(1A*) | 1 | 0 | 0 |
| 12. 1A(2A) | 1 | 0 | 0 |
| 14. 1A(3E) | 1 | 0 | 0 |
| 16. 1A*(1A) | 1 | 0 | 0 |
| 17. 1A*(1A*) | 6 | 0 | 0 |
| 19. 1A*(2A) | 19 | 0 | 0 |
| 21. 1A*(3A) | 1 | 0 | 0 |
| 22. 2A(1A) | 1 | 0 | 0 |
| 23. 2A(1A*) | 2 | 0 | 0 |
| 24. 2A(1D) | 8 | 1 | 0 |
| 25. 2A(2A) | 16 | 0 | 0 |
| 39. 3A(1A) | 2 | 0 | 0 |
| 40. 3A(2A) | 1 | 0 | 0 |
| Total | 65 | 3 | 68 |

# Appendix III

## The Latin Sources

*Vulgate*: chapter 12.10–16.1

Ordinary face indicates verses, or parts of verses, that were used or adapted by the poet (if his source was the Vulgate); italics indicate verses, or parts of verses, that are not used by the poet. The text is taken from Weber (1975) but punctuation has been added.

12.10 *Et factum est*, quarto die Holofernis fecit cenam servis suis, *et dixit ad Bagao eunuchum: Vade, et suade Hebraeam illam, ut sponte consentiat habitare mecum.*

12.11 *Foedum est enim apud Assyrios, si femina inrideat virum, agendo ut inmunis transeat ab eo.*

12.12 *Tunc introivit Bagao ad Iudith, et dixit: Non vereatur bona puella introire ad dominum meum, ut honorificetur ante faciem eius, et manducet cum eo, et bibat vinum in iucunditate.*

12.13 *Cui Iudith respondit: Quae ego sum, ut contradicam domino meo?*

12.14 *Omne quod erit ante oculos eius bonum et optimum, faciam. Quicquid autem illi placuerit, hoc mihi erit optimum omnibus diebus vitae meae.*

12.15 *Et surrexit*, et ornavit *se vestimento suo*, et ingressa *stetit ante faciem eius.*

12.16 *Cor autem Holofernis concussum est: erat enim ardens in concupiscentia eius.*

12.17 *Et dixit ad eam Holofernis: Bibe nunc, et accumbe in iucunditate, quoniam gratiam invenisti coram me.*

12.18 *Et dixit Iudith: Bibam, domine, quoniam magnificata est anima mea hodie prae omnibus diebus meis.*

12.19 *Et accepit, et manducavit, et bibit coram ipso, ea quae paraverat illi ancilla eius.*

12.20 Et iucundus factus est Holofernis ad illam, bibitque vinum nimis multum quantum numquam biberat in vita sua.
13.1 Ut autem sero factum est, festinaverunt servi illius ad hospitia sua, *et conclusit Bagao ostia cubiculi, et abiit.*
13.2 Erant autem omnes fatigati a vino:
13.3 eratque Iudith sola in cubiculo.
13.4 Porro Holofernis iacebat in lecto, nimia ebrietate sopitus.
13.5 *Dixitque Iudith puellae suae ut staret foras ante cubiculum, et observaret.*
13.6 Stetitque Iudith ante lectum, orans *cum lacrimis, et labiorum motu in silentio,*
13.7 dicens: Confirma me, Domine Deus Israhel, *et respice in hac hora ad opera manuum mearum, ut, sicut promisisti, Hierusalem civitatem tuam erigas*: et hoc, quod credens per te posse fieri, cogitavi, perficiam.
13.8 *Et haec cum dixisset, accessit ad columnam, quae erat ad caput lectuli eius*, et pugionem *eius, qui in ea ligatus pendebat*, exsolvit.
13.9 Cumque evaginasset illud, adprehendit comam capitis eius, *et ait*: *Confirma me, Domine Deus Israhel in hac hora.*
13.10 Et percussit bis in cervicem eius, et abscidit caput eius, *et abstulit conopeum eius a columnis*, et evolvit corpus eius truncum.
13.11 *Et post pusillum exivit*, et tradidit caput Holofernis ancillae suae, et iussit ut mitteret illud in peram suam.
13.12 Et exierunt duae, *secundum consuetudinem suam, quasi ad orationem*, et transierunt castra, *et gyrantes vallem*, venerunt ad portam civitatis.
13.13 Et dixit Iudith a longe custodibus murorum: Aperite portas, quoniam nobiscum est Deus, qui fecit virtutem in Israhel.
13.14 *Et factum est*, cum audissent viri vocem eius, vocaverunt presbyteros civitatis.
13.15 Et concurrerunt ad eam omnes, a minimo usque ad maximum: *quoniam speraverunt eam iam non esse venturam.*
13.16 *Et accendentes luminaria*, congyraverunt circa eam universi: *illa autem ascendens in eminentiori loco, iussit fieri silentium. Cumque omnes tacuissent,*
13.17 dixit Iudith: *Laudate Dominum Deum nostrum, qui non deseruit sperantes in se*:

13.18 *et in me ancillam suam adimplevit misericordiam suam, quam promisit domui Israhel*: et interfecit in manu mea hostem populi sui in hac nocte.
13.19 Et proferens de pera caput Holofernis, ostendit illis, dicens: Ecce caput Holofernis, principis militiae Assyriorum, *et ecce conopeum illius, in quo recumbebat in ebrietate sua, ubi et per manum feminae percussit illum Dominus Deus noster.*
13.20 *Vivit autem ipse Dominus, quoniam custodivit me angelus eius, et hinc euntum, et ibi commorantem, et inde huc revertentem*, et non permisit me ancillam suam Dominus coinquinari, sed sine pollutione peccati *revocavit me vobis gaudentem in victoria* sua, *in evasione mea, in liberatione vestra.*
13.21 *Confiteamur illi omnes, quoniam bonus, quoniam in saeculum misericordia eius.*
13.22 *Universi autem adorantes Dominum, dixerunt ad eam: Benedixit te Dominus in virtute sua, quia per te ad nihilum redegit inimicos nostros.*
13.23 *Porro Ozias, princeps populi Israhel, dixit ad eam: Benedicta es tu filia a Domino Deo excelso, prae omnibus mulieribus super terram.*
13.24 *Benedictus Dominus, qui creavit caelum et terram, qui te direxit in vulnere capitis principis inimicorum nostrorum:*
13.25 *quia hodie nomen tuum ita magnificavit, ut non recedat laus tua de ore hominum, qui memores fuerint virtutis Domini in aeternum, pro quibus non pepercisti animae tuae, propter angustias et tribulationem generis tui, sed subvenisti ruinae ante conspectum Dei nostri.*
13.26 *Et dixit omnis populus: Fiat, fiat.*
13.27 *Porro Achior vocatus venit, et dixit ei: Deus Israhel, cui tu testimonium dedisti quod ulciscatur de inimicis suis, ipse caput omnium incredulorum incidit in hac nocte in manu mea.*
13.28 *Ut probes quia ita est, ecce caput Holofernis, qui in contemptu superbiae suae Deum Israhel contempsit, et tibi interitum minabatur, dicens: Cum captus fuerit populus Israhel, gladio perforari praecipiam latera tua.*
13.29 *Videns autem Achior caput Holofernis, angustiatus prae pavore, cecidit in faciem suam super terram, et aestuavit anima eius;*

13.30 *postea vero quam, resumpto spiritu, recreatus est, procidit ad pedes eius, et adoravit eam, et dixit*:
13.31 *Benedicta tu Deo tuo in omni tabernaculo Iacob, quoniam in omni gente, quae audierit nomen tuum, magnificabit Deus Israhel super te.*
14.1 *Dixit autem Iudith ad omnem populum*: *Audite me, fratres, suspendite caput hoc super muros nostros*;
14.2 et erit, cum exierit sol accipiat unusquisque arma sua, et exite cum impetu, *non ut descendatis deorsum, sed quasi* impetum facientes.
14.3 *Tunc exploratores necesse erit ut* fugiant ad principem suum excitandum ad pugnam.
14.4 *Cumque duces eorum cucurrerint ad tabernaculum Holofernis, et invenerint eum truncum in suo sanguine volutatum, decidet super eos timor.*
14.5 *Cumque cognoveritis fugere illos, ite post illos securi, quoniam Dominus conteret eos sub pedibus vestris.*
14.6 *Tunc Achior videns virtutem, quam fecit Deus Israhel, relicto gentilitatis ritu, credidit Deo, et circumcidit carnem praeputii sui, et adpositus est ad populum Israhel, et omnis successio generis eius usque in hodiernum diem.*
14.7 Mox autem ut ortus est dies, *suspenderunt super muros caput Holofernis*, accepitque unusquisque vir arma sua, et egressi sunt cum grandi strepitu et ululatu.
14.8 Quod videntes exploratores, ad tabernaculum cucurrerunt.
14.9 *Porro hi qui in tabernaculo erant*, *venientes*, et ante ingressum cubiculi perstrepentes, excitandi gratia, inquietudinem arte moliebantur, ut non ab excitantibus, sed a sonantibus Holofernis evigilaret.
14.10 Nullus enim audebat cubiculum virtutis Assyriorum pulsando aut intrando aperire.
14.11 Sed cum venissent duces eius et tribuni, et universi maiores exercitus Assyriorum, *dixerunt cubiculariis*:
14.12 *Intrate, et excitate illum, quoniam egressi mures de cavernis suis, ausi sunt provocare ad proelium.*
14.13 Tunc ingressus *Bagao cubiculum eius, stetit ante cortinam, et plausum fecit manibus suis*: suspicabatur enim illum cum Iudith dormire.

14.14 *Sed cum nullum motum iacentis sensu aurium caperet, accessit proximans ad cortinam, et elevans eam*, videns iacens cadaver absque capite Holofernis in suo sanguine tabefactum iacere super terram, et clamavit voce magna *cum fletu*, et scidit vestimenta sua.
14.15 *Et ingressus tabernaculum Iudith, non invenit eam, et exilivit foras ad populum,*
14.16 et dixit: *Una mulier hebraea fecit confusionem in domo regis Nabuchodonosor*: ecce enim Holofernis iacet in terra, et caput ipsius non est in illo.
14.17 *Quod cum audissent principes virtutis Assyriorum, sciderunt omnes vestimenta sua, et intolerabilis timor et tremor cecidit super eos*, et turbati sunt animi eorum valde.
14.18 *Et factus est clamor inconparabilis in media castra eorum.*
15.1 Cumque omnis exercitus decollatum Holofernem audisset, fugit mens et consilium ab eis, et solo tremore et metu agitati, fugae praesidium sumunt:
15.2 *ita ut nullus loqueretur cum proximo suo, sed inclinato capite, relictis omnibus, evadere Hebraeos, quos armatos super se audierant, fugientes per vias camporum et semitas collium.*
15.3 Videntes itaque filii Israhel fugientes illos. *Descenderunt clangentes tubis, et ululantes post ipsos.*
15.4 *Et quoniam Assyrii non adunati, in fuga ibant praecipites: filii autem Israhel* uno agmine persequentes, debilitabant omnes, quos invenire potuissent.
15.5 *Misitque Ozias nuntios per omnes civitates et regiones Israhel.*
15.6 *Omnis itaque regio, omnisque urbs, electam iuventutem misit armatam post eos*, et persecuti sunt eos in ore gladii *quousque pervenirent ad extremitatem finium suarum.*
15.7 *Reliqui autem qui erant in Bethulia*, ingressi sunt castra Assyriorum, et praedam, quam fugientes Assyrii reliquerant, abstulerunt, et honestati sunt valde.
15.8 Hii vero, qui victores reversi sunt ad Bethuliam, omnia quaeque erant illorum, abstulerunt secum, *ita ut non esset numerus in pecoribus in iumentis, et universis mobilibus eorum, ut a minimo usque ad magnum omnes divites fierent de praedationibus eorum.*

15.9 *Ioacim autem, summus pontifex, de Hierusalem venit in Bethuliam cum universis presbyteris suis, ut videret Iudith.*
15.10 *Quae cum exisset ad illum, benedixerunt illam omnes una voce, dicentes: Tu gloria Hierusalem, tu laetitia Israhel, tu honorificentia populi nostri:*
15.11 *quia fecisti viriliter, et confortatum est cor tuum, eo quod castitatem amaveris, et post virum tuum, alterum non scieris: ideo et manus Domini confortavit te, et ideo eris benedicta in aeternum.*
15.12 *Et dixit omnis populus: Fiat, fiat.*
15.13 Per dies autem triginta, vix collecta est spolia Assyriorum a
populo Israhel. 15.14 Porro autem universa, quae Holofernis peculiaria fuisse probata sunt, dederunt Iudith in auro, *et argento, et vestibus*, et gemmis, *et omni supellectile*, et tradita sunt illi omnia a populo.
15.15 *Et omnes populi gaudebant cum mulieribus, et virginibus, et iuvenibus, in organis, et citharis.*
16.1 Tunc cantavit canticum hoc Domino Iudith ...

## *Old Latin*

Only those verses containing the part of the narrative found in the O.E. poem are given, and italics mark those OL readings which differ from the Vulgate and which may have influenced the poem. The text is taken from Sabatier (1751), but readings from Bodleian MS Auctar. E., infra 1–2 [A.] and Munich MS 6239 [M.] which differ from Sabatier's text, and yet appear to be closer to the poet's source, are given in square brackets.

12.10 Et factum est, quarto die fecit Olofernis coenam famulis suis solis, et neminem vocavit ad coenam de necessariis: et dixit Bagoe spadoni, qui erat super omnia ipsius: Vade nunc ad mulierem illam Hebræam, quæ est apud te, et suade ei, ut veniat manducare et bibere nobiscum ...
12.15 Et surgens, ornavit se vestibus, et *omni muliebri ornatu*. Et accessit ancilla ejus, et stravit illi contra Olofernem in terra stragula, quæ acceperat à Bagoa spadone in quotidianum usum, ut manducaret discumbens super ea. Et introiens Judith, discubuit ...

12.20 Et jocundatus est Olofernis super eam, et bibit multum vinum, quantum nunquam biberat ulla die ex qua natus est.
13.1 Et ut sero factum est, satagerunt servi ejus abire, et Bagoas conclusit tabernaculum à foris, et dimisit adstantes à facie domini sui, et abierunt omnes in cubilia sua:
13.2 erant enim omnes fatigati et *soporati*, quoniam plurimus factus erat potus:
13.3 derelicta est autem sola Judith in tabernaculo.
13.4 Et Olofernis prociderat supra lectum suum erat enim solutus à vino ...
13.6 Et stetit Judith ad caput ejus, et dixit in corde suo [in corde suo: *omitted by* A. and M.]:
13.7 Domine Deus [M.: *domine domine deus*] omnium virtutem, respice in hac hora ad opera manuum mearum, ut exaltetur Hierusalem, quia nunc est tempus suscipiendi hæreditatem tuam: et fac cogitationem meam in quassationem gentium, quæ insurrexerunt super nos.
13.8 Et accedens ad columnam tabernaculi, quæ erat ad caput Olofernis, deposuit pugionem ejus ab illa.
13.9 Et accedens ad lectum, comprehendit comam capitis ejus, et dixit: Domine confirma me Deus Israël in hodierno die:
13.10 et percussit in cervice ejus bis [M: *semel et iterum*]in virtute sua, et abstulit caput ejus ab illo, et involvit corpus ejus *à toro* [M.: *de toro in terra*] ipsius, et abstulit conopeum ejus à columnis.
13.11 Et post pusillum exiit, et tradidit ancillæ suæ caput Olofernis, et misit illud in peram *escarum suarum*.
13.12 Et exierunt duæ simul, secundùm consuetudinem suam, quasi ad orationem; et transeuntes castra, gyraverunt totam vallem illam, et ascenderunt montem, et venerunt ad portam Bethuliæ.
13.13 Et dixit Judith à longe eis qui custodiebant in turribus: Aperite, aperite nunc portam; nobiscum est Deus noster, qui dedit virtutem in Israël, et potestatem adversùs inimicos, sicut hodie fecit et facturus est.
13.14 Et factum est, cùm audissent viri civitatis vocem ejus, festinaverunt descendere ad portam civitatis suæ, et convocaverunt majores natu plebis.
13.15 Et concurrerunt omnes, à minimo usque ad maximum: quoniam mirum erat eis reversam illam.

13.16 Et aperuerunt portas, et susceperunt eas; et incendentes ignem ad lumen, congyraverunt illam:
13.17 quæ dixit ad eos voce magna: Laudate Deum, laudate Dominum nostrum,
13.18 qui non abstulit misericordiam suam à domo Israël: sed quassavit inimicos nostros per manum meam in hac nocte.
13.19 Et proferens caput ejus de pera, ostendit, et dixit eis: Ecce caput Olofernis principis virtutis Assyriorum, et ecce conopeum, in quo recumbebat in ebrietate sua, et percussit illum Dominus in manu feminæ.
13.20 Vivit Dominus, qui custodivit me in via mea qua profecta sum, quoniam seduxit eum facies mea in perditionem ipsius, et non fecit peccatum mecum in coinquinatione, et in confusione ...
14.2 et cùm lucere coeperit, et exierit sol in terram, sumat unusquisque vestrûm arma bellica sua, et exeat omnis vir in fortitudine potens extra civitatem, et date priores impetum in illos, tanquam descendentes in campum ad bellum adversùs custodiam filiorum Assur.
14.3 Et mox ut descendetis in campum, accipient illi arma sua, et ibunt in castra sua ...
14.7 Et postquam factum est diluculum, subierunt, et suspenderunt caput Olofernis in muro, et accepit omnis vir arma sua, et exierunt secundùm ordinem ad ascensum montis.
14.8 Filii verò Assyriorum, ut viderunt illos, miserunt ad duces, et ad tribunos suos, et ad omnes principes.
14.11 Et venerunt ad tabernaculum Olofernis et dixerunt ad Bagoe, qui erat super omnia ejus ...
14.13 Et introivit Bagoas, et pulsavit januam quæ ante tabernaculum erat: suspicabatur enim illum adhuc cum Judith dormire.
14.14 Postquam verò nullus respondebat, aperuit, et introivit in cubiculum, et invenit illum jacentem nudum in testudine, et caput ejus sublatum ab eo: et exclamavit voce magna cum lacrymis et *luctu*, et scidit vestimenta sua ...
14.16 et dixit: Neglexerunt heri servi ejus, et fecit confusionem una mulier Hebræa in domo regis Nabuchodonosor, quoniam ecce Olofernis in terra jacet, et caput ipsius non est in eo.
14.17 Et audierunt verba hæc presbyteri Assyriorum, sciderunt tunicas suas, et conturbata est anima eorum valde ...

15.1 Et ut audierunt ii qui in tabernaculis erant, admirati sunt, et inquisierunt quid esset facti: et incidit in illis timor et tremor ...
15.3 Tunc filiorum Israël omnis vir bellator diffusus est super illos ...
15.6 Et postquam audierunt filii Israël, omnes simul incubuerunt in illos, et conciderunt illos usque Choba. Similiter autem et qui in Hierusalem erant, venerunt ex omni montana; renuntiata sunt enim illis quæ facta sunt inimicis eorum: et qui in Galaad, et qui in Galilæa erant, consecuti sunt eos, et interfecerunt illos plagâ magnâ, quousque transirent Damascum et terminos eorum.
15.7 Reliqui autem qui inhabitabant Bethuliam, incubuerunt in castra Assyriorum, et spoliaverunt eos, et locupletati sunt valde.
15.8 Filii autem Israël reversi à cacumine montis, dominati sunt reliquorum, et vicos, et civitates, et omnes campos obtinuerunt, et multa spolia possederunt; multitudo enim fuit magna ...
15.13 Et spolia collegit populus multa per dies triginta.
15.14 Et dederunt Judith tabernaculum Olofernis, et omne argentum, et lectum, et apparatum illius: et cùm accepisset Judith, imposuit super mulas suas, et junxit currus suos, et congessit illa simul.

# Glossary

The glossary is arranged alphabetically; *æ* is treated as a separate letter and follows *a*, and *ð/þ* follows *t*. The prefix *ge-* has in all cases been disregarded in the ordering. All words used in the text are dealt with, and a complete list of forms and line references is given (except for the use of *ond*). Where the spellings of a word vary, all the variations are noted (including *ð/þ*), and the most frequent spelling supplies the form of the head-word. Emended forms are indicated by italics, and editorial additions by square brackets. Irregular forms, or forms (especially of strong verbs) which may cause difficulty to the student, are cross-referenced to the head-words under which they are treated. The symbol ~ indicates that the head-word form should be supplied. Unless otherwise indicated, the indicative mood of verb forms is understood. Where a line number is followed by 'n.' there is a note to that form either in the textual notes or in the Commentary. The abbreviations used are conventional. The following symbols attempt to give some guide to restricted usage and register: † is used where the occurrence of a word or a sense is confined to poetry, (†) where a word or a sense occurs mainly or with disproportionate frequency in poetry; ‡ indicates *hapax legomenon*, (‡) a word or a sense of more than one occurrence in the text which is confined in usage to *Judith*; ¶ is used of a word whose occurrence is otherwise almost entirely confined to prose.

### A

**ā,** *adv.*, always, 7 [*see* **āwa**].

**ā-bregdan**, *s.v.(3)*, draw, *pret. 3 sg.* ābrǣd, 79.

**ac**, *conj. (following a neg. clause in 60, 119; with adversative function in 60, 119, 183, and connective-adversative function in 209)*, but, but then, 60, 119, 183, 209n.

**ā-cweðan**, *s.v.(5)*, utter, speak; word ācweðan, make a speech, *pret. 3*

*sg.* (ond þ word) ācwæð, 82, 151, 283.
**āfor**, *adj.*, fierce, ferocious, *nsm.* ~, 257n.
**āgan**, *pret. pr.*, *(1)* have, *pret. 3 sg.* āhte, 3, 6, 344, *pret. 2 pl.* 196, *pret. 1 sg. neg.* nāhte, 91, *(2)* possess, own, 339.
**ā-gēotan**, *s.v.(2)*, drain, empty, *infl. pp.* āgotene, 32n.
**ā-gifan**, *s.v.(5)*, give, bestow; on hond ~, hand over, *pret. 3 sg.* āgeaf, 130, *pret. 3 pl.* āgēafon, 341.
**ā-hōn**, *s.v.(7d)*, hang, *pp.* āhongen, 48.
**āhte**, *see* **āgan**.
**aldor**, *see* **ealdor**, *m.*
**aldre**, *see* **ealdor**, *n.*
**ā-lecgan**, *w.v.(1)*, lay, position, *pret. 3 sg.* ālēde, 101.
**al-walda** (†), *m. n-stem*, omnipotent ruler, God, *gs.* alwaldan, 84.
**ān**, *num.*, *adj.*, one, *gsm.* ānes, 324n, *dsf.* ānre 64, *gp.* ānra, 95 (*see* **gehwylc**).
**anbyht-scealc** †, *m. a-stem*, rctainer, servant, *np.* anbyhtscealcas, 38.
**āninga**, (†) *adv.*, at once, 250.
**ā-rētan**, *w.v.(1)*, gladden, delight, *pp.* ārēted, 167.
**ār-fæst**, *adj.*, benevolent, gracious, *nsm.* ~, 190.
**arod** ¶, *adj. (w.* tō *and dat.)*, ready *(for)*, readily inclined *(to)*, *nsm.* ~, 275n.
**ā-secgan**, *w.v.(3)*, say, relate, *inf.* ~, 330.
**Assȳrias**, *prop. n.*, the Assyrians, *gp.* Assīria, 232, 309, Assȳria, 265, *dp.* Assȳrium, 218.
**ā-swebban** (†), *w.v.(1)*, 'put to sleep', kill, *infl. pp.* āswefede, 321.
**atol** (†), *adj.*, terrible, *asm.* atolne, 246; *(as noun)*, *asm. wk.* atolan, 75n.
**āwa** (†), *adv.*, ever, always, *(in set phrase)* āwa tō aldre, for ever and ever, 120 [*see* **ā**, **ealdor**, *n.*].
**ā-weccan**, *w.v.(1)*, awake, *inf.* ~, 258, 273.

### Æ

**ǣdre** (†), *adv.*, quickly, at once, 64, 95, 246n.
**ǣfre**, *adv.*, ever, 114.
**æfter**, *prep. w. dat.*, *(1) (local)*, along, 18, *(2) (orig. local, denoting the direction of effort, w. vb. of striving)*, towards, for, 65n., *(3) (temporal)*, after, 117.
**æf-ðonca**, *m. n-stem*, grudge, *ap.* æfðoncan, 265.
**ǣg-hwylc**, *pron.*, each (one), every (one), *asm.*

ǣghwylcne, 50, *dsm.* ǣghwylcum, 166.

**ælf-scīne** †, *adj.*, beautiful as an elf, marvellously attractive, *nsf.* ælfscīnu, 14n.

**æl-mihtig**, *adj.*, almighty, *nsm.* ~, 300; *(as noun)*, the Almighty, *dsm. wk.* ælmihtigan, 7, 345.

**ǣnig**, *pron.*, any, *nsm.* ~, 329.

**ǣr**, *adv.*, *(stressed)*, before, previously *(giving pluperf. sense)*, 65, 143, 214.

**ǣr**, *conj.*, *(unstressed)*, before, 76.

**ǣrest**, *adv. (superl. of* **ǣr***)*, first, 14.

**ǣr-ðon-ðe** ¶, *conj.*, before, 252.

**æsc-plega** ‡, *m. n-stem*, spear-play, battle, *ds.* æscplegan, 217.

**æsc-rōf** †, *adj.*, spear-brave, brave in battle, *npm.* æscrōfe, 336.

**æt**, *prep. w. dat.*, *(1) (of place)*, in, 123, 175, 197, 217, 288, *(2) (of time)*, at, 272, 345, *(3) (at the hands of a person)*, from, 3.

**ǣt**, *n. a-stem*, food, prey, *gs.* ǣtes, 210.

**æt-somne**, *adv.*, together, 255.

**æt-ȳwan**, *w.v.(1)*, display, *inf.* ~, 174.

**æðele**, *adj.*, noble, *nsf.* ~, 256; *(as noun), nsf.* ~, 176.

**B**

**bā**, *see* **bēgen**.

**baldor** †, *m. a-stem*, prince, king, *ns.* ~, 9, 49, 338.

**bælc** †, *m. i-stem,* pride, *ns.* ~, 267.

**ge-bǣran**, *w.v. (1)*, behave, conduct *(oneself)*, *or* cry out in joy, enjoy *(oneself)*, *pret. 3 pl.* gebǣrdon, 27n.

**bǣron**, *see* **beran**.

**be**, *prep. w. dat.*, *(1) (of physical means)*, by, 99, *(2) (of means, after vb. of calling, as sign of identification)*, by, 81.

**beado** †, *f. wō-stem*, conflict, battle, *ds.* beaduwe, 175, beadowe, 213.

**beado-rinc** †, *m. a-stem*, warrior, *gp.* beadorinca, 276.

**bēah**, *m. a-stem*, ring, armlet, bracelet, *gp.* bēaga, 340, *dp.* bēagum 36.

**bēah-hroden** †, *adj.*, ring-adorned, *npf.* bēah-hrodene, 138.

**beald**, *adj.*, bold, *npm.* bealde, 17.

**bealo-full** (†), *adj.*, evil, *nsm.* ~, 63; *(as noun?)*, *nsm. wk.* bealofulla, 48, *asm. wk.* bealofullan,

100, *gsm. wk.* bealo-fullan, 248.

**bearhtm**, *m. a-stem*, (†) tumult, clamour, *ds. (as adv.)*, 39n.

**bearn**, *n. a-stem*, child, son, *as* ~, 84, *np.* ~, 24, *gp.* bearna, 51, *dp.* bearnum, 33.

**be-æftan** ¶, *adv.*, behind, 112.

**be-bēodan**, *s.v. (2), w. dat.*, command, *pret. 3 sg.* bebēad, 38, 144.

**be-cuman**, *s.v. (4)*, come, arrive, *pret. 3 sg.* becōm, 310, pass, *pret. 3 pl.* becōmon, 134.

**bed**, *n. ja-stem*, bed, *as.* ~, 48, *gs.* beddes 63, *ds.* bedde, 72, 278.

**bed-rest**, *f. jō-stem*, bed, *ds.* bedreste, 36.

**bēgen**, *num.*, both, *(1) adj.*, *nf.* bā, 133, *gf. (in attrib. to a pl. poss. adj. and a noun)* bēgea, 128n., *(2) as noun*, *nm.* bēgen, 207.

**be-hēafdian** ¶, *w.v. (2)*, be-head, *pp.* behēafdod, 289.

**bēhð** ‡, *f. ō-stem*, sign, proof, *ds.* bēhðe, 174n.

**be-līðan** †, *s.v. (1), w. gen.*, deprive of *(life)*, *infl. pp.* belidenne, 280n.

**be-nǣman**, *w.v. (1), w. dat.*, deprive of *(life)*, *inf.* ~, 76.

**benc** (†), *f. i-stem*, bench (in hall), *dp.*, bencum, 18.

**benc-sittende** †, *m. nd-stem, pl.*, bench-sitters, hall-retainers, *ap.* ~, 27.

**beorht**, *adj.*, *(1) (of things)*, bright, shining, *gp.* beorhtra, 340, *dsf. wk.* beorhtan, 326, *(2) (of people)*, beautiful, vir-tuous?, *nsf. wk.* beorhte 254, *asf. wk.* beorhtan 58n., *dsf. wk.* beorhtan 340.

**beorn** †, *m. a-stem*, man, warrior, *np.* beornas, 213, 267, *gp.* beorna, 254.

**beran**, *s.v. (4)*, carry *(w. words for armour or weapons* = 'to advance to battle'*)*, *infl. inf.* tō berenne, 131, *pret. 3 pl.* bǣron,201, *pp.* boren, 18, *imp. pl.* berað, 191.

**be-smītan**, *s.v. (1)*, be-smirch, defile, *inf.* ~, 59.

**be-ðeccan**, *w.v. (1)*, cover, protect, *infl. pp.* be-ðeahte, 213.

**Bēthūlia**, *prop. n.*, Bethulia, *as.* Bēthūliam, 138n., 326.

**be-windan**, *s.v. (3)*, coil about with, *pp.* be-wunden, 115.

**ge-bīdan**, *s.v. (1)*, attain, reach, *infl. pp.* ge-bidenne, 64.

**biddan**, *s.v. (5)*, ask, *inf.* ~, 84, 187.

**(ge-)bindan**, *s.v. (3)*, bind, fetter, *pp.* gebunden, 115.

**binnan** ¶, *prep. w. dat.*, within, 64.

**blāc**, *adj.*, pale, pallid, *asm.* blācne, 278n.

**blāc-hlēor** †, *adj.*, of pale, or fair complexion, *nsf.* ~, 128.

**blǣd**, *m. a-stem*, *(1)* life, *as.* ~, 63, *(2)* (†) glory, *as.* ~, 122. – Cpd.: wuldor-.

**blīcan** (†), *s.v. (1)*, shine, gleam, *inf.* ~, 137.

**blīðe**, *adj.*, *(1)* happy, glad, *nsm.* ~, 58, *npm.* ~, 159, *(2)* pleased with, benevolently disposed towards, *nsm.* ~, 154.

**blōdig**, *adj.*, bloody, gory, *asn.* ~, 126, 174.

**(ge-)blondan** (†), *s.v. (7d)*, steep in, corrupt, *pp.* geblonden, 34.

**bodian**, *w.v. (2)*, announce, *inf.* ~, 251, *pret. 3 pl.* bodedon, 244.

**bolla** ¶, *m. n-stem*, bowl, *np.* bollan, 17.

**bord**, *n. a-stem*, (†) shield, *ap.* ~, 192, 317, *dp.* bordum, 213.

**boren**, *see* **beran**.

**brād-swyrd** †, *n. a-stem*, broadsword, *ap.* ~, 317n.

**bregdan**, *s.v. (3)*, draw *(sword)*, *pret. 3 pl.* brugdon, 229. – Cpd.: ā-, tō-.

**brego** (†), *m. u-stem*, chief, lord, *ns.* ~, 39, 254.

**brēme**, *adj.*, famous, *nsm. wk. (as noun?)* brēma, 57.

**brēost**, *f. ō-stem, n. a-stem*, breast, chest, *dp.* brēostum, 192.

**bringan**, *w.v. (1)*, bring, *pret. 3 pl.* brōhton, 335.

**ge-bringan**, *w.v. (1)*, bring, *(foll. by* on *w. dat.)* bring to, put into, *pret. 3 sg.* gebrōhte, 125, *pret. 3 pl.* gebrōhton, 54n., *pp.* gebrōht, 57.

**brōga**, *m. n-stem*, danger, horror, *gs.* brōgan, 4.

**brugdon**, *see* **bregdan**.

**brūn**, *adj.*, † polished, gleaming, *apm.* brūne, 317.

**bryne**, *m. i-stem*, fire, burning, *ds.* ~, 116n.

**brytta** (†), *m. n-stem*, giver, dispenser, *ns.* ~, 30, 93, *as.* bryttan, 90.

**ge-bunden**, *see* **bindan**.

**būne**, *f. n-stem*, cup for drinking, goblet, *np.* būnan, 18.

**būr-geteld** (‡), *n. a-stem*, private inner bedchamber of a tent, *as.* ~, 276, *gs.* būrgeteldes, 248, *ds.* būrgetelde, 57n.

**burh**, *f. mut.*, (walled) town, *gs.* byrig, 137, *ds.* byrig, 149, 203, 326, *gp.* burga, 58. – Cpd.: medo-, scild-.

**burh-lēode**, *m. i-stem, pl.*, citizens, townspeople, *gp.* burglēoda, 187, *dp.* burhlēodum, 175.

**burh-sittende** (†), *m. nd-stem, pl.*, city dwellers, townspeople, *np.* ~, 159.

**būtan**, *prep. w. dat.*, without, 120.

**(ge-)byldan**, *w.v. (1)*, embolden (?), *infl. pp.* gebylde, 268n.

**byrig**, *see* **burg**.

**byrne**, *f. n-stem*, coat of mail, corslet, *as.* byrnan, 337, *ap.* byrnan, 327.

**byrn-hom** ‡, *m. a-stem*, coat of mail, corslet, *ap.* byrnhomas, 192n.

**byrn-wiga** †, *m. n-stem*, mailed warrior, *gp.* byrnwigena, 39.

**byrn-wiggende** †, *m. nd-stem, pl.*, mailed warriors, *np.* ~, 17.

**bysmer-līce**, *adv.*, ignominiously, 100n.

## C

**camp**, *m., n. a-stem*, battle, fight, *ds.* campe, 200.

**cēne**, *adj.*, brave, *npm.* ~, 332, *gp.* cēnra, 200.

**cirman**, *w.v. (1)*, shout, cry out, *inf.* ~, 270.

**cirran**, *w.v. (1)*, turn back, *pret. 3 pl.* cirdon, 311.

**cnēoris**, *f. jō-stem*, tribe, race, *ns.* ~, 323.

**cohhetan** ‡, *w.v. (1)*, clear the throat (noisily and frequently)?, *inf.* ~, 270n.

**collen-ferhð** †, *adj.*, elated, bold, *npf.* collenferhðe, 134.

**comp-wīg** ‡, *n. a-stem*, battle, fray, *ds.* compwīge, 332.

**ge-cost** (†), *adj.*, tried, trusty, *npn.* gecoste, 231.

**cuman**, *s.v. (4)*, come, *pret. 3 sg.* cōm, 50, *pret. 3 pl.* cōmon, *(w. inf. of motion)* 11; ~ eft tō, come back to, return *pp.* cumen, 146, 168. – Cpd.: ofer-.

**cumbol** †, *n. a-stem*, banner, standard, *dp.* cumblum, 332.

**cumbol-wiga** (‡), *m. n-stem*, warrior, *as.* cumbolwigan, 259, *ap.* cumbolwigan, 243n.

**ge-cunnian**, *w.v. (2)*, investigate, inquire, *inf.* ~, 259.

**cwic**, *adj.*, living, alive, *gp.* cwiccra, 235, 311, 323.

**cyn(n)**, *n. ja-stem*, race, tribe, people, *gs.* cynnes, 52, 310, *ds.* cynne, 226, *gp.* cynna, 323.

**cyne-rōf** †, *adj.*, royally (*or* very?) brave (*or* famous), *npm.* cynerōfe, 200, 311n.

**cyning**, *m. a-stem*, king, *ns.* ~, 190, *gp.* cyninga, 155.

**cȳðan**, *w.v. (1)*, make known, *inf.* ~, 56, 243, *pp.* gecȳðed, 155.

**cȳðð**, *f. ō-stem*, native land, home, *ds.* cȳððe, 311.

**D**

**dæg**, *m. a-stem*, day, *as.* ~, 28.

**dæg-red**, *n. a-stem*, dawn, *as.* ~, 204.

**dæg-weorc** (†), *n. a-stem*, day's work, *ds.* dæg-weorce, *266*n.

**dǣl**, *m. i-stem*, part, *ns.* ~, 292, 308.

**dēad**, *adj.*, dead, *nsm.* ~, 107.

**dēað**, *m. a-stem*, death, *ds.* dēaðe, 31, 196.

**dēma**, *m. n-stem*, judge, ruler, *ns.* ~, 59n., 94, *gs.* dēman, 4.

**(ge-)dēman**, *w.v. (1)*, condemn, sentence, *pp.* gedēmed, 196.

**dēofol-cund** ‡, *adj. (as noun)*, devilish, diabolical, *nsm. wk.* dēofolcunda, 61.

**dēð**, *see* **dōn**.

**dōgor**, *n. es/os-stem*, day, *ds.* dōgore, 12.

**dolh-wund** ‡, *adj.*, (mortally) wounded, *nsm.* ~, 107.

**dōm**, *m. a-stem*, glory, renown, *ns.* ~, 266, *as.* ~, 196, *ds.* dōme, 299.

**dōm-līce** †, *adv.*, gloriously, 318.

**dōn**, *anom.*, do, *pres. 3 sg.* dēð, 95.

**dorste**, *see* **durran**.

**drēam**, *m. a-stem*, joy, *ap.* drēamas, 349.

**(ge-)drēfan**, *w.v. (1)*, afflict, disturb, *pp.* gedrēfed, 88.

**drencan**, *w.v. (1)*, make drunk, *pret. 3 sg.* drencte, 29. – Cpd.: ofer-.

**drēogan**, *s.v. (2)*, endure, suffer, *pret. 2 pl.* drugon, 158.

**druncen**, *adj. (pp.)*, drunk, *nsm.* ~, 67, 107.

**dryhten**, *m. a-stem*, *(1)* (†) lord, *ns.* ~, 21, *(2)* Lord, God, *ns.* ~, 61, 92, 198, 299, *ds.* dryhtne, 342, 346. – Cpd.: wine-.

**dryht-guma**, *m. n-stem*, † retainer, warrior, *ap.* dryhtguman, 29.

**duguð**, *f. ō-stem*, (†) band of select troops, élite host, *as. or gs.* duguðe, 31n., *gp.* dugeða, 61. – Cpd.: ealdor-.

**durran**, *pret. pr.*, dare, *pret. 3 sg.* dorste, 258.

**dynian**, *w.v. (2)*, make a din, racket, rowdy noise, *pret. 3 sg.* dynede, 23, *pret. 3 pl.* dynedan, 204.
**dȳre**, *adj.*, valuable, precious, *apm.* ~, 318.
**(ge-)dȳrsian** ‡, *w.v. (2)*, exalt, honour, glorify, *pp.* gedȳrsod, 299.

**E**

**ēac**, *adv.*, also, 295, swylce ēac, as well as, in addition to, 18, 337, 343, 348.
**ēad** (†), *n. a-stem*, prosperity, happiness, *gs.* ēades, 273.
**ēad-hrēðig** †, *adj.*, triumphant, blessed, *npf.* ēadhrēðige, 135.
**ēadig**, *adj.*, happy, blessed, *asf. wk.* ēadigan, 35.
**eald**, *adj.*, old, *npm.* ealde, 166, *apm.* 265; *superl.*, chief, most senior,*ap. wk.* yldestan, 10, *dp. wk.* yldestan, 242.
**eald-fēond** †, *m. nd-stem*, ancient enemy, *dp.* ealdfēondum, 315n.
**eald-hettende** ‡, *m. nd-stem, pl.*, ancient enemies, *ap.* ~, 320.
**eald-genīðla** †, *m. n-stem*, ancient enemy, *ap.* ealdgenīðlan, 228.
**ealdor**, *m. a-stem*, prince, chief, *ns.* ~, 38, 58, aldor, 32n.; Lord, God, *ns.* ~, 88, 124.
**ealdor** (†), *n. a-stem*, *(1)* life, *as.* ~, 185, *ds.* ealdre, 76, *(2)* age, āwa to aldre, for ever and ever, always, 120, to wīdan aldre, for ever, always, 347.
**ealdor-duguð** †, *f. ō-stem*, chief leaders, flower of the nobility, *gs.* ealdorduguðe, 309.
**ealdor-þegn** (†), *m. a-stem*, senior officer, chief thane, *dp.* ealdorþegnum, 242.
**eal(l)**, *(1) adj.*, all, *(stressed, except at* 8, 16, 338, 341*)*, *nsf.* eall, 323, *asm.* ealne, 28n., *asf.* ealle, 31n. *(or npm. as noun)*, 237, *asn.* eal, 331, 338, *gsn.* ealles, 341, *dsn.* eallum, 176, *npm.* ealle, 16, 269, *apm.* ealle, 10, *gp.* ealra, 81, *dp.* eallum, 8, 217; *(2) as noun*, all, *npm.* ealle, 253.
**ealles**, *adv.*, entirely, 108.
**eall-gylden** (†), *adj.*, all-golden, entirely made of gold thread, *nsn.* ~, 46.
**earn**, *m. a-stem*, eagle, *ns.* ~, 210.
**ēastan**, *adv.*, from the east, 190.
**ēaðe**, *adv.*, easily, *superl.* ēaðost, 75, 102.

**ēað-mēdu**, *f. ō-stem*, humility, *dp. (w. sg. sense)* ēaðmēdum, 170.

**Ebrēas**, *prop. n.*, the Hebrews, *np.* ~, 218, *gp.* Ebrēa, 253, 262, 298.

**Ebrisc**, *adj.*, Hebrew, *npm.* Ebrisce, 241, 305.

**ecg**, *f. jō-stem*, (†) edge (of sword, *dp.* ecgum, 231.

**ecg-plega** ‡, *m. n-stem*, sword-play, *as.* ecgplegan, 246.

**ed-wīt**, *n. a-stem*, abuse, scorn, *as.* ~, 215.

**eft**, *adv.*, back, again, 146, 169 *(see* **cuman***)*.

**egesa**, *m. n-stem*, terror, *ns.* ~, 252.

**eges-ful(l)**, *adj.*, terrible, dreadful, *nsm.* egesful, 21, egesfull, 257.

**eglan**, *w.v. (1)*, *w. dat.(of pers.)*, trouble, plague, *inf.* ~, 185.

**ēhtan**, *w.v. (1)*, *w. gen.*, pursue, harry, *pret. 3 pl.* ēhton, 237.

**ellen**, (†) *n. a-stem*, courage, strength, *ds.* elne, 95.

**ellen-dǣd** †, *f. i-stem*, valorous deed, *gp.* ellendǣda, 273.

**ellen-rōf** (†), *adj.*, daring, courageous *nsf.* ~, 109, 146.

**ellen-þrīste** ‡, *adj.*, audacious, boldly daring, *npf.* ~, 133.

**ellor** †, *adv.*, elsewhere, 112.

**el-ðēod**, *f. ō-stem*, foreign people, *gp.* elðēoda, 237.

**el-ðēodig**, *adj.*, foreign, *gp. (as noun)* elðēodigra, 215.

**ende**, *m. ja-stem*, end, *as.* ~, 64, *ds.* ~, 120, 272, 345.

**ēodon**, **ge-ēodon**, *see* **gān**, **gegān**.

**eorl**, *m. a-stem*, (†) man (of noble birth), warrior, *np.* eorlas, 273, 336, *gp.* eorla, 21, 257.

**eornoste** (†), *adv.*, fiercely, resolutely, 108, 231.

**eorðe**, *f. n-stem*, earth, *ds.* eorðan, 65.

**ēow**, *see* **ðū**.

**ēowan**, *w.v. (1)*, show, *pret. 3 pl.* ēowdon, 240. – Cpd.: æt-ȳwan.

**ēower**, *poss. adj.*, your *(pl.)*, *npm.* ēowere, 195.

**ēðel**, *m. a-stem*, native land, home, *ds.* ēðle, 169.

**ēðel-weard** †, *m. a-stem*, guardian of the homeland, *np.* ēðelweardas, 320.

## F

**fāg**, *adj.*, decorated, gleaming, *dsm.* fāgum, 104, *dp.* fāgum, 194, 264, 301 (or 'blood-stained'?).

**faran**, *s.v. (6)*, go, march, *pret. 3 sg.* fōr, 297, *pret. 3 pl.* fōron, 202.

**fæder**, *m. r-stem*, father, *ns.* ~, 5.

**fǣge** (†), *adj.*, fated, doomed to death, *npm.* ~, 19, *apm.* ~, 195; *(as noun), dp.* fǣgum, 209. – Cpd.: slege-.

**fæger**, *adj.* fair, beautiful, *nsn.* ~, 47.

**fægre**, *adv.*, fairly, fittingly, 300.

**fǣr-spel** †, *n. a-stem*, sudden bad news, *as.* ~, 244.

**fæste**, *adv.*, firmly, tightly, 99.

**fæsten**, *n. ja-stem*, stronghold, *ds.* fæstenne, 143.

**fæsten-geat** ‡, *n. a-stem*, fortress gate, *gs.* fæstengeates, 162.

**fǣtels** ¶, *m. a-stem*, pouch, bag, *ds.* fǣtelse, 127.

**ge-feah**, *see* **ge-fēon**.

**ge-feallan**, *s.v. (7c)*, fall, fall down, *pret. 3 sg.* gefēol, 67, gefēoll, 280, 307.

**feax**, *n. a-stem*, hair, *as.* ~, 281, *ds.* feaxe, 99.

**fēng**, *see* **fōn**.

**ge-feoht**, *n. a-stem*, battle, *ds.* gefeohte, 189, 202.

**feohtan**, *s.v. (3)*, fight, *pret. 3 sg.* feaht, 291, *pret. 3 pl.* fuhton, 262.

**ge-feohtan**, *s.v. (3)*, gain, win (by fighting), *pp.* gefohten, 122.

**ge-fēon**, *s.v. (5), w. gen.*, rejoice, *pret. 3 sg.* gefeah, 205.

**fēond**, *m. nd-stem*, foe, enemy, *np.* fȳnd, 195, *ap.* fȳnd, 319n. – Cpd.: eald-.

**fēond-sceaða** †, *m. n-stem*, dire foe, bitter enemy, *as.* fēondsceaðan, 104.

**feorran**, *adv.*, from far away, 24.

**fēorða**, *adj.*, fourth, *dsn.* fēorðan, 12.

**fēran**, *w.v. (1)*, go, travel, *(inf. in periphrasis:* cōmon ... fēran*)*, came, 12.

**ferhð-glēaw** †, *adj.*, prudent, wise, *asf.* ferhð-glēawe, 41.

**fetigan**, *w.v. (2)*, fetch, *inf.* ~, 35.

**fēðe-lāst** †, *m. a-stem*, step, walking-track, *ds.* fēðelāste, 'with pace', 'at speed', 139n.

**findan**, *s.v. (3)*, find, *pret. 3 sg.* funde, 2, 278, *pret. 3 pl.* fundon, 41.

**fīras** †, *m. ja-stem, pl.*, men, *gp.* fīra, 24, 33.

**flān**, *m. f.(?)*, arrow, *gp.* flāna, 221.

**flēam**, *m. a-stem*, flight, *as.* ~, 291.

**flēogan**, *s.v. (2)*, *(1)* fly, *inf.* ~, 221, *pret.3 sg.* flēah, 209, *(2)* flee, *pret. 3 pl.*

flugon *(? or intrans.* **flēon**, flee*)*, 296n.

**flēoh-net**, *n. ja-stem*, fly-net, mosquito net, *ns.* ~, 47n.

**flet-sittende** †, *m. nd-stem pl.*, hall-sitters, warriors feasting in the hall, *dp.* fletsittendum, 19, 33.

**flōr**, *f. u > ō-stem*, floor, *as.* flōre, 111n.

**ge-fohten**, *see* **ge-feohtan**.

**folc**, *n. a-stem*, people, nation, army, *ns.* ~, 162, 262, 292, *gs.* folces, 12, *ds.* folce, 143, 176. – Cpds.: here-, sige-.

**folc-stede** †, *m. i-stem*, battle-field, *ds.* ~, 319.

**folc-toga** †, *m. n-stem*, leader, chief, commander, *gs.* folctogan, 47, *ap.* folctogan, 194.

**folde** (†), *f. n-stem*, earth, ground, *ds.* foldan, 281.

**folm** (†), *f. ō-stem*, hand, *ds.* folme, 80, *dp.* folmum, 99.

**fōn**, *s.v. (7c)*, **fōn on fultum**, give help to, come to the aid of, *pret. 3 sg.* fēng, 299n.

**for**, *prep. w. dat.*, in front of, before, 192.

**for-bīgan**, *w.v. (1)*, bring low, humble, *pp.* forbīged, 267.

**for-ceorfan** ¶, *s.v. (3)*, cut through, *pret. 3 sg.* forcearf, 105.

**for-drīfan**, *s.v. (1)*, drive, compel, *pret. 3 sg.* fordrāf, 277.

**fore-genga**, *m. n-stem*, ‡ attendant, *ns.* ~, 127n.

**fore-mǣre**, *adj.*, outstanding, *asm.* foremǣrne, 122.

**for-gifan**, *s.v. (5)*, grant, *imp. sg.* forgif, 88.

**for-gildan**, *s.v. (3)*, repay, *pp.* forgolden, 217.

**forht-līce**, *adv.*, fearfully, 244.

**for-lǣtan**, *s.v. (7e)*, let go; in forlǣtan, let in, *inf.* forlǣton, 150n., *pret. 3 pl.* forlēton, 170.

**for-lēosan**, *s.v. (2)*, lose, *inf.* ~, 63.

**fōron**, *see* **faran**.

**forð**, *adv.*, *(1) (of motion)*, forth, forwards, 111, 139, 191, 202, 221, *(2) (of time)*, henceforth, 120.

**for-ðylman**, *w.v. (1)*, envelop, wrap round, *pp.* forðylmed, 118.

**for-weorðan**, *s.v. (3)*, perish, *inf.* ~, 288.

**for-wyrd**, *f. i-stem*, destruction, *ns.* ~, 285.

**ge-fræg(e)n**, *see* **ge-frignan**.

**(ge-)frætw(i)an**, *w.v. (2)*, adorn, ornament, *pp.* gefrætewod, 171, 328.

**frēa** (†), *m. n-stem*, lord, the Lord, *ns.* ~, 300.
**fremman**, *w.v. (1)*, do, *pret. 3 pl.* fremedon, 37.
**ge-fremman**, *w.v. (1)*, commit, perpetrate, *pret. 3 sg.* gefremede, 181; tiðe ~, grant a plea, *pret. 3 sg.* gefremede, 6.
**frēorig** †, *adj.*, cold, shivering, *nsm.* ~, 281.
**ge-frignan**, *s.v. (3), (w. acc. and inf.)*, hear, learn, *pret. 1 sg.* gefrægen, 7, gefrægn, 246.
**ge-friðian**, *w.v. (2)*, protect, defend, *pret. 3 sg. (indic. or subj.)* gefriðode, 5.
**frōfor**, *f. ō-stem*, joy, comfort, *gs.* frōfre, 83, *ds.* frōfre, 296.
**from-līce**, *adv.*, promptly, rapidly, 41, 220, boldly, 301.
**frum-gār** †, *m. a-stem*, leader, chief, *ap.* frumgāras, 195.
**frymð**, *f. ō-stem, (pl. w. collective sense)*, creation, *gp.* frymða, 5, 83, 189.
**fugel**, *m. a-stem*, bird, *ns.* ~, 207, *dp.* fuglum, 296.
**fuhton**, *see* **feohtan**.
**fūl**, *adj.*, foul, loathsome, *nsm.wk.* fūla, 111.
**full**, *adj.*, full, *npm.* fulle, 19. – Cpds.: bealo-, eges-, þrym-, wom-.
**fultum**, *m. a-stem*, help, aid, *as.* ~, 186, 300 *(see* **fōn***)*.
**fylgan**, *w.v. (1), w. dat.*, serve, attend to, *inf.* ~, 33n.
**fyllan**, *w.v. (1)*, cut down, *inf.* ~, 194n. *(or subj. pres. 1 pl.)*.
**fyll(o)**, *f. īn-stem*, fill, feast, *gs.* fylle, 209.
**fȳnd**, *see* **fēond**.
**fyrd-wīc**, *n. a-stem, (pl. w. sg. sense)*, camp, *dp.* fyrdwīcum, 220n.
**fyrn-geflit** †, *n. a-stem*, old quarrel, age-old grudge, *ap.* fyrngeflitu, 264.
**fyrst**, *m. i-stem*, period, space of time, *as.* ~, 324.
**fȳsan** (†), *w.v. (1)*, hasten, *subj. pres. 2 pl.* ~, 189n.

### G

**gāl-ferhð** ‡, *adj.*, lustful, lascivious, *nsm.* ~, 62.
**gāl-mōd** ‡, *adj. (as noun)*, lustful, lascivious, *nsm. wk.* gālmōda, 256.
**gān**, *anom.*, go, *inf.* ~, 149, *pret. 3 pl.*, ēodon, 15, 55, 132, 243.
**ge-gān**, *anom.*, *(1)*, arrive at, reach, *pp.* gegān, 140, 219, *(2)*, gain, win, *pret. 3 pl.* geēodon, 331.
**ge-gāngan**, *s.v. (7d)*, go, *inf.* ~, 54.

**gār** (†), *m. a-stem*, spear, javelin, *ap.* garas, 224. – Cpd.: frum-.

**gār-gewinn** †, *n. i-stem*, clash of spears, spear-contest, *gs.* gārgewinnes, 307.

**gǣst**, *m. es/os-stem, (1)* spirit, life, *gs.* gǣstes, 279, *(2)* spirit, the soul, *ns.* ~, 112, *(3)* Spirit, the Holy Ghost, *ns.* ~, 83.

**ge**, *conj.*, and, 166.

**gē**, *see* **ðū**.

**geaf**, *see* **gifan**.

**gearo**, *adj.*, ready, *asf.* gearwe, 2 *(or adv.* **gearwe**, readily*)*.

**gearo-þoncol** ‡, *adj.*, ready-witted, wise, *dsf.* gearo-þoncolre, 341.

**(ge-)gearwian**, *w.v. (2)*, prepare, *pp.* gegeare-wod, 199.

**geat**, *n. a-stem*, gate, *as.* ~, 151. – Cpd.: fæsten-, weal-.

**gegnum** †, *adv.*, directly, straightaway *(w. vb. of motion)*, 132.

**geōmor** (†), *adj.*, sad, gloomy, *nsm.* ~, 87.

**geōmor-mōd** (†), *adj.*, sad at heart, despondent, *dsn.* gēomormōdum, 144.

**geond**, *prep. w. acc.*, throughout, 156.

**geong**, *adj.*, young, *npm.* geonge, 166.

**georn**, *adj.*, eager, desirous, *nsm.* ~, 210.

**georne**, *adv.*, eagerly, 8.

**gēsne** (†), *adj.*, *(1)* deprived of, *asm.* ~, 279, *(2)* dead, *nsm.* ~, 112.

**gifan**, *s.v. (5)*, give, *pret. 3 sg.* geaf, 342. – Cpds.: ā-, for-.

**gifeðe** (†), *adj.*, granted, *nsm.* ~, 157.

**gifu**, *f. ō-stem*, gift, *gp.* gifena, 2.

**gildan**, *s.v. (3)*, repay, *pret. 3 pl.* guldon, 263. – Cpd.: for-.

**gingre**, *f. n-stem (comp. of* **geong***)*, ‡ handmaid, female servant, *dsf.* gingran, 132n.

**ginn** (†), *adj.*, spacious, wide, *dsm. wk.* ginnan, 2, *dsf. wk.* ginnan, 149.

**girwan**, *w.v. (1)*, prepare, ~ **up,** serve up (?), *inf.* ~, 9n.

**glæd-mōd** (†), *adj.*, glad at heart, cheerful, *npf.* glædmōde, 140.

**glēaw**, *adj.*, prudent, wise, *nsf.* ~, 13, *asf.* glēawe, 333; *(as noun), nsf. wk.* glēawe, 171. – Cpd.: ferhð-.

**glēaw-hȳdig** †, *adj.*, wise of thought, shrewd, *nsn.* ~, 148.

**god**, *m. a-stem*, God, *ns.* ~ 83, 123, 183, 189, 299, *gs.* godes, 186, *ds.* gode, 271n. *(or* gōde*)*.

**gōd**, *n. a-stem*, good, virtue, *ds.* gōde, 271n. *(or* gode*)*, *gp.* gōda, 32.

**gold**, *n. a-stem*, gold, *ds.* golde, 171, 328, 338.

**gold-gifa** †, *m. n-stem*, gold-giver, lord, *as.* goldgifan, 279.

**gold-wine** †, *m. i-stem*, gold-friend, lord, *ns.* ~, 22.

**gram**, *adj.*, fierce, angry, *npm.* grame, 224, 238.

**(ge-)gremman**, *w.v. (1)*, enrage, *pp.* gegremede, 305.

**grēot** (†), *n. a-stem*, dust, dirt, earth, *as.* ~, 307.

**grīstbitian**, *w.v. (2)*, gnash the teeth, *inf.* ~, 271.

**grund**, *m. a-stem*, *(1)* earth, world, *ds.* grunde, 2, *(2)*, region, *ap.* grundas, 348.

**guldon**, *see* **gildan**.

**guma** (†), *m. n-stem*, man, *np.* guman, 305, *gp.* gumena, 9, 22, 32, 62, 66, 91, 148, 186, 328. – Cpds.: dryht-, þēod-.

**gūð** (†), *f. ō-stem*, war, battle, *ds.* gūðe, 123, 305.

**gūð-fana** ¶, *m. n-stem*, battle-standard, banner, *dp.* gūðfanum, 219n.

**gūð-freca** †, *m. n-stem*, warrior, *np.* gūðfrecan, 224.

**gūð-sceorp** ‡, *n. a-stem*, armour, *as.* ~, 328.

**gylian**, *w.v. (1)*, yell, *pret. 3 sg.* gylede, 25.

**gyrnan** ¶, *w.v. (1)*, yearn for, desire, *pret. 3 sg.* gyrnde, 346.

**gyst-ern**, *n. a-stem*, guest-house, *ds.* gysterne, 40.

**gȳt**, *adv.*, yet, 182, þā gȳt, 107.

**gyte-sǣl** ‡, *mf. i-stem*, merriness from tippling, festive mood, *dp.* gyte-sālum, 22.

## H

**habban**, *w.v. (3)*, *(used as auxiliary w. pp.)*, have, *pres. 3 sg.* hafað, 197, *pret. 3 sg.* hæfde, 64, 122, 260, *pret. 3 pl.* hæfdon, 140, 219, 318.

**hālig**, *adj.*, holy, *nsf. wk.* hālige, 56, *asf. wk.* hālgan, 260, *dsf. wk.* hāligan, 203; *(as noun)*, *dsf.* hāligre, 98n., *nsf. wk.* hālige, 160.

**hām**, *(1) m. a-stem*, home, *ds.* ~, 121n.; *(2) adv.*, home, homewards, ~, 131.

**hand**, *f. u-stem*, hand, *as.* ~, 198, hond, 130.

**hār**, *adj.*, grey, *apf.* hāre, 327.

**hātan**, *s.v. (7a)*, order, command, *pret. 3 sg.* hēt, 9, 32, 34, 147, 171, *pret. subj. 3 sg.* hēte, 53.

**hāte**, *adv.*, hotly, 94n.

**hæfde**, **-on**, *see* **habban**.

**hæft**, *n. a-stem*, sword-hilt, sword?, *ds.* hæfte, 263n.

**(ge-)hæftan**, *w.v. (1)*, chain, imprison, *pp.* gehæfted, 116.

**hæleð** (†), *m. þ-stem*, man, *np.* ~, 56, 177, 203, 225, 302, *ap.* ~, 247, *gp.* hæleða, 51.

**hǣðen**, *adj.*, heathen, *gsm.* hǣðenes, 179, *asm. wk.* hǣðenan, 98, 110; *(as noun), gp.* hǣðenra, 216.

**hē**, **hēo**, **hit**, *pers. pron.*, he, she, it, *nsm.* hē, 4, 60, 63, 65, 66, 68, 95, 106, 117, 118, 184, 276, 280, *asm.* hyne, 13, 51, 96, 99, 277, *(as refl.)* 44, *gsm. (as poss. adj.)* his, 16, 31, 36, 57, 63a, 63b, 64, 68, 279, 281, 282, 349, *dsm.* him 53, 60, 96, 183, 185, *(as poss. pron. w. parts of the body)* 106, 110; *nsf.* hēo, 2, 3, 6, 75, 102, 105, 145, 344, 346, *asf.* hīe, 4, 170n., hī, 94, 150 *(or ap.?)*, *gsf.* hyre, 99n., *(as poss. adj.)* 127, 130n., 172, *dsf.* hyre, 5, 97, 123, 124, 149, 175, 334, 342; *asn.* hit, 130, hyt, 174; *np.* hīe, 10, 15, 19, 30, 31, 37, 40, 54, 134, 136, 138, 140, 168, 220, 235, 241, 321, hī, 27, 160, 269, 289, 301, 334, 340, *gp. (as poss. adj.)* heora, 38, 56, hyra 128, 251, 264, 268, 272, 274, 290, 315, *dp.* him, 38, 208, 209, 216, 240, 244, 252 *(or ds.?)*, 274, 290n., 291n., 297, 299, 322.

**hēafod**, *n. a-stem*, head, *ns.* ~, 110, *as.* ~, 126, 173, 179.

**hēafod-gerīm** ‡, *n. a-stem*, head-count, total number, *gs.* hēafodgerīmes, 308.

**hēafod-weard**, *m. a-stem*, chief guard, *or* bodyguard, *np.* hēafodweardas, 239n.

**hēah**, *adj.*, high, *asm.* hēanne, 161, *dsn. wk.* hēan, 43; *superl.* hēhst, highest, greatest, *nsm. wk.* hēhsta, 94, hȳhsta, 308, *gsm. wk.* hēhstan, 4a, 4b.

**healdan**, *s.v. (7c)*, hold, keep, guard, *pret. 3 pl.* hēoldon, 142n.

**healdend**, *m. nd-stem*, leader, *ns.* ~, 289.

**healf**, *adj.*, half, *asm* healfne, 105.

**hēan**, *adj.*, low, of low rank, *asm.* hēanne, 234n.
**hēan(ne)**, *see* **hēah**.
**hēap**, *m. a-stem*, crowd, throng, *dp.* hēapum, 163.
**heard**, *adj.*, *(1)* hard, toughened (of weapons), *asm.* heardne, 79n., *dp.* heardum, 263, *(2)* tough, brave (of people), *(as noun)*, *gp.* heardra, 225. – Cpds.: nīð-, stede-.
**hearde**, *adv.*, painfully, severely, 116, 216.
**hearra** †, *m. n-stem,* lord, *ds.* hearran, 56n.
**heaðo-rinc** †, *m. a-stem*, warrior, *gs.* heaðorinces, 179, *np.* heaðorincas, 212.
**hēawan**, *s.v. (7b)*, cleave, hew, *pret. 3 pl.* hēowon, 303.
**ge-hēawan**, *s.v. (7b)*, cut down, slay, *inf.* ~, 90, *pp.* gehēawen, 288, 294.
**hēhst(an)**, *see* **hēah**.
**hell**, *f. jō-stem*, hell, *gs.* helle, 116n.
**helm**, *m. a-stem,* helmet, *as.* ~, 337, *ap.* helmas, 193, 317, 327, *dp.* helmum, 203.
**help**, *f. ō-stem*, help, *ds.* helpe, 96.
**hēo**, *see* **hē**.
**heofon**, *m. a-stem*, heaven, *(pl. w. sg. meaning), dp.* heofonum, 343.
**hēoldon**, *see* **healdan**.
**heolfrig** (‡), *adj.*, bloody, gory, *asn.* ~, 130n., 316.
**heolstor**, *adj.*, dark, hidden, secret, *dsm. wk.* heolstran, 121n.
**heora**, *see* **hē**.
**heorte**, *f. n-stem*, heart, *ns.* ~, 87.
**heoru-wǣpen** ‡, *n. a-stem*, deadly weapon, sword, *dp.* heoruwǣpnum, 263.
**hēowon**, *see* **hēawan**.
**hēr**, *adv.*, here, 177, 285, 288.
**hēr-būende** †, *m. nd-stem, pl.*, those dwelling here (on earth), *gp.* hēr-būendra, 96.
**here**, *m. ja-stem*, army, host, *ns.* ~, 161, *gs.* heriges, 293, *ds.* herige, 135.
**here-folc** (‡), *n. a-stem*, army, *gs.* herefolces, 234, 239.
**here-rēaf** ¶, *n. a-stem*, spoils of war, booty, *as.* ~, 316.
**here-wǣða** (‡), *m. n-stem*, warrior, *gs.* herewǣðan, 126, 173.
**her-pað** ¶, *m. a-stem*, passage for an army, war-path, *as.* ~, 302.
**hēt(e)**, *see* **hātan**.
**hete-þoncol** ‡, *adj.*, hostile, *asm.* heteþoncolne, 105.
**hī**, **hīe**, *see* **hē**.
**hige** (†), *m. i-stem*, mind, heart, *ns.* ~, 87.

**hige-rōf** †, *adj.*, brave-hearted, *npm.* higerōfe, 302.

**hige-þoncol** †, *adj.*, thoughtful, *dsf.* hige-þoncolre, 131.

**hild** †, *f. jō-stem*, battle, *as.* h*i*lde, *251*n., *ds.* hilde, 293.

**hilde-lēoð** ‡, *n. a-stem*, war-song, *as.* ~, 211.

**hilde-nǣdre** †, *f. n-stem*, 'battle-adder', arrow, *ap.* hildenǣdran, 222n.

**him**, *see* **hē**.

**hin-sīð** (†), *m. a-stem*, the journey hence, death, *ds.* hinsīðe, 117.

**his**, **hit**, *see* **hē**.

**hlāford**, *m. a-stem*, lord, *ds.* hlāforde, 251.

**hlanc**, *adj.*, lean, gaunt, *nsm. wk. (as noun?)*, hlanca, 205.

**(ge-)hlæstan**, *w.v. (1)*, load, burden, *infl. pp.* ge-hlæste, 36.

**hlihhan**, *s.v. (6)*, laugh, *pret. 3 sg.* hlōh, 23.

**hlimman** †, *s.v. (3)*, re-sound, reverberate, *pret. 3 pl.* hlummon, 205.

**hlūde**, *adv.*, loudly, 205, 223, 270.

**hlȳdan**, *w.v. (1)*, roar, *pret. 3 sg.* hlȳdde, 23.

**hlynnan**, *w.v. (1)*, roar, clamour, *pret. 3 sg.* hlynede, 23.

**hogian**, *w.v. (2)*, intend, *pret. 3 pl.* hogedon, 250, 273.

**Hōlofernus**, *prop. n.*, Holofernes, *n.* ~, 21, 46, *a.* ~, 7n., *g.* ~, 180, 250, Hōlofernes, 336.

**hond**, *see* **hand**.

**hopian** ¶, *w.v. (2)*, hope, *inf.* ~, 117.

**horn-boga** †, *m. n-stem*, bow curved like a horn, or tipped with horn, *dp.* hornbogan, 222n.

**hosp**, *m. a-stem*, scorn, contempt, *as.* ~, 216.

**hraðe**, *adv.*, quickly, 37.

**hrægl**, *n. a-stem*, clothing, cloths, *as.* ~, 282.

**hrǣw**, *n. es/os-stem*, corpse, *ap.* ~, 313.

**hrefn**, *m. a-stem*, raven, *ns.* ~, 206.

**hrēoh**, *adj.*, disturbed, distraught, *nsm.* ~, 282.

**hrēowig-mōd** †, *adj.*, grieving at heart, *npm.* hrēowigmōde, 289.

**hreðer** †, *m.n. a-stem*, heart, *ds.* hreðre, 94.

**hring**, *m. a-stem*, ring, orna-ment, *dp.* hringum, 37.

**ge-hroden** †, *pp. (of* **hrēo-dan**, *s.v. (2))*, adorned, *infl.* ~, gehrodene, 37.

**hrōf**, *m. a-stem*, roof, *ds.* hrōfe, 67.

**hū**, *adv.*, how, 25, 75, 160, 175, 259.

**hund**, *m. a-stem*, hound, dog, *as.* ~, 110.

**hup-seax**, *n. a-stem*, hip-dagger, short sword, *ap.* ~, 327.

**hūru**, *adv.*, certainly, indeed, 345.

**hwā**, *indef. pron.*, any one, *asm.* hwæne, 52.

**ge-hwā**, *indef. pron.*, each one, every one, *asm.* gehwæne, 186.

**hwealf**, *adj.*, hollowed, curved, *dpf.* hwealfum, 214.

**hwearf** †, *m. a-stem*, crowd, *dp.* hwearfum, 249n.

**hweorfan**, *s.v. (3)*, travel, pass, *pret. 3 sg.* hwearf, 112.

**hwīl**, *f ō-stem*, a (long) time, *as.* hwīle, 214.

**ge-hwylc**, *pron. (as noun, w. gen.)*, each, every, *gsn.* gehwylces, 32, ānra ~, every one, *asm.* gehwylcne, 95.

**hȳhsta**, *see* **hēah**.

**hyht**, *m. i-stem*, hope, *ns.* ~, 98.

**hyht-wyn(n)** ‡, *f. jō-stem*, hope of bliss, *gp.* hyht-wynna, 121.

**hyldo**, *f. īn > ō-stem*, grace, favour, *gs. (or as.?)* ~, 4n.

**hyne**, **hyra**, *see* **hē**.

**ge-hȳran**, *w.v. (1)*, hear, *inf.* ~, 24, *pret. 3 pl.* gehȳrdon, 160.

**hyrde**, *m. ja-stem*, shepherd, guardian, *ns.* ~, 60.

**hyre**, *see* **hē**.

**hyrned-nebba** †, *m. n-stem*, horny-beaked one, raven, *ns.* ~, 212.

**hyrst** (†), *f. i-stem*, trappings, armour, *ap.* hyrsta, 316.

**hyt**, *see* **hē**.

## I

**ic**, *pers. pron.*, I, *ns.* ~, 7, 83, 89, 91, 152, 185, 186, 246, *ds.* mē, 85, 86, 88, 90n., 93, *np.* wē, 287, *gp.* ūre, 285, *dp.* ūs, 181, 184.

**ides** (†), *f. jō-stem*, woman, *ns.* ~, 14, 109, 128, 146, *as.* idese, 55, 58, *ds.* idese, 340, *np.* idesa, 133.

**in**, *prep.*, *(1) w. acc. (of motion)*, into, 276, *(w.* gemong*)* 193, 225, *(2) w. dat. (of location or situation)*, in, 2, 116, 121, 143, 206, 255, 344.

**in**, *adv.*, in, 150, 170.

**inn**, *n. a-stem*, room, *ds.* inne, 70.

**inne**, *see* **ðær**.

**inwid(d)**, *adj. (as noun)*, evil, wicked, *nsm. wk.* inwidda, 28n.

**irnan**, *s.v. (3)*, run, *pret. 3 pl.* urnon, 164.

**Iūdith**, *prop. n.*, Judith, *n.* ~, 13, 123, 132, *144*n., 168, 256, 341, *a.* Iūdithðe, 40, *g.* Iūdithe, 333.

**L**

**lāgon**, *see* **licgan**.

**land-būende**, *m. nd-stem, pl.*, † land-dwellers, native people, *np.* ~, 226, *dp.* londbūendum, 314.

**lang**, *adj.*, long, *comp.* lengra, *gsn.* lengran, 184.

**lange**, *adv.*, long, 158, 346, *comp.*, leng, 153.

**lār**, *f. ō-stem*, advice, guidance, *as.* lāre, 333.

**lāst** (†), *m. a-stem*, track, (him) on ~(e) *(w. dat.)*, behind, after (*them*), *as.* ~, 209, 291, *ds.* lāste, 297. – Cpd.: fēðe-.

**late**, *adv.* tardily, 275, *see* **sīð.**

**lāð**, *adj.*, hateful, odious, *nsm.* ~, 45, *asm.* lāðne, 72, 101, *dsn.* lāðum, 226, *gsn. wk.* lāðan, 310n.; *(as noun)*, hated one, foe, *gp.* lāðra, 297, 303; *superl.*, lāðost, *(in predicate)* 322, *gsm. wk.* lāðestan, 178n.; *(as noun)*, *dpm. wk.* lāð-estan, 314.

**lǣdan**, *w.v. (1)*, lead, bring, *inf.* ~, 42, *pret. 3 sg.* lǣdde, 129, *pret. 3 pl.* lǣddon, 72, 325.

**læg**, *see* **licgan**.

**lǣtan**, *s.v. (7e)*, let, cause, make *(w. acc., and inf. of vb. of motion)*, *pret. 3 pl.* lēton, 221. – Cpd.: for-.

**lǣðð**, *f. ō-stem*, affliction, injury, *gp.* lǣðða, 158n., *dp.* lǣððum, 184.

**ge-lēafa**, *m. n-stem*, faith, belief, *as.* gelēafan, 6, 89, 344, *ds.* gelēafan, 97.

**lēan**, *n. a-stem*, reward, *gs.* lēanes, 346. – Cpd.: sigor-.

**lēap**, *m. a-stem*, trunk, carcass, *ns.* ~, 111n.

**lēas**, *adj. w. gen.*, lacking, devoid of, *nsm.* ~, 121.

**leng**, **lengra**(**n**), *see* **lang**/**-e**.

**lēode**, *m. i-stem*, *pl.*, people, *gp.* lēoda, 178, *dp.* lēo-dum, 147. – Cpd.: burg-.

**lēod-hata**, *m. n-stem*, tyrant, *as.* lēodhatan, 72.

**lēof**, *adj.*, dear, beloved, *dsm. wk.* lēofan, 346; *(as noun)*, *nsf.* ~, 147.

**lēoht**, *adj.*, bright, shining, *asm.* lēohtne, 191.

**lēoma**, *m. n-stem*, light, *as.* lēoman, 191.

**lēton**, *see* **lǣtan**.

**licgan**, *s.v. (5)*, lie (slain, unconscious), *inf.* ~, 278, *pres. 3 sg.* līð, 288, *pret. 3 sg.* læg, 106, 111, 293, *pret. 3 pl.* lāgon, 30.

**līf**, *n. a-stem*, life, *gs.* līfes, 184, 280, *ds.* līfe, 322.

**lind**, *f. ō-stem*, † shield, *ap.* linde, 191, 303, *dp.* lindum, 214.

**lind-wīg** ‡, *mn. a-stem*, shield-army, *or* military prowess, *ns. (or as.?)* ~, 297n.

**lind-wiggende** †, *m. nd-stem, pl.*, shield-warriors, *np.* ~, 42.

**list** (†), *mf. i-stem*, skill, *dp. (used as adv.)* listum, skilfully, 101.

**līð**, *see* **licgan**.

**ge-lōme**, *adv.*, frequently, 18.

**lond-**, *see* **land-**.

**losian**, *w.v. (2)*, perish, *inf.* ~, 287.

**lungre** †, *adv.*, quickly, at once, 147, 280.

**lust**, *m. a-stem*, joy, *dp. (used as adv. w.* on*)* lustum, 161n.

**lybban**, *w.v. (3)*, live, *pret. 3 pl.* lyfdon, 296. – Cpd.: unlyfigende.

**lyft**, *f. i-stem*, air, cloud, *ap.* lyfte, 347.

**ge-lystan**, *w.v. (1)*, *w. gen. (of thing)*, desire, *pret. 3 sg.* gelyste, 306.

**lȳt-hwōn**, *adj. ( as noun)*, *w. gen.*, few, *ns.* ~, 310.

## M

**mādm**, *m. a-stem*, treasure, *ap.* mādmas, 318, *gp.* mādma, 329, māðma, 340.

**magan**, *pret. pr.*, *(w. inf.)*, can, be able, *pres. 1 sg.* mæg, 152, *pres. 2 pl.* magon 177, *pret. 3 sg.* mihte 102, *pret. 3 pl.* mihton, 235, mihten, 24n., 136, *subj. pres 3 sg.* mæge, 330n., *subj. pret 3 sg.* mihte, 49, 75.

**mago-þegn** †, *m. a-stem*, retainer, *np.* mago-þegnas, 236.

**man**, *see* **mon**.

**gemang**, *see* **gemong**.

**manian**, *w.v. (2)*, urge, exhort, *pret. 3 sg.* manode, 26.

**manna**, *m. n-stem*, man, *as.* mannan, 98, 101.

**māra**, *see* **micel**.

**māðm**, *see* **mādm**.

**mæg(e)**, *see* **magan**.

**mægen**, *n. a-stem*, force, might, *ns.* ~, 253, 261.

**mægen-ēacen** †, *adj.*, mighty, powerful, *nsn.* ~, 292.

**mægð** (†), *f. þ-stem*, woman, *ns.* ~, 78, 125, 145, 254, *as.* ~, 35, 43, 165, 260, *gs.* ~, 334, *np.* ~, 135.

**mǣgð**, *f. ō-stem*, tribe, nation, *gp.* mǣgða, 324.

**mǣre**, *adj.*, famous, illustrious, *dsm. wk.* mǣran, 3; *superl. nsf.* mǣrost, 324. – Cpd.: fore-.

**mǣrð**, *f. ō-stem*, glory, *as.* mǣrðe, 343.
**mǣst**, *see* **micel**.
**mē**, *see* **ic**.
**mēce** (†), *m. ja-stem*, sword, *as.* ~, 78, *ds.* ~, 104.
**mēd**, *f. ō-stem*, reward, *as.* mēde, 343, *ds.* mēde, 334.
**medo-burh** †, *f. ath.*, city with a mead-hall, *ds.* medobyrig, 167n.
**medo-wērig** (‡), *adj.*, 'weary from drinking', dead-drunk, *or* hung-over, *apm.* medowērige, 229n., *dpm.* medowērigum, 245.
**medu-gāl** †, *adj.*, drunk with mead, *nsm.* ~, 26n.
**mēowle** (†), *f. n-stem*, woman, *ns.* ~, 56, *as.* mēowlan, 261.
**metod** (†), *m. a-stem*, Creator, God, *ns.* ~, 154, *gs.* metodes, 261.
**micel**, *adj.*, much, great, *dp.* miclum, 10, 70; *comp.* māra, *asf.* māran, 92, *(as noun, w. part. gen.) apm.* māre, *329*n.; *superl.* mǣst, *asf.* mǣste, 3, *nsm. wk.* mǣsta, 292; *(as noun w. part. gen.), asn.* mǣst, 181.
**mid**, *prep. w. dat.*, *(1)* together with, along with (*things*), 287, *(2) (manner; often in semi-adv. phrases)*, with, 59 (2x), 88, 95, 97 (2x), 170, 184, *(3) (instrument)*, with, by means of, 29, 89, 272.
**middan**, *see* **onmiddan**.
**mihte, -en, -on**, *see* **magan**.
**mihtig**, *adj.*, mighty, *nsm.* ~, 92, 198. – Cpd.: æl-.
**milts**, *f. jō-stem*, grace, mercy, *as.* miltse, 349, *gs.* miltse, 85, 92.
**mīn**, *poss. adj.*, my, *asf.* mīne, 198n., *dsn.* mīnum, 94, *gp.* mīnra, 90.
**mōd**, *n. a-stem*, heart, spirit, *ns.* ~, 167, *ds.* mōde, 57, 93, 97, 154, 282. – Cpds.: gāl-, gēomor-, glæd-, hrēowig-, stīð-, styrn-, swīð-, torht-, þancol-, þearl-.
**mōdig**, *adj.*, *(1)* courageous, *gsf.* mōdigre, 334, *(2)* proud, arrogant, *nsm.* ~, 26n.; *(as noun), nsm. wk.* mōdiga 52.
**molde**, *f. n-stem*, earth, *gs.* moldan, 343.
**mon(n)**, *m. mut.*, man, *ds.* men, 167, *gp.* monna, 52, 181, manna, 235; *(as indef. pron.)*, one, they, *ns.* ~, 291n., 329.
**mōnað**, *m. þ-stem,* month, *gs.* mōnðes, 324.
**ge-mong**, *n. a-stem*, throng, crowd, *as.* ~, 193, 303, gemang, 225.

**morgen-colla** ‡, *m. n-stem*, morning slaughter, *as.* morgencollan, 245n.
**morgen-tīd**, *f. i-stem*, morning, *as.* ~, 236.
**morðor**, *n. a-stem*, violent crime, great wickedness, *gs.* morðres, 90, *gp.* morðra, 181.
**mōtan**, *pret. pr.*, may, be allowed to, *(1) (w. inf.)*, *pret. 3 sg. (indic. or subj.)* mōste, 185, *subj. pres. 1 sg.* mōte, 89; *(2) (w. ellipsis of inf. of motion)*, *subj. pres. 3 sg.* mōte, 118.
**mund** (†), *f. ō-stem*, hand, *dp.* mundum, 229.
**mund-byrd**, *f. i-stem*, protection, *as.* ~, 3.
**murnan**, *s.v. (3)*, grieve, *inf.* ~, 154.
**ge-myndig**, *adj.*, mindful, *nsf.* ~, 74.
**myntan**, *w.v. (1)*, think, suppose, *pret. 3 pl.* mynton, 253.

N

**nāhte**, *see* **āgan**.
**ge-nam**, *see* **ge-niman**.
**nama**, *m. n-stem*, name, *ds.* naman, 81.
**nān**, *indef. pron. (as noun, w. part. gen.)*, none, *nsm.* ~, 257, *asm.* nānne, 68, 233.
**nǣfre**, *adv.*, never, 91.
**nǣnig**, *indef. pron. (as noun w. part. gen.)*, none, *nsm.* ~, 51.
**næs**, *see* **wesan**.
**næs**, *m. a-stem*, cliff, *as.* ~, 113.
**ne**, *adv., (immediately prec. vb.)*, not, 20, 59, 117, 153, 183, 233, 274, 345.
**ne**, *conj.*, nor, 234.
**nēah**, *adj.*, near, *superl.*, nēhsta, *dsm.* nēhstan (sīðe), for the last (time), 73.
**nēah**, *adv.*, near, 287, *comp.* nēar, nearer, 53.
**ge-neahhe** (†), *adv.*, frequently, 26.
**nēa-lǣcan**, *w.v. (1)*, approach, *pret. 3 sg.* nēalǣhte, 34, 261.
**nēhsta**, *see* **nēah**, *adj.*.
**nēar**, *see* **nēah**, *adv.*.
**nemnan**, *w.v. (1)*, name, call, *inf.* ~, 81.
**nēosan**, *w.v. (1)*, *w. gen.*, go to *(a place)*, *inf.* ~, 63.
**neowol**, *adj.*, steep, *asm.* neowelne, 113.
**nergend** (†), *m. nd-stem*, Saviour, *as.* ~, 81, *gs.* nergendes, 73, *ds.* nergende, 45.
**nest**, *n. a-stem*, provisions, food, *as.* ~, 128.
**nēðan** (†), *w.v. (1)*, venture, *pret. 3 sg.* nēðde, 277.
**niht**, *f. mut.*, night, *ns.* ~, 34, *ds.* nihte, 64; *gs., (as*

*adv.)*, by night, nihtes, 45.

**niman**, *s.v. (4)*, take, seize, *infl. inf.* tō nimanne, 313.

**ge-niman**, *s.v. (4)*, take hold of, grip, *pret. 3 sg.* genam, 77, 98.

**nīð**, *m. a-stem*, *(1)* violence, trouble, *gp.* nīða, 34, *dp.* nīðum, 287; *(2)* † battle, *ds.* nīðe, 53.

**nīð-heard** †, *adj.*, daring, bold in battle, *nsm.* ~, 277.

**nīð-hycgende** †, *m. nd-stem, pl.*, evil schemers, *or* those intent on battle, *ap.(or np.)* ~, 233n.

**(ge-)nīwian**, *w.v. (2)*, renew, *pp.* genīwod, 98.

**nō**, *adv.*, *(emphatic)* not at all, 117.

**nū**, *adv.*, now, 92, 186, [287n.]; nū ðā *(stressed* nū, *cf. M.E. nouthe)*, now, 86.

**nȳd**, *f. i-stem*, need, necessity, *ns.* ~, 277.

**nymðe**, *conj.*, unless, 52.

**nyste**, *see* **witan**.

**(ge-)nyðerian** ¶, *w.v. (2)*, humble, bring low, *pp.* genyðerad, 113.

## O

**of**, *prep. w. dat.*, *(1) (motion)*, *(a) (out of)*, from, 79, 119, 149, 203, 230, ūt of, out of, 70, 135; *(b) (away from)*, from, 222; *(2) (with the idea of origin)*, from, 335.

**of-dūne** ¶, *adv.*, down, 290.

**ofer**, *prep. w. acc. (of motion)*, over, *(1) (of time)*, throughout, 28, *(2) (of place)*, over, across, 161.

**ofer-cuman**, *s.v. (4)*, overcome, *inf.* ~, 235.

**ofer-drencan** ¶, *w.v. (1)*, to make drunk, inebriate, *pret. 3 sg. (or pp. npm.)*, oferdrencte, 31n.

**ofer-winnan**, *s.v. (3)*, conquer, defeat, *pp.* oferwunnen, 319.

**ofost-līce**, *adv.*, quickly, 150, 169.

**ofst**, *f. ō-stem*, haste, *dp.* ofstum, 10, 70, *(as adv.)* quickly, 35.

**on**, *prep.*, *(1) w. acc. (a) (motion)*, in, 209b, 291a, 291b, 300 *(see* **fōn***)*, 307, 312, into, 130, on, 145, onto, 111; *(b) (aspect or direction)*, on, (wlitan) 50, 51, (starian) 178, *(c) (time)*, in, 236, on, 204, at, 306; *(d) (semi-adv. phrase)*, on symbel, always, 44; *(2) w. dat. (a) (location), (i) (physical)*, in, on, 5, 54n, 57a, 65, 66, 127, 167, 209a, 278, 294, 297, 319, 321, *332*n., 343a, 343b; *(ii) (mental)*, in, 13, 57b, 69, 93, 94, 97, 154, 282; *(b)* *(state)*, in, 22, 30, 106, 161n.; *(c) (means)*, by, 266; *(d) (w. vb. of taking)*, from, 314; *(e) (semi-adv. phrase)*, on gerihte, straightaway, 202.

**on**, *adv.*, in, 129.

**on ... middan**, *see* **onmiddan**.

**on-bryrdan**, *w.v. (1)*, inspire, *pret. 3 sg.* onbryrde, 95.

**ond (and?)**, *conj. (abbrev. 7)*, and, 52 times, *(1) (joining similar units)*, (both) ... and, 163, 164a, 164b, *(2) (linking disparate units)*, 47n., *(3) (adversative, w. sense shading into* but*)*, 51n.

**ōnettan**, *w.v. (1)*, hasten, hurry, *pret. 3 sg.* ōnette, 162, *pret. 3 pl.* ōnettan, 139.

**on-gēan**, *prep. w. acc.*, towards, 165.

**on-ginnan**, *s.v. (3)*, begin, *(w. inf.), pret. 3 sg.* ongan, 80, 281, *pret. 3 pl.* ongunnon, 42 *(pleonastic)*, 270.

**on-gitan**, *s.v. (5)*, realise, learn, *pret. 3 pl.* ongēaton, 168, 238.

**on-hǣtan**, *w.v. (1)*, inflame, *pp.* onhǣted, 87.

**on-innan**, *prep. w. acc.*, among, 312.

**on-lēon (†)**, *s.v. (1 > 2), w. dat. (of pers.) and gen. (of thing)*, grant, *pret. 3 sg.* onlēah, 124.

**on ... middan**, *prep. w. dat.*, upon, 68.

**on-ufan ¶**, *prep. w. dat.*, upon, 252.

**on-wæcnan**, *s.v. (6)*, awake, *subj. pret. 3 sg.* onwōce, 77.

**on-wrīðan ¶**, *s.v. (1)*, unwrap, *inf.* ~, 173.

**orc**, *m. a-stem*, pitcher, jug, *np.* orcas, 18.

**ōret-mæcg (†)**, *m. ja-stem*, warrior, *ap.* ōretmæcgas, 232.

**or-feorme †**, *adj. w. dat.*, alienated, estranged *(from)*, *npm.* ~, 271.

**or-sāwle**, *adj.*, lifeless, *nsm.* ~, 108.

**oð**, *conj.*, until, 140, 292.

**ōðer**, *adj.*, other (of two), second, *dsm.* ōðre, 109.

**oð-þæt**, *conj.*, until, 30, 33n., 134, 238.

**oððe**, *conj.*, or, 259, 339.

**oð-þringan (†)**, *s.v. (3), w. dat. (of pers.) and gen. (of thing)*, take (by force), *pret. 1 sg.* oðþrong, 185.

## R

**rǣd**, *m. a-stem*, *(1)* wisdom, *ds.* rǣde, 97n.; *(2)* plan, design, *gp.* rǣda, 68.

**ræfnan**, *w.v. (1)*, do, carry out, *pret. 3 pl.* ræfndon, 11.

**rǣswa** †, *m. n-stem*, leader, chief, *np.* rǣswan, 12n. *(or ds.)*, 178.

**rēad**, *adj.*, red (?), *dsn.* rēadum, 338n.

**recene**, *adv.*, quickly, 188.

**(ge-)rēnian**, *w.v. (2)*, adorn, *infl. pp.* gerēnode, 338.

**rēocende**, *pres. part. (as adj.)*, reeking, steaming, *nap.* ~, 313.

**rest**, *f. jō-stem*, bed, couch, *ds.* reste, 54n., 68. – Cpd.: bed-.

**restan**, *w.v. (1)*, *(1)* rest, *pret. 3 sg.* reste, 44; *(2)* lie dead, *pret. 3 pl.* reston, 321.

**rēðe**, *adj.*, fierce, raging, *apm.* ~, 348.

**rīce**, *adj.*, high (of rank), noble, powerful, *asm.* rīc[n]e, *234*n., *nsm. wk.* rīca, *(as noun?)* 20, 44, *dsm. wk.* rīcan, 11; *(as noun)*, *nsm. wk.* rīca, 68.

**rīce**, *n. ja-stem*, kingdom, *ds.* ~, 343.

**riht**, *adj.*, true, *dsm.* rihte, 97.

**ge-riht**, *n. a-stem*, direct route, *(in semi-adv. phrase)* on gerihte, straight on, 202.

**rinc** (†), *m. a-stem*, warrior, *gp.* rinca, 54, 338. – Cpds.: beado-, heaðo-.

**roder**, *m.a-stem*, heaven, *ap.* roderas, 348, *dp.* roderum, 5.

**rōf** (†), *adj.*, brave, *npm.* rōfe, 20, *gp.* rōfra, 53. – Cpds.: æsc-, cyne-, hige-, sige-.

**rond-wiggende** †, *m. nd-stem, pl.*, shield-warrior, *np.* ~, 11, 20, *gp.* rand-wiggendra, 188.

**rūm**, *m. a-stem*, opportunity, *ns.* ~, 313.

**rūm**, *adj.*, broad, spacious, *apm.* rūme, 348.

**rūme** (†), *adv.*, abundantly, 97.

**rūn**, *f. ō-stem*, consultation, *ds.* rūne, 54.

## S

**sacu**, *f. ō-stem*, conflict, battle, *ds.* sæcce, 288.

**salowig-pād** †, *adj.*, dark-coated, *nsm. wk.* salowigpāda, 211.

**sār**, *adj.*, grievous, painful, *gp.* sārra, 182.

**sæcce**, *see* **sacu**.

**(ge-)sǣgan**, *w.v. (1)*, destroy, *pp.* gesǣged, 293.

**(ge-)sǣlan**, *w.v. (1)*, † bind, fetter, *pp.* gesǣled, 114.

**sǣte**, **sǣton**, *see* **sittan**.

**scǣron**, *see* **sceran**.

**sceacan**, *s.v. (6)*, hasten, *inf.* ~, 291.

**sceal**, *see* **sculan**.

**scealc** (†), *m. a-stem*, retainer, warrior, *np.* scealcas, 230. – Cpd.: anbyht-.

**scearp**, *adj.*, sharp, *asm.* scearpne, 78.
**scēað**, *f. ō-stem*, sheath, *ds.* scēaðe, 79, *dp.* scēaðum, 230.
**sceaða**, *m. n-stem*, enemy, *gp.* sceaðena, 193. – Cpd.: fēond-.
**sceolde**, *see* **sculan**.
**ge-sceō[p]**, *see* **ge-scyppan**.
**scēotend** †, *m. nd-stem*, shooter, warrior, *np.* ~, 304.
**sceran**, *s.v. (4)*, cut through, *pret. 3 pl.* scǣron, 304.
**scild**, *m. a-stem*, shield, *np.* scildas, 204.
**scild-burh** †, *f. ath.*, shield-wall, *as.* ~, 304.
**scīr**, *adj.*, bright, gleaming, *apm.* scīre, 193.
**scīr-mǣled** ‡, *adj.*, brightly decorated, *apn.* ~, 230.
**sculan**, *pret. pr.*, *(w. inf.)*, have to, must, *pres. 3 sg.* sceal, 119, *pres. 1 pl.* sculon, 287, *pret. 3 sg.* sceolde, 63.
**scūr**, *m. a-stem*, shower *(† fig. of weapons in battle)*, *ap.* scūras, 221, *dp.* scūrum, 79n.
**scȳne** (†), *adj.*, bright, fair, *apf.* ~, 316. – Cpd.: ælf-.
**ge-scyppan**, *s.v. (6)*, create, *pret. 3 sg.* gesceōp, *347*n.
**scyppend**, *m. nd-stem*, Creator, God, *gs.* scyppendes, 78.
**sē**, **sēo**, **þæt**, *(1) dem. adj.*, the, that, *nsm.* sē, 9, 20, 25, 28, 32, 44, 48, 52, 57, 61, 68, 76, 94, 111, 205, 206, 252, 254, 256, 292, 308, 338, *nsf.* sēo, 34, 56, 125, 160, 171, 176, 254, 256, 323, *nsn.* þæt (ꝥ), 110, *asm.* þone, 75, 98, 100, 104, 106, 110, ðone, 71, 258, 259, *asf.* þā 35, 43, ðā, 55, 58, 111, 165, 236, 260, 306, *asn.* þæt (ꝥ), 82, 151, 276, 283, ðæt, 204, *gsm.* þæs, 4a, 4b, 47, 126, 173, 248, 293, ðæs, 102, 151, 178, *gsf.* þǣre, 137, *gsn.* þæs, 162, 234, ðæs 239, *(with vb. taking gen.)* þæs, 60, 346a, *dsm.* þām, 345b, ðām, 3, 7, 11, 119, 121, 127, 135, 217, 294, 314, 319, 345a, 346, *dsf.* þǣre, 286, 340, ðǣre, 149, 167, 203, 326, *dsn.* þām, 43, 176, ðām, 15, 40, 70, 141, 143a, 143b, 152, 255, 266, 335, *isn.* þȳ, 12, þē, 53, þon, 92, *np.* þā, 133, 273, ðā, 208, 236, 331, *ap.* ðā, 10, *gp.* þāra, 158, 276, *dp.* þām, 175, 242, ðām, 220, 283;
*(2) dem. pron.*, that, *nsn.* þæt (ꝥ) 12, 155, 216, *asn.* þæt (ꝥ), 19, 24n., 59, 182, 241, 331, 340,

ðæt, 10, *gsn. (with v. taking gen.)* þæs, 205, ðæs, 20, *(semi-adv., with expressions of reward, thanks, rejoicing)* for that, þæs, 346b, ðæs, 5, 341, *(in comb. with* ðe, *as conj.)* since, þæs, 13, because, þæs, 344, *dsn.* ðām *(in adv. phrase* to ðām*)* to such a degree, sufficiently, 275, *np.* þā *(in comb. with* ðe, *as rel. pron.)*, those who, þā, 214, 322, ðā, 238, 296, *dp.* ðām, 9;

*(3) rel. pron.*, that, which, *asn.* þæt (ꝥ), 338.

**searo-ðoncol** †, *adj.*, discerning, shrewd, *nsf.* ~, 145; *(as noun)*, *gp.* searoþoncelra, 330.

**sēcan**, *w.v. (1)*, seek, try to get, *pres. 3 sg.* sēceð, 96.

**ge-sēcan**, *w.v. (1)*, come to visit, *pret. 3 sg.* gesōhte, 14.

**secg** †, *m. ja-stem*, man, *np.* secgas, 201.

**secgan**, *w.v. (3)*, tell, ascribe, *inf.* ~, 152, *pret. 3 sg.* sægde, 341n. – Cpd.: ā-.

**sendan**, *w.v. (1)*, send, *pret. 3 pl.* sendon, 224, *subj. pres. 3 sg.* sende, 190n.

**sēo**, *see* **sē**.

**ge-sēon**, *s.v. (5)*, see, *inf.* ~, 136.

**sīd** (†), *adj.*, broad, vast, *asf.* sīde, 337.

**sige-folc** †, *n. a-stem*, victorious people, *ds.* sigefolce, 152.

**sige-rōf** †, *adj.*, triumphant, *np.* sigerōfe, 177.

[**sige**]-**þūf** ‡, *m. a-stem*, banner of victory, *ap.* [sige]þūfas, *201*n.

**sige-wong** †, *m. a-stem*, field of victory, *ds.* sigewonge, 294.

**sigor** (†), *m. es/os-stem*, victory, *as.* ~, 89, *gs.* sigores, 124, *ds.* sigore, 298n.

**sigor-lēan** †, *n. a-stem*, reward for victory, *as.* ~, 344.

**sīn** (†), *poss. pron.*, his, her, *dsf.* sīnre,132n., *dsn.* sīnum, 99, *apm.* sīne, 29n.

**sinc** (†), *n. a-stem*, treasure, *gs.* sinces, 30, 339.

**singan**, *s.v. (3)*, sing, *pret. 3 sg.* sang, 211.

**sittan**, *s.v. (5)*, sit, *inf.* ~, 15, *pret. 3 pl.* sǣton, 141; onufan ~, descend upon, set upon, *subj. pret. 3 sg.* sǣte, 252. – Cpds.: benc-, burh-, flet-sittende.

**sīð**, *m. a-stem*, *(1)* journey, *as.* ~, 145, *(2)* time, occasion, *ds.* sīðe, 73, 109. – Cpd.: hin-.

**sīð**, *adv.*, late; sīð ond late, at last, 275.

**ge-sīð**, *m. a-stem*, retainer, comrade, *np.* gesīðas, 201. – Cpd.: wēa-.
**sīð-fæt**, *m. a-stem,* expedition, venture, *ds.* sīðfate, 335.
**slǣp**, *m. a-stem*, sleep, *ds.* slǣpe, 247.
**slēan**, *s.v. (6)*, strike, *pret. 3 sg.* slōh, 103, 108, *pret. 3 pl.* slōgon, 231.
**ge-slēan**, *s.v. (6)*, strike down, *infl. pp.* geslegene, 31.
**slege-fǣge** ‡, *adj.*, death-doomed, destined to be slaughtered, *apm.* ~, 247.
**snel**, *adj.,(as noun)*, keen, eager, *gp.* snelra, 199.
**snotor**, *adj.*, wise, shrewd, *nsf. wk.* snotere, 125, *asf. wk.* snoteran, 55.
**snūde** (†), *adv.*, quickly, 55n., 125, 199.
**ge-sōhte**, *see* **ge-sēcan**.
**somod**, *adv.*, *(1) (association in joint action)*, together, 288, *(2) (with* eall*)*, all together, 269, *(3) (association of similar objects or circumstances)*, and, also, too, 163, 282.
**sorg**, *f. ō-stem*, sorrow, woe, *gp.* sorga, 182, *dp.* sorgum, 88.
**sōð**, *adj.*, true, *asm.* sōðne, 89, 344.
**sparian**, *w.v. (2)*, spare, *pret. 3 pl.* sparedon, 233.
**spōwan**, *s.v. (7f)*, *impers. w. dat.*, avail, help, *pret. 3 sg.* spēow, 274.
**ge-spōwan**, *s.v. (7f)*, *impers. w. dat.*, prosper, succeed, *pret. 3 sg.* ge-spēow, 175.
**sprecan**, *s.v. (5)*, speak, *pret. 3 sg.* spræc, 160, 176.
**standan**, *s.v. (6)*, stand, *pret. 3 pl.* stōdon, 267.
**starian**, *w.v. (2)*, gaze, *inf.* ~, *179*n.
**stēap**, *adj.*, deep, *npm.* stēape, 17.
**stede-heard** ‡, *adj.*, firmly fixed, very hard (?), *apm.* stedehearde, 223n.
**steppan**, *s.v. (6)*, march, advance, *pret 3 pl.* stōpon, 39, 69, 200, 212, 227.
**sterced-ferhð** †, *adj.*, stout-hearted, determined, *npm.* stercedferhðe, 55, 227.
**stīð-mōd**, *adj. (as noun)*, fierce-hearted, *nsm. wk.* stīðmōda, 25.
**strǣl**, *m. a-stem*, arrow, *ap.* strǣlas, 223.
**strēam**, *m. a-stem*, *pl.*, † sea, *ap.* strēamas, 348.
**ge-stȳran**, *w.v. (1)*, *w. dat. (of pers.) and gen. (of thing)*, restrain, *pret. 3 sg.* gestȳrde, 60.
**styrman**, *w.v. (1)*, † storm, rage *(of people)*, *pret. 3*

*sg.* styrmde, 25, *pret. 3 pl.* styrmdon, 223.
**styrn-mōd** ‡, *adj.*, stern-hearted, *npm.* styrnmōde, 227.
**sum**, *indef. pron.*, one, a certain one (of many), *(as noun w. part. gen.)*, *nsm.* ~, 275n., *asm.* sumne, 148.
**sundor-yrfe** †, *n. ja-stem*, private property, personal possessions, *gs.* sundoryrfes, 339.
**sūsl**, *n. a-stem*, torment, misery, *ds.* sūsle, 114.
**swā**, *(1) adv.*, *(a) with following adj. (verse and clause non-initial)*, so, to such an extent, 67, 126, 130; *(b) with following clause introduced by* oðþæt *(verse and sentence initial)*, so, in this manner ( ... until), 28, 32, 236; *(2) conj. (verse-clause initial; sentence non-initial*), as *(at head of b-verse)* 38, 95, 123, 143, 197, 277; so that 102; *correl.* swā *(adv.)* ... swā *(conj.)*, so ... that, 67-8n.
**swātig**, *adj.*, † bloody, *asm.* swātigne, 337.
**swaðu**, *f. ō-stem*, track, wake, *ds.* swaðe, 321.
**swǣsendo**, *n. ja-stem*, *pl.*, banquet, *ap.* ~, 9.
**swegel** (†), *n. a-stem*, heaven, *gs.* swegles, 80, 88, 124, 344, 349.
**swēora**, *m. n-stem*, neck, *as.* swēoran, 106.
**sweorcend-ferhð** ‡, *adj.*, sombre, gloomy, *npm.* sweorcendferhðe, 269n.
**sweord**, *n. a-stem*, sword, *as.* ~, 337, *ds.* sweorde, 89, 288, *ap.* swyrd, 230, *dp.* sweordum, 194, 294, swyrdum, 264, 301, 321. – Cpd.: brād-.
**swēot** †, *n. a-stem*, army, *ns.* ~, 298.
**sweotole**, *adv.*, openly, 177.
**sweotol-lice**, *adv.*, clearly, 136.
**swīma**, *m. n-stem*, swoon, *ds.* swīman, 30, 106.
**swīð-līc**, *adj.*, violent, *asn.* ~, 240.
**swīð-mōd** (†), *adj.*, arrogant, *nsm.* ~, 30, 339.
**swīðre**, *comp. adj.*, right *(hand)*, *dsf.* swīðran, 80.
**(ge-)swiðrian**, *w.v. (2)*, destroy, bring to an end, *pp.* geswiðrod, 266.
**(ge-)swutelian** ¶, *w.v. (2)*, reveal, *pp.* geswutelod, 285.
**swylc**, *pron.*, such, *asm.* swylcne, 65.
**swylce**, *(1) adv.*, swylce ēac, in addition to, as well as, 18, 337, 343, 348, *(2) conj.*, as if *(w. subj.?)*, 31n.

**swyrd**, *see* **sweord**.
**swyrd-geswing** ‡, *n. a-stem*, sword-stroke, *as. (or pl.?)* ~, 240.
**swȳðe**, *adv.*, greatly, 88; *comp.*, swȳðor, 182.
**sȳ**, *see* **wesan**.
**sylf**, *pron.*, self, own, *(1) (w. noun which it immediately follows)*, *asn.* ~, 204; *(2) (w. pers. pron. in dat.)*, *dsf.* sylfre, 335; *(3) (w. poss. pron.)*, *gsm.* sylfes, 349, *gp.* sylfra, 285.
**symbel**, *adj.*, continual, *asn. (in semi-adv. phrase)* on ~, always, 44.
**sym(b)el**, *n. a-stem*, feast, *ds.* symle, 15.
**syndon**, *see* **wesan**.
**ge-synto**, *f. ō-stem*, deliverance, *gp.* gesynta, 90.
**syððan**, *(1) adv.*, after, 114; *(2) conj.*, when, after, 160, 168 *(w. sense shading into* because*)*, 189n., 218.

## T

**(ge-)tācnian**, *w.v. (2)*, show, signal, *pp.* getācnod, 197, 286.
**tēon**, *s.v. (2)*, pull, *pret. 3 sg.* tēah, 99.
**teran**, *s.v. (4)*, tear, *inf.* ~, 281.
**tīd**, *f. i-stem*, time, *as.* ~, 306n., *ds.* tīde, 286. – Cpd.: morgen-.
**tilian**, *w.v. (2)*, supply, *inf.* ~, 208.
**tīr** †, *m. a-stem*, glory, *ns.* ~, 157, *as.* ~, 197, *gs.* tīres, 93, 272.
**tīð**, *f. ō-stem*, boon, favour, *as.* tīðe, 6, *see* gefremman.
**tō**, *prep.w. dat., (1) (motion) (a) (w. vbs. of coming, going, etc. marking end reached by that which moves)*, to, 11, 40, 141, 147, 169, 189, 202, 213, 220, 281, 311, *(w. ellipsis of inf. of motion in a command)*, 9, *(b) (w. vbs. of leading and fetching, marking end reached by that which is moved)*, to, 36, 43, 72, 326; *(2) (extent)*, to, 275; *(3) (result)*, for, as, 295, 296; *(4) (marking end to which object or action is directed)*, *(a) (w. vb. denoting destination)*, to, 196, *(b) (w. vb. of address)*, to, 152, 176, 283, *(c) (w. vb. denoting preparation)*, for, 200, *(d) (marking object of a feeling)*, in, 7, 345, *(e) (marking purpose)*, *(i) (of action)*, for, 54, 96; *(ii) (of object)*, as, 174, 334, *(5) (marking juxtaposition)*, at, 15, 16, *(6) (time)*, *(a) (during which something takes place)*,

in, 322, *(b) (during which something continues)*, for, tō ... aldre, 120, 347; *(7) w. infl. inf.*, to, 131, 313.

**tō-brēdan**, *s.v. (3)*, *w. dat.*, shake off, cast off *(sleep)*, *inf.* tōbrēdon, 247.

**tō-gēanes**, *prep. w. dat.*, towards, 149.

**tohte** †, *f. n-stem*, battle, *ds.* tohtan, 197.

**torht** (†), *adj.*, beautiful, *or* noble, *asf. wk.* torhtan, 43.

**torht-līc** †, *adj.*, glorious, *nsm.* ~, 157.

**torht-mōd** †, *adj.*, glorious, *nsm.* ~, 6, 93.

**torn** (†), *n. a-stem*, grief, *as.* ~, 272.

**torne** †, *adv.*, grievously, 93n.

**tōð**, *m. mut.*, tooth, *dp.* tōðon, 272.

**tō-weard**, *adj.*, imminent, approaching, *nsm.* ~, 157, *nsf.* ~, 286.

**træf** †, *n. a-stem*, (‡) tent, *as.* ~, 268, *ds.* træfe, 43n., 255.

**trum**, *adj.*, firm, *asm.* trumne, 6.

**twēogan**, *w.v. (2)*, *w. gen. (of object of doubt)*, doubt, *pret. 3 sg.* twēode, 1, 345.

**Þ**

**ðā**, *dem. adj.*, *see* **sē**.

**ðā**, *(1) adv.*, then, *(spelled* þa *when clause initial, except at 21; elsewhere,* ða*, except at 280)*, *(a) (clause initial, followed by) (i) (finite part of* wesan *or* weorðan*)*, 21, 57, 73, 97, 159, 199, 272, 275, *(ii) (nominal sub. phrase)*, 125, 171, 323, *(iii) (pron. sub. of* gefrignan *clause)*, 246n.; *(b) (clause non-initial, preceded by)*, *(i) (non-alliterating vb.; in b-verse, except at 122, 176, 278)*, 34, 55, 61, 64, 67, 77, 80, 98, 103, 107, 108, 122, 132, 146, 176, 278, *(ii) (pers. pron. sub.; in b-verse, except at 15, 301)*, 15, 54, 138, 220, 269, 280, 289, 301, *(iii) (conj.* ond, *foll. by adv., in b-verse)*, 41, 147, 169, *(iv) (other constructions)*, 2, 7, 94, 130; *(c)* þā gȳt, 107, *see* **gȳt,** *(d)* nū ðā, 86, *see* **nū**.

*(2) conj.*, when, *(spelled* þa*, followed by pron. subj. and vb.)*, 3, 145.

**ge-ðafian**, *w.v. (2)*, permit, consent to, *inf.* ~, 60.

**ðām**, *see* **sē**.

**þancol-mōd** †, *adj.*, thoughtful, wise, *asf.* þancolmōde, 172.

**þanonne**, *adv.* from that place, 132, ðonan, 118.

**þāra**, *see* **sē**.

**þǣr**, *(1) adv.*, there, *(clause initial, with VS order)* þǣr, 17, 46, 307, *(clause non-initial)* ðǣr, 2, 113, 119, 284, ðǣr inne, therein, 50; *(2) conj.*, where *(with SV order)* þær, 40, 63; þǣr ... inne, wherein, 44-5n.

**þǣre**, **þæs**, *see* **sē**.

**þæt**, *dem. adj. and pron.*, *see* **sē**.

**þæt**, *conj.*, that, *(always spelled ꝥ), introd. (1) noun clauses, (a) as subj.*, 156, 286, *(b) as obj.*, 56, 93, 118, 153, 168, 188, 208, 240, 254, 276; *(2) adv. clauses, (a) of purpose*, in order that, 48, *(b) of result*, so that, 24n. *(or dem. pron.?)*, 105, 106, 110, 136n.; *(3) ambiguous clauses*, 4 *(2a or 2b)*, 27 *(1b or 2b)*, 89 *(1b or 2a)*, 184 *(1b or 2a)*.

**þe**, *(1) indeclinable relative particle, (verse initial and spelled* þe, *except at 346), (a)* who, 50, 71, 96, 124, 181, 258, 284, 342, 347, which, 127n., 158, 346, that, 235, *(b) (after noun denoting time)*, in which, 287; *(2) conj.*, because, 6 *(cf. þæs ðe, 344)*.

**ðe**, *in comb. w.* þā, þæs *(spelled ðe)*, *see* **sē**.

**þē**, *see* **sē**.

**þēah**, *(1) adv.*, however, ðēah, 257; *(2) conj.*, though, ~, 20.

**þearf**, *f. ō-stem*, need, *as.* þearfe, 3, 92.

**ðearf**, *see* **ðurfan**.

**þearfende**, *pres. part. (as adj.)*, needy, *dsf.* þearfendre, *85*n.

**þearle**, *adv.*, *(1) w. adj. or pp.*, *(a) (where there is an idea of pain)*, sorely, grievously, 86, *(b) (where there is no idea of pain)*, very, 74, 268, *(2) w. vb.*, *(a) (of action)*, vigorously, 262, *(b) (of desire)*, very much, 306.

**þearl-mōd** (‡), *adj.*, *(1)* strict, firm, *nsm.* ~, 91, *(2) (ironically, or pejoratively)*, severe *or* tyrannical, *nsm.* ~, 66n.

**ðēaw**, *m. wa-stem*, habit, *dp.* ðēawum, 129.

**þegn**, *m. a-stem*, *(1)* officer, *ap.* ðegnas, 10, *(2)* warrior, *np.* þegnas, 306. – Cpds.: ealdor-, mago-.

**þēgon**, *see* **þicgan**.

**þencan**, *w.v. (1)*, intend, mean, *pret. 3 sg.* þōhte, 58, *pret. 3 pl.* þōhton, 208.

**þenden** (†), *conj.*, while, 66.

**þēoden** (†), *m. a-stem*, *(1)* lord, *ns.* ðēoden, 66, *gs.*

þēodnes, 268, *ds.* þēodne 11, *(2)* Lord, God, *ns.* ~, 91, *gs.* þēodnes, *165*n., *ds.* þēodne, 3.

**þēod-guma** (‡), *m. n-stem*, warrior, *np.* ~, 208, ðēodguman, 331.

**þēowen** ¶, *f. jō-stem*, female servant, handmaid, *ns.* ~, 74n.

**þes**, *dem. adj.*, this, *asm.* þysne, 90, *dsf.* ðysse, 66n., *ism.* ðȳs, 2, *isn.* þȳs, 89, *gp.* þyssa, 187.

**þicgan**, *s.v. (5)*, consume, drink, *pret. 3 pl.* þēgon, 19.

**þīn**, *poss. adj.*, your *(sg.)*, *gsf.* þīnre, 85, 91.

**ðīnen** ¶, *f. jō-stem*, female servant, handmaid, *as.* ðīnenne, 172.

**þing**, *n. a-stem*, thing, deed, *as.* ~, 153, *gs.* ðinges, 60.

**þōhte, þōhton**, *see* **þencan**.

**þolian**, *w.v. (2)*, endure, suffer, *pret. 3 pl.* þoledon, 215, *pres. part.* þoligende, 272.

**ðonan**, *see* **þanonne**.

**ge-ðonc**, *m. a-stem*, mind, *ds.* geðonce, 13.

**þonc-wyrðe**, *adj.*, memorable, gratifying, *asn.* ~, 153.

**þone**, *see* **sē**.

**þonne**, *conj. (after comp.)*, than, 329.

**þrāg** (†), *f. ō-stem*, time, *as.* þrāge *(in semi-adv. phrase* ealle *~)*, continuously, 237.

**ðrēat**, *m. a-stem*, group, troop, *ds.* ðrēate, 62, *dp.* ðrēatum, 164.

**þringan**, *s.v. (3)*, *(of people)*, throng, press forward, *inf.* ~, 249, *pret. 3 pl.* þrungon, 164. – Cpd.: oð-.

**(ge-)ðringan**, *s.v. (3)*, *intrans. (of time)*, rush, hasten, *pp.* geðrungen, 287.

**þrym**, *m. ja-stem*, *(1)* band, host, *dp.* ðrymmum, 164, *(2)* force, might, *ds.* þrymme, 331, *(3)* splendour, majesty, *ns.* ðrym, 86, *(4) (ambiguous)*, *gs.* þrymmes, 60.

**þrym-ful** (†), *adj.*, glorious, illustrious, *nsf.* ~, 74n.

**þrym-līc**, *adj.*, magnificent, *apn.* ~, 8.

**ðrȳ-nes**, *f. jō-stem*, the Trinity, *gs.* ðrȳnesse, 86.

**ðū**, *pers. pron.*, you, *as.* ðē, 83, *np.* gē, 153, 158, 177, 188, 196, *ap. (used refl.)* ēow, 188, *dp.* ēow, 152, 154, 156, 197.

**ge-ðungen**, *adj. (pp. of ðēon)*, excellent, *nsf.* ~, 129.

**þurfan**, *pret. pr.*, *(w. inf.)*, need, *pres. 3 sg.* ðearf,

117, *subj. pres. 2 pl.* þyrfen, 153.

**þurh**, *(1) prep. w. acc.*, *(always spelled* þurh*)*, *(a) (local)*, through, 151, 303, *(b) (means, instrument, agency)*, through, by means of, 186, 198, 333, 349; *(2) adv.* through, 49n.

**þus**, *adv.*, so, to such an extent, *(w. adj.)*, 93.

**þūsend-mǣlum** (†), *adv.*, in thousands, 165.

**þȳ**, *see* **sē**.

**þyder**, *adv.*, to there, 129.

**þyrfen**, *see* **þurfan**.

**þȳs**, **þyssa**, etc., *see* **þes**.

**þȳstre**, *adj.*, dark, gloomy, *nsf.* ~, 34.

**þȳstru**, *f. īn-stem*, darkness, *dp.* þȳstrum, 118.

U

**under**, *prep.*, under, beneath, *(1) w. acc. (of motion)*, 113; *(2) w. dat. (a) (of position)*, 67, 219, 332, *(b) (marking protection)*, covered by, in, 203.

**un-lǣd**, *adj. (as noun)*, miserable, wicked, *gsm. wk.* unlǣdan, 102.

**un-lyfigende**, *pres. part. (as adj.)*, lifeless, dead, *gsm.* unlyfigendes, 180, *dp.* unlyfigendum, 315.

**unnan**, *pret. pr.*, *w. dat. (of pers.) and gen. (of thing)*, grant, *pret. 3 sg.*, ūðe, 123, 183.

**ge-unnan**, *pret. pr.*, *w. dat. (of pers.) and gen. (of thing)*, grant, *imp. sg.* geunne, 90.

**un-rōt**, *adj.*, dejected, gloomy, *npm.* unrōte, 284.

**un-sōfte**, *adv.*, ungently, 228.

**un-swǣslīc** ‡, *adj.*, unpleasant, *asm.* unswǣslīcne, 65.

**un-sȳfre**, *adj. (as noun)*, unclean, filthy, *nsm. wk.* unsȳfra, 76.

**up**, *adv.*, up, 9n.

**ūre**, *poss. adj.*, our, *nsm.* ~, 289.

**ūre**, *poss. pron.*, *see* **ic**.

**ūrig-feðera** †, *adj.*, wet-winged, *nsm.* ~, 210.

**urnon**, *see* **irnan**.

**ūs**, *see* **ic**.

**ūt**, *adv.*, out, 70, 135.

**ūte**, *adv.*, outside, 284.

**ūðe**, *see* **unnan**.

W

**wald**, *m. u > a-stem*, forest, *ds.* walde, 206.

**waldend**, *m. nd-stem*, Ruler, God, *ns.* ~, 5, 61.

**wand**, *see* **windan**.

**wann**, *adj.*, dark, black, *nsm. wk.* wanna, 206.

**gewāt**, *see* **gewītan**.

**wæccende**, *pres. part. (as adj.)*, watchful, vigilant, *npm.* ~, 142.

**wǣgon**, *see* **wegan**.

**wæl-gīfre** †, *adj.*, greedy for slaughter, blood-thirsty, *nsm.* ~, 207, *dp.* wælgīfrum, 295.

**wæl-scel** ‡, *(?)*, heaps of slain?, deadly noise?, *as.* ~, 312n.

**wǣpen**, *n. a-stem*, weapon, *ap.* ~, 290. – Cpd.: heoru-.

**wǣr-loga** (†), *m. n-stem*, treacherous person, traitor, *as.* wǣrlogan, 71n.

**wǣron**, **wæs**, *see* **wesan**.

**wē**, *see* **ic**.

**wēa-gesīð**, *m. a-stem*, companions in misery, criminal associates, *np.* wēagesīðas, 16n.

**ge-wealdan**, *s.v. (7c)*, *w. gen.*, control, manage, *inf.* ~, 103.

**weal-geat** †, *n. a-stem*, city gate, *ds.* wealgate, 141n.

**weall**, *m. a-stem*, wall, city wall, *as.* ~, 161, *gs.* wealles, 151, *ap.* weallas, 137.

**weard**, *m. a-stem*, Guardian, God, *as.* ~, 80. – Cpds.: ēðel-, hēafod-.

**weard**, *f. ō-stem*, watch, *as.* wearde, 142.

**weard**, *in comb. w. wið*, 99, *see* **wið**.

**wearð**, *see* **weorðan**.

**wegan**, *s.v. (5)*, carry, *pret. 3 pl.* wǣgon, 325.

**wel**, *adv.*, *(1) (in accordance with good conduct)*, well, properly, 27; *(2) (as regards result)*, well, effectively, 103.

**wēnan**, *w.v. (1)*, *w. gen.*, think, suspect, *subj. pret. 3 sg.*, wēnde, 20.

**weorpan**, *s.v. (3)*, throw, fling, *pret. 3 pl.* wurpon, 290.

**weorðan**, *s.v. (3)*, become, be, *pret. 3 sg.* wearð, 21, 57, 97, 155, 166, 199, 216, 265, 275, *pret. 3 pl.* wurdon, 159. – Cpd.: for-.

**ge-weorðan**, *s.v. (3)*, come to be, *(impersonal w. acc. of pers.)* turn out, *pp.* geworden, 260n.

**(ge-)weorðian**, *w.v. (2)*, honour, favour, *pp.* geweorðod, 298.

**weorð-mynd**, *f. ō-stem*, honour, *as.* weorðmynde, 342.

**wer**, *m. a-stem*, man, *np.* weras, 71, 142, 163, 241.

**wērig-ferhð** †, *adj.*, tired at heart, *npm.* wērigferhðe, 290, *apm.* wērigferhðe, *249*n.

**werod**, *n. a-stem*, host, *ns.* ~, 199, *gp.* weroda, 342.

**wesan**, *anom.*, be, *pres. 3 sg.* ys, 86, 93, 154, 156, 285, *(stressed)* 286, *pres.*

*3 pl.* syndon, 195, *pret. 3 sg.* wæs, 12, 46, 56, 73, *(stressed)* 113n., 146, 161, 168, 272, 313, *neg. pret. 3 sg.* næs, 107, 257, *pret. 3 pl.* wǣron *(unstressed)*, 17, 31n. *(subj.?)*, 225, *(stressed)* 238, 255, 284, 304, 322n., *subj. 3 sg.* sȳ, 346.

**wīd**, *adj.*, *(of duration of time)*, long, *dsn. wk.* wīdan, *(in poetic idiom)* tō wīdan aldre, for ever, 347n.

**wīde**, *adv.*, widely, far and wide, 156.

**wīdl**, *m.n. a-stem*, filth, corruption, *ds.* wīdle, 59.

**wīf**, *n. a-stem*, woman, *ns.* ~, 148, *np.* ~, 163.

**wiga** (†), *m. n-stem*, warrior, *gp.* wigena, 49. – Cpds.: byrn-, cumbol-.

**wiggend** (†), *m. nd-stem*, *as.* ~, 258, *np.* ~, 69, 141, 312, *dp.* wiggendum, 283. – Cpds.: byrn-, lind-, rond-.

**wiht**, *adv.*, *(in neg. clause)*, at all, 274.

**willa**, *m. n-stem*, enjoyment, *ds.* willan, 295.

**wīn**, *n. a-stem*, wine, *ds.* wīne, 29, 67.

**wind**, *m. a-stem*, wind, *as.* ~, 347.

**windan**, *s.v. (3)*, roll, *pret. 3 sg.* wand, 110. – Cpd.: be-.

**wine-dryhten** †, *m. a-stem*, lord and friend, *as.* ~, 274.

**wīn-gedrinc** (†), *n. a-stem*, wine-drinking, *ds.* wīngedrince, 16.

**wīn-hāte** ‡, *f. n.-stem*, invitation for drinks, *as.* wīnhātan, 8.

**wīn-sæd** †, *adj.*, glutted with wine, *npm.* wīnsade, 71.

**witan**, *pret. pr.*, know, *pret. 3 pl.* w[i]stan, *207*n., *pret. 3 sg. neg.* nyste, 68.

**ge-wītan**, *s.v. (1)*, set out, set off, *pret 3 sg.* gewāt, 61n., 145, *pret. 3 pl.* gewitan, 290.

**wīte**, *n. ja-stem*, torture, punishment, *dp.* wītum, 115.

**gewit-loca** (†), *m. n-stem*, mind, *ds.* gewitlocan, 69.

**wið**, *prep.*, *(1) w. acc. (marking association)*, with, 260n.; *(2) w. gen. (a) (of motion)*, towards, 162, 248, *(b) (of action in opposition to)*, against, 4, *(c) in comb. w.* weard *(of motion)*, towards, 99n.

**wiðer-trod** †, *n. a-stem*, *either* retreat, flight, *or*

retirement, withdrawal, *as.* ~, 312n.
**wlanc** (†), *adj.*, *(1)* proud, *nsf.* ~, 325, *(2)* proud, *or* lusting, *or* merry, *npm.* wlance, 16n.
**wlītan** (†), *s.v.* *(1)*, look, see, *inf.* ~, 49.
**wlitig**, *adj.*, beautiful, splendid, *gsf.* *wk.* wlitegan, 137, *dsn.* *wk.* wlitegan, 255.
**wolcen**, *n.* *a-stem*, cloud, *gp.* wolcna, 67.
**wolde**, *see* **wyllan**.
**wom**, *m.n.* *a-stem*, sin, *ds.* womme, 59.
**wom-full** †, *adj.*, foul, *nsm.* ~, 77.
**word**, *n.* *a-stem*, speech, *as.* ~, 82, 151, 283, *dp.* wordum, 241.
**ge-worden**, *see* **ge-weorðan**.
**worhte, -on**, *see* **wyrcean**.
**worn** (†), *m.* *a-stem*, crowd, *dp.* wornum, 163.
**woruld**, *f.* *i-stem*, world, *as.* ~, 156, *ds.* worulde, 66.
**woruld-būende** †, *m.* *nd-stem*, *pl.*, those who dwell on earth, *gp.* woruldbūendra, 82.
**ge-wrecan**, *s.v.* *(5)*, avenge, *imp.* *sg.* gewrec, 92.
**wreccan**, *w.v.* *(1)*, arouse, wake up, *pret.* *3 pl.* wrehton, 228, 243.
**wuldor**, *n.* *a-stem*, *(1)* glory, *ns.* ~, 347, *as.* ~, 342, *gs.* wuldres, 59, *ds.* wuldre, 344; *(2)* *(of God)*, glorious Lord, *ns.* ~, 155.
**wuldor-blǣd** ‡, *m.* *a-stem*, glorious success, *ns.* ~, 156.
**wulf**, *m.* *a-stem*, wolf, *ns.* ~, 206, *dp.* wulfum, 295.
**wunden-locc** †, *adj.*, curly-haired, *or* with braided locks, *nsf.* ~, 77n., 103, 325n.
**wundor**, *n.* *a-stem*, wonderful thing, *dp.* wundrum, 8.
**wunian**, *w.v.* *(2)*, dwell, remain, live, *inf.* ~, 119, *pret.* *3 sg.* wunode, 67.
**wurdon**, *see* **weorðan**.
**wurpon**, *see* **weorpan**.
**wyllan**, *anom.* *(w. inf.)*, wish, will, *pres.* *1 sg.* wylle, 84, 187, *pret.* *3 sg.* wolde, 59, 183.
**wyrcean**, *w.v.* *(1)*, *(1)* work, strive *(for)*, *pret.* *3 sg.* worhte, 65n.; *(2)* make, *pret.* *3 pl.* worhton, 302; *(3)* issue, *inf.* ~, 8.
**wyrm**, *m.* *i-stem*, worm, snake, *dp.* wyrmum, 115.
**wyrm-sele** ‡, *m.* *i-stem*, hall of worms, snake-infested hall, *ds.* ~, 119.

## Y

**ȳcan**, *w.v.* *(1)*, add to, increase, *inf.* ~, 183.
**yldesta**, *see* **eald**.

**ymbe**, *prep. w. acc.*, *(local)*, *(1) (marking object which is enclosed)*, around, about, 47, *(marking object which forms a centre for others)*, around, about, 268.
**yrre**, *adj.*, angry, enraged, *npm.* ~, 225.
**ys**, *see* **wesan**.